PRAISE FOR LOOK—IT'

Anna has written the book I wish I had when I first started to write. Apart from being extraordinarily detailed, it draws on the experience and expertise of others in the book writing and publishing space, which adds tremendous value for the reader. A very good book that every aspiring author needs to read.

— ANDREW GRIFFITHS, COACH, AUTHOR, SPEAKER

Anna has written the bible of self-publishing for Australian non-fiction authors. As someone who has been in business book publishing, written 25 books and mentored over 200 business owners, consultants and entrepreneurs, *Look—It's Your Book* is the ultimate guide to EVERYTHING you need to know about the book writing, publishing and marketing journey.

— JAQUI LANE, THE BOOK ADVISER

This is a marvellous resource for newbies and veterans alike. So much practical and useful detail about the myriad ways one can create, publish, distribute, and market a book today.

— VIRGINIA LLOYD, PUBLISHING MENTOR, AUTHOR

Look—It's Your Book sidesteps confusing online research and expensive trial and error—it's essential reading for anyone with a book in them and the zeal to make it happen.

— TESS MCCABE, BOOK DESIGNER

Written in an entertaining and warm tone, this is an extremely useful resource for first-time, and even second- and third-time self-publishers. A stellar book.

— TINA MORGANELLA, EDITOR, AUTHOR

Self-publishing can be a minefield, especially for a first-time author, and *Look—It's Your Book!* demystifies the process with humour, heart and a heap of tips, advice and actionable strategies. If you want to bring your book to market (without the stress) and start making sales right away, it's the only guide to self-publishing you'll ever need.

— RACHEL SMITH, JOURNALIST, RACHEL'S LIST

This is such a valuable resource for any writer. It's rigorous and well researched, and has a lot of depth and character to it. If you have always wanted to write a book, but still have a lot of questions about how, then start here with the lovely Anna and her go-to experts and experiences of the Australian publishing industry.

— KELLY IRVING, BOOK COACH AND EDITOR

In *Look—It's Your Book*, Anna has done a rare thing— identified a gap in the available information and completely filled it. Finally, there is a one-stop resource that I can direct my self-publishing clients to and be confident that, after they have read it, they'll be fully prepared to embark on creating their own book.

— LORNA HENDRY, BOOK DESIGNER, EDITOR, WRITER

Anna has prepared a most useful publication for those who really want to author a successful book. It is thorough and detailed and brings together the experience of many who have done it all before.

— GARRY BROWNE, THE PERSONAL BRAND CATALYST

Finally want to write that book you've been dreaming about for years? Well, stop dreaming and read this book if you want to make it happen.

— MARK JONES, AUTHOR, *BELIEFONOMICS*

LOOK—IT'S YOUR BOOK!

WRITE, PUBLISH & PROMOTE YOUR NON-FICTION BOOK: A SELF-PUBLISHING GUIDE FOR AUSTRALIAN WRITERS

ANNA FEATHERSTONE

CAPEABLE PUBLISHING

First published in Australia in 2022 by CapeAble Publishing

PO Box 556 Port Macquarie NSW 2444

ISBN: 978-0-6453422-2-2

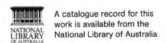

A catalogue record for this work is available from the National Library of Australia

Cover design: Tess McCabe

Printed by: Ligare

❀ Created with Vellum

CONTENTS

PART IV
MARKETING YOUR BOOK

PART V
LEVERAGE YOUR BOOK

For Darcy, Zac and Josie.
Keep writing your own lives,
weaving dreams, making change, creating magic.
You have so much heart and all of mine.
Lava you.

HOW TO USE THIS BOOK

Web links

In the paperback version of this book, URLs are not included in the text to avoid distraction and enhance readability. What I have done though, is prepare a free file for you that you can access at www.annafeatherstone.com. This list has all the links (to people, organisations, companies and resources) you will need. They are listed by chapter. I hope it saves your fingers from having to type all the URLs in from scratch.

Companion Workbook

A companion workbook is available for sale on my site at www.annafeatherstone.com. The workbook includes checklists, worksheets, reminders, sample marketing material, and extra information and motivation to help you get your book done and dusted!

Key terms and abbreviations used throughout the book

- ALLi: The Alliance of Independent Authors
- ASA: Australian Society of Authors
- CAL: Copyright Agency
- ELR: Educational Lending Right (discussed in detail in Chapter 50)
- Indie: Used as another way to describe self-publishing authors
- PLR: Public Lending Right (discussed in detail in Chapter 50)
- POD: Print on demand
- SEO: Search engine optimisation
- SPN: Small Press Network
- TOC: Table of contents (list of your book's chapters and subheadings)
- Trad: As in 'traditional' author or publishing company (i.e., non-indie)

A book stops time, but people and companies keep moving

People, products and companies change. Throughout this book you will find short case studies, interviews and mentions of authors, consultants, companies and products. These spotlights are just that—a look at a specific time in their experience and/or product offering. Depending on when you are reading this book, their circumstances, ownership and offerings may well have changed and they might be up to all sorts of different things, as may be their competitors. I want to thank them though, for their generosity in sharing their story at this moment in time.

Affiliate disclosure

Just because people, products and companies have been interviewed and/or mentioned in this book, it doesn't mean I endorse them, just as it doesn't mean similar services or experts not mentioned are any less worthy. Please do your own research before engaging services. I will add fresh links and information on my website over time as I hear recommendations from readers.

However, there are some services that have been of extra benefit to me and which I believe may add value to other self-publishers. In these cases, I have joined them as an affiliate. This means if you click on the associated link, I may receive a micro-percentage of any resulting sale to help with the running costs of my site. It doesn't mean you will end up paying more for the service and sometimes it might even mean you get a discount. Chapter 55 in this book discusses how as an author, you can use affiliate programs too.

A THANK YOU

I thank, respect and honour the past, present and future Traditional Custodians and Elders of this land and especially the people of the Birpai nation on whose land I live, work and receive sustenance and massive inspiration from. I also acknowledge Aboriginal and Torres Strait Islander peoples as the land's first storytellers. I wish I, and all of us, had listened, learned and cherished sooner.

Aboriginal and Torres Strait Islander peoples, please be aware that this book does contain the names of people who have passed away.

∽

This book is based on my accumulated experience of writing, publishing, marketing and distributing four non-fiction books (as well as one traditionally published one). But I didn't just magically know how to do it. It took a lot of experimentation, humbling mistakes and, most importantly, learning from others.

I'd therefore like to thank the following passionate and generous sharers of knowledge for all their trailblazing, tips and encouragement along the way:

Orna Ross, the team (and writing community) at ALLi
Joanna Penn, The Creative Penn
Ricardo Fayet of Reedsy
Dave Chesson of Kindlepreneur, Publisher Rocket and Atticus
Dave Gaughran
Stephanie Chandler and Karl W Palachuk
Valerie Khoo and Allison Tait, The Australian Writers Centre (AWC)

INTRODUCTION

Since my mid-30s I've barely read a novel. Instead, I've clear-felled my way through a small forest's-worth of non-fiction (don't worry, I literally planted thousands of trees on a farm to make up for it). My quest for real-life knowledge, meaning and actionable ideas is insatiable.

Why? Although a great novel transports my mind to fascinating fictional places, I still get the bulk of my enjoyment from learning about real-life places, people, problems, opportunities, and solutions.

Whether you want to know the sleeping habits of cicadas, how to mix a glaze for ceramics, the story behind a true crime, the financial advice followed by self-made millionaires, the life story of the local barista, the latest business tips for career success, or the top gluten-free Tibetan recipes using chilli ... there is a non-fiction book for you.

Or maybe there isn't, and that's why you're reading this book: because you're ready to write it.

Go you!

And go me! I saw a gap in the market for budding Australian self-publishers and hope these words will help fill it and fill it well.

The idea started when I was on a self-publishing journey with my books *Small Farm Success Australia*, *Honey Farm Dreaming* and *Honeycomb Kids*. I couldn't find a simple, independent Australian resource to show me how to get my books out into the world, but I did find an overwhelming expanse of information. There were so many websites, mailing lists, groups, courses,

US- and UK-based experts, local and international companies—and so many dodgy operations vying for eyeballs, headspace and my wallet—that I got sucked into an information vortex. I don't want that for you.

This is my fifth book, four of which have been self-published. I've had literary agents in Sydney and New York, sold foreign-language rights, had bookstore windows, appeared in national media, given many talks, and one of my books even became 'required reading' for a national VET/TAFE course. It doesn't mean I know everything about the constantly evolving world of self-publishing, but I know the road to successful indie publishing can be longer and more complex than the actual writing of the book!

I want this book to collapse time for you and vault you over challenges, minefields, and quicksand traps so you can get to the finish line faster, with you and your book in the best possible shape. It's not the only resource on self-publishing you will benefit from—consider it part of your arsenal—but the benefits of learning from the Australian experts interviewed in this book and the extra material I provide online will help you get going and set your course.

Why I started writing this book, and what drove me to finish it, even when I felt sapped by inertia or had an overflowing life buffet on my plate, is that I truly believe that information delivered using the right words, through the right medium, can change lives and therefore the world.

I hope these words help you on your writing and publishing journey, so you can enhance your world and that of others, too.

Oh, but if you're reading this book as a form of procrastination, do yourself a favour: close it. Get back to writing! You can always read it later.

PART I
WRITING AND EDITING

1

WHY WRITE A NON-FICTION BOOK?

W elcome! Let's start with why you're here. We all have different reasons for wanting to write, and these reasons have a huge impact on how we approach our book projects. So, why are you itching to put thoughts into words?

To inform

You want to add to the body of knowledge on a certain topic or share information that will help people become more confident and capable. And perhaps you don't want certain information to be lost, and the only way to do that is to write it down—to leave a legacy, even. One motivation behind writing my memoir *Honey Farm Dreaming* was to share the organic balm recipes I'd developed over more than a decade. What's inspiring you to convey your information to readers?

 I think writing a book is a work of service. My book can go to places that I can't and can serve people I may never meet. It's a labour of love.

— DR PAIGE WILLIAMS, *BECOMING ANTIFRAGILE*

You're an expert

You're literally an expert. You're a leader in your field. You're the person people turn to for information and advice. Or you're new to a field but want to be an expert in it, and it's seeing the topic through fresh eyes and sharing your experiences along that path to expertise that will really help your work create impact.

Experts aren't just professors, scientists and top-level advisors. Perhaps you have a high level of knowledge or skill in using natural dyes for eyelash tinting, surviving an army deployment, or crafting with palm fronds.

Or have you been fired ten times? Completed your family tree going back eight generations? Dated a new person every day for a month? Or had to cook for a family where every person in it has a different food intolerance?

Getting to the level of 'subject-matter expert' means you have probably made plenty of mistakes along the way, and sharing what went wrong can be just as valuable to your readers as sharing what went right.

To be a writer

From a young age, you've always wanted to be a writer. Books, words, and ideas are your oxygen. To be a writer is your lifelong dream.

Or, let's be truthful, perhaps you don't feel like you were born to be a writer, but you do want to 'have written' a book, and to feel the sense of accomplishment and the acknowledgement that comes from being a writer. Yes, they're two very different motivations, but both can be the impetus you need to get started on—and finish—your book.

You might already be a writer, for example, a journalist or copywriter, wanting to take that step from short to long form, to be able to go deep rather than be bound by the word limits, interests and audience of a daily paper or monthly magazine.

Whatever it was that led you to pick up this book, the one thing I can guarantee is that if you put the words down and get your non-fiction book finished, you won't just be a writer, you'll be an author. And that is a remarkable achievement for anybody.

 Journalists make great authors, but some never attempt to write a book due to fear. Part of that fear is linked to the fact that though we're experts at finding experts and quoting them, we're not used to thinking of ourselves as 'the' expert. Yes, the best books are based on solid research, but we journalists need to be prepared to do more, we must persuade the reader that now, with all the research we have done, we can also claim authority in the field we're writing about.

— KATH WALTERS, BOOK COACH

To entertain

You love spouting juicy facts and seeing people's eyes light up at your way of explaining oddities and mundanities. You love making people laugh, inspiring them, motivating them, leaving them feeling better than when you met them. Now you're ready to entertain them in book form too ... and maybe even from the stage or live streaming during your book launch and ongoing appearances.

For family

You want to write something for your family, about your family, or to make sense of your family or self. Perhaps you discovered the link between an ancestor and a local crime, feel driven to capture your turbulent teenage years in writing, to set the record straight, or to inspire people in your extended family or even yet-to-be-born descendants.

 If you have a great idea for a story, or feel you have lived an amazing life, I urge you to write it down. It doesn't have to be great literature, it only has to be your lived experience told in your own way. Too many of us leave this world with our stories locked inside us, forever lost to future generations.

— VALERIE PARV, TRAD AND INDIE AUTHOR

Perhaps there's some special knowledge or photos you don't want lost, or you want to capture the feelings, facts, scents, spirit, or craziness of your clan. A book can be a great way to do this.

To find and connect with your tribe

Writing and publishing a book opens doors as you contact, meet and engage with people who are interested in your area of expertise. It's a wonderful way to find your tribe.

As a side project

Writing a book is a way to make use of the hours before, after, or even on your way to work. And if you're retired, you can fit writing in between being active in your community or helping with grandkids. Because you can write from anywhere in the world and at any time of the day or night, writing a book makes the perfect side hustle. The process of writing may even help you decompress from the stresses of everyday life.

Because there's a market for it

Ebook sales skew towards fiction due to 'whale' readers (people who read a ton of books online) downloading cheaper romance and series fiction to their ereaders. However, according to a 2018 article in *Forbes Magazine*, the value of adult non-fiction sales has far outpaced fiction sales since 2013. The *Ebook Industry News* feed has current statistics.

To generate more cash from your content

If you've been blogging for a while, have hundreds of letters from your grandma, are sitting on a baker's dozen of dessert recipes or have a nice stash of articles under your belt that you've written for LinkedIn, Medium, or Substack, you might be interested in compiling all those words into a book.

It won't be as easy as a simple cut-and-paste, but you're likely to already have a lot of the material you need to successfully produce a book in a shorter-than-usual amount of time.

To make serious money

Yes! You want to make some serious coin from your book. You want to cash in on your years of expertise and live the life of your dreams! Unfortunately —reality check alert—though you might hope that writing will be your gravy train, most authors don't make a living, or even a profit, solely from one book.

You could be 'the little engine that could'—and my wish for you is that you are—but you will be the one responsible for getting your train from idle to a smooth forward motion and then on to bullet train speed.

You will either need to capture the zeitgeist and get everything just right with your timing, niche, writing quality and marketing, or you will need to buckle in for the long haul, taking the time to progress through the many steps that are needed to establish yourself as an author who has the long shelf life and loyal fan base needed to bring in the big bucks. You'll need to keep writing and publishing in your area of expertise, whether that be business, history, cooking, health, wellness, travel, parenting or whatever your specialty is. Over time, that can all add up to a successful publishing career.

It's all about setting expectations—realistic ones—and staying the course. I knew writing would never make me rich, but I realised it could supplement whatever other income I made. I also knew that if I did the work and did it well, long after I had finished work on the books, I would continue to be paid for them. I've also found that writing each book leads to other income-generating opportunities, time and time again.

For some authors, earning an income from royalties doesn't matter so much. You may, for example, be confident that investing in your book will pay off in spades by generating new high-value consulting or speaking work. But if you are writing a local history, the odds are that your main—and perhaps only!—payment for investing in the writing and production of the book will be self-satisfaction, positive reader responses and knowing that the rich history you love and value will not be lost to future generations of your community.

And you know what? If your book pays off more in intangibles like self-satisfaction and ends up contributing more to your community than it does to your own pocket, I think that is more than okay. It's actually wonderful.

Writing a book exposes us to all types of riches, including ones that might not be financial, but are priceless nonetheless.

To benefit your business

Perhaps you've seen other business thought leaders bring out books and felt a twinge of envy, or thought, 'I can do that, and do it better, too!' But there's a saying in the industry: 'Writing a book is the most expensive business card you will ever produce'.

However, the good news is that when done well, it can restart or turbocharge your career and open new opportunities for you and your company. You'll be able to leverage your book with clients, convert prospects, increase your credibility, and make inroads with people who are willing to pay for your expertise.

A chef's cookbook might bring more business to your restaurant or cook up opportunities for a paid newspaper recipe column or premium cooking classes. An up-and-coming executive might use a book to launch themselves on the international speaking circuit, or a retired athlete might use a book to inspire kids to follow their dreams.

By way of a very small example, my book *Small Farm Success Australia* not only led to Australia-wide media coverage and ongoing sales, but also saw Box Hill Institute engage me as a paid consultant on a new national TAFE course—an out-of-the-blue opportunity that would never have found its way to my door otherwise, and a chance to share my experiences with a whole new audience of people who were ready to push the boundaries with farms of their own. Exercising my writing muscles on the books gave me the experience and confidence to pitch and write articles for *The Guardian* and *The Sydney Morning Herald*, amongst others. And producing the books led to me running a Self-Publishing Mini Masterclass for Rachel's List, which led to this book, which enabled me to meet and interview some awesome people. And no doubt there are plenty of other opportunities to come.

 Unwritten books don't unlock leads.

— KATH WALTERS, BOOK COACH

Many of the business leaders I've interviewed speak not just of book sales as the mark of success, but of the doors that the book has opened for them in their speaking careers and the new business it has generated for their companies.

You might also use your book to cross-sell another product. For example, if you make artisan cheese, you might produce a recipe book to show readers how to use it in dinner creations, or even how to make it in their own homes.

A book or extract from it can also be used as a lead magnet to get people to sign up to your email list or monthly newsletter. People are happy to opt in to marketing when they perceive value—and you deliver it.

A book can also help build loyalty and create added value and long-term relationships with customers.

Yes, writing a non-fiction book can open many doors for your business, but there's a catch—it needs to be a good book. It needs to explain a core process, idea, or value well, and be written in a way that gives life to your intellectual property.

> Thought leader stuff is still important, but more and more people are talking about contributing their ideas; activating change, igniting a movement, advancing an idea; sharing their lived experience to help others fulfill their potential; changing lives and making meaningful connections and feeling that our experiences are valid and that we belong in the world
>
> — KELLY IRVING, EDITOR AND BOOK COACH

So, you know your stuff, you've spent years in the trenches listening, learning, doing, mastering, developing, evolving, and improving the way you do things to become an expert. You've developed your own way of getting things done, or have a unique take, and you want to share that information with the world. In business, this is called intellectual property (IP). In publishing, it's called gold.

> My books have raised my profile as a consultant globally, generating an enormous amount of lucrative consulting work.
>
> — PHILIP SHELPER, LOYALTY & REWARD CO

For an organisation or charity

Do you want to celebrate a major project, applaud your team of volunteers, or record your association's history or colourful contributors? A book can be a great way to inspire and inform people about your charity or get them truly invested in the work of a foundation.

As an example, *Heartbreak in the Himalayas* by Dr Ray Hodgson is a self-published book that does this wonderfully, illuminating the challenges of health care in Nepal and connecting with hearts and minds to drive the donations Ray and his team at Australians for Women's Health need to fund necessary services.

Curiosity

Writing a non-fiction book is a great way to follow your curiosity, as you'll be doing reams of research on a topic that fascinates you.

When you write a book on a subject that gives you tingles, you won't leave any stone unturned in your pursuit of it. How often in life do we get a chance to potentially earn an income by following our interests, our heart, and head?

Writing a book that piques your interest is immensely pleasurable and it will involve interviewing people and experts who you might never have had access to otherwise.

Penning a curiosity-driven book gives you permission to ask, and try to answer, all your burning questions. Want to know what treatments work best for PTSD? Or which continent has the most caves suitable for diving? Or the leadership principles of Australians working in senior management positions in global tech companies? The answers are there to be found. You'll likely find yourself, too, in the process.

> I was speaking with a university professor friend about my desire to do a PhD on the topic of how to maintain engagement, relevance and reputation through various stages of life and career. My friend, tongue in cheek, advised me I'd be better off writing a book on the subject. And so, the seed for the book took hold.
>
> — GARRY BROWNE, THE PERSONAL BRAND CATALYST AND AUTHOR, *BRAND NEW, BRAND YOU*

Exploring your deep curiosity about a subject also gives you a compelling reason to keep going. Often, when an author is trying to write 'what the market wants', it means their heart isn't necessarily in it, and it's easy to give up. When you're writing because you're fascinated, it gives you a natural spring of energy to tap into so that you can get the job done.

Passion

A deep passion for my kids led me to research and write my second book, which was my first self-published title.

Honeycomb Kids: Big Picture Parenting for a Changing World and to Change the World came out in 2012, receiving a testimonial from Professor Tim Flannery, whose path I would never have expected to cross while I was raising my three kids (and a few hundred animals) on my little patch of farmland in rural New South Wales.

The book was ahead of its time in many ways. It explored hundreds of practical ideas and activities to help kids, their families and local communities become more resilient in the face of likely challenges, including pandemics (COVID was nowhere on the horizon at the time!), climate change, competition for resources, increasing costs of living, social unrest, and plenty more. What drove me to write it was a mix of passion and curiosity. It was information I really wanted to know, and although there were books out there about raising happy and smart kids, there were none about raising kids given the stark realities of the global context.

That's one of the topics I'm passionate about. What about you? Are you passionate about better political and business leadership, or handcrafted lederhosen? The LGBTQI community or unsolved crimes? DIY miniature pony carts or mentoring refugee families? Are you passionate about pain relief, breakdancing, corneas, or capsicums? Depression, yoga, quantum computing, or herbal remedies for queasy tummies?

Find your passion and you have found your book. It will also fuel you to finish it.

To clear your head

One reason I wrote my memoir *Honey Farm Dreaming* was to simply clear my head. I had so many memories swirling around, living rent-free in my brain's hippocampus, that I was running out of space for new opportunities, visitors, information and experiences. I needed to declutter.

I didn't want to just dump them out and completely forget them though; after all, the sad times, heady moments, recipes, plant knowledge and fantastic memories were borne of hard work and happy times. I just didn't want to be lugging them around with me anymore.

The process of writing the book freed me to move on, to commence a new chapter in my life story. I'm so glad I did, and I had a lot of fun in the process. Are you ready to clear your head too?

Prestige

Author. It really does have a ring to it. That's because it's a word that signals a finish line, completion, achievement. Most people who want to write a book, could write a book, 'have a book in them', are 'thinking about writing a book', 'could write a much better book than that', never make it to the end. They don't complete the task.

Not you though.

You know that being an author will in some way complete you. That even if it's not a bestseller, the process of producing it will change you for the better and might even change what people know and think about you.

You know that being an author is a bit like being able to say you summited Everest. Many have dreams of it, some make it to Base Camp, but only a few enjoy the sensation and kudos of hitting the Himalayan heights and eventually relishing the view from the top.

You know that prestige is earned, not given. You're ready to earn it.

For the buzz

You're ready to write this book just for the fun of it. To see if you can do it. It's a challenge you're approaching with optimism and a, 'Well, why not? Why not me?' attitude.

And really, why not!?

I'm getting a buzz right now just from penning these words. There's adrenalin flowing between my fingertips and my soul. It's like the feel-good endorphins I get when I've been out walking or have learnt a little more about the world and my place in it. A natural high.

It's one word at a time, dopamine hit after dopamine hit. And when you've finally finished … bliss. Contentment. So, why not?

Into the unknown

Although most writers have a plan about what they want to achieve by writing a book, some people just write a book because they can't *not* write a book … they get excited about putting something out into the universe and taking that big leap of faith without knowing exactly where or to whom it will lead.

 One intangible value of writing a book is how it transforms you as a person. It impacts your overall life, and brings joy, knowledge, depth and a sense of worth for yourself and other people, too.

— KELLY IRVING, BOOK COACH AND EDITOR

To unlock new opportunities

Yes, writing and publishing a non-fiction book can lead to benefits to your financial and overall wellbeing. It can also lead to new ideas for further books and products, paid articles in other publications, job and consulting offers and jaunts. It may even bring you fame, if that's your thing, or lead to traditional publishing deals and media opportunities.

But if you don't write that book, you'll never know what opportunities await.

To practise writing

What better way to get better at writing than to write?

Writing a book is exercise, not just for your fingers, but also for your mind. The more you write, the more you learn how to achieve word and mental flow. Invariably, you read other people's work during your research. By reading more, whether it be articles or other non-fiction books, you'll absorb different styles of writing and technical knowledge relating to grammar, spelling, punctuation and how to bring information to life. You'll also become a better writer through the process of working with your editor.

You're practical and left-brain led

Not every writer has an imagination that conjures up fairies in skyscrapers, serial-killing kindergarten teachers, and seahorse-led invasions of luxury underwater hotel suites. Leave that to the fiction writers. Stop fighting your practicality and use it to your advantage. Write non-fiction, you can always try fiction later.

Because it matters

Here's the biggie: your words can change a life. It might only be your life you change, but it might also be the lives of countless others. If you reach just one person, and either motivate, inspire, inform, educate, protect, or engage them, you have left a mark, made an impact, created a legacy.

Make it a good one.

Take a moment right now to think about your motivation for writing your book. Write your reasoning down. And then stick it up high somewhere where you will see it regularly. It will ground and inspire you when your energy wanes.

However, while there are loads of great reasons to write a non-fiction book, there are also some reasons not to go down that road.

WHY NOT TO WRITE A NON-FICTION BOOK

It would be better as fiction

Some memoirs are written as fiction to allow authors to spice things up without fear of boring readers to death, feeling too exposed, or being sued. It allows you to use some core truths from your experience, while giving readers a potentially more enjoyable or entertaining read and might also help you stay out of court.

In the book *How to be an Author: The Business of Being a Writer in Australia* ©2021 published by Fremantle Press, authors Georgia Richter and Deborah Hunn advise, 'Extra care should be taken when writing narrative non-fiction. You may think you have a premise for a true crime book based on a story you have heard around town. You'll need more solid evidence than pub and online gossip to avoid a defamation case. Is real evidence there? How will you go about uncovering it? Do you have the skills and resources to do so? Before you get in too deep, ask whether you should instead turn this story into crime fiction, altering recognisable details with creative touches.'

Or, if you have an inspirational or instructional message, it might be more effectively written as a 'parable', rather than as a straight directive. Examples of books like these include *Who Moved My Cheese* by Spencer Johnson and *The Celestine Prophecy* by James Redfield, the latter of which, interestingly, was originally self-published. It was only after Redfield had sold more than 100,000 copies out of the boot of his car that Warner Books offered him a publishing deal. It has since gone on to sell more than five million copies.

Your subject is too controversial

The ramifications of sharing your views so publicly might lead to career or personal blowback. Though controversy can be a wonderful thing for a book, do you have enough emotional fortitude and support to face a backlash? And if it's controversial, is it because it spreads hate speech or vitriol? If so, maybe line up therapy before you line up a printer.

You've neither the time nor headspace

We've all been there. But if you can find time for social media or TV, you do have the snatches of time you need to start and keep writing your book. You don't need to do a Tolstoy and pen north of half a million words. Your book doesn't need to even be 20,000 words if it delivers what the reader needs. Writing a book can be done in manageable chunks, one word at a time.

You can't afford to

It doesn't cost anything to write except your time. By the end of this book, you'll also have learnt how to keep publishing costs to a minimum, even potentially crowdfunding your book. So, the question you really need to ask is: 'Can I afford not to write it?'

Your heart is not in it

Some people do things in life because they think it is expected of them, or because they see others doing it and think it means they must do it too. If this is you, here's a timely reminder: life is way too short and the book writing process way too long to bother. Do something else with your time.

You 'can't' write

'We're not all Willie Shakes,' says my daughter, referring to the penner of *A Midsummer Night's Dream*, *Hamlet*, and *Othello*. And—newsflash—we don't need to be. Identify your weaknesses, then work out a way to make the most of your strengths. Improve your writing through practice, courses and working with editors. Write your book by chatting out loud into a voice recorder, or work with a ghostwriter. Can't write? Collaborate.

 I remember getting a phone call from the editor who basically said, 'It looks like it's been written by a dyslexic, heroin-addicted chimpanzee ... but your content is fantastic. We can fix bad writing, but we can't create content'.

— ANDREW GRIFFITHS, BOOK WRITING COACH, AUTHOR
AND SPEAKER

Another format may be better

Your book idea might be better as an article, podcast, blog, presentation, course, masterclass, documentary, TV or radio segment, YouTube channel, reality TV show, App or virtual reality set up in the Metaverse. Of course, you can always pursue these in addition to your book, but perhaps the book format is not needed at all.

For example, if you are trying to help people on the road to fitness, are they best served by a 300-page book, or a weekly online program, or app, or all three?

Years ago, my daughter ran sweaty and puffing into the house, 'Are you okay?' I asked. Her reply: 'I'm being chased by zombies!'

That's how I came to learn about the *Zombies, Run!* app which has multiple seasons and more than 300 episodes/missions. Its immersive storyline is written by British authors, including Naomi Alderman and Rebecca Levene, with guest contributions from writers including Margaret Atwood.

Mobile-based, it's classed as an 'exergame' in the mobile health category, and is an extraordinarily high grossing Health & Fitness app. It is interval training with a fun twist. Would it have worked as a non-fiction fitness book? No. So ... might your book be better if it wasn't a book at all?

Whatever you decide, writing a non-fiction book is rewarding in more ways than one. And once you've made a commitment to yourself that you're going to get it done, the next big question to tackle is: what to write. But let's start with a case study, to see what a commitment to self-publishing in Australia can achieve.

~

INSIDE ADVICE: KIM MCCOSKER
SELF-PUBLISHER, *4 INGREDIENTS*

Kim has self-published more than 40 titles since 2006, and more under license to other organisations. Her publishing enterprise has sold more than 9 million copies!

Why self-publishing?

I thought I had a great idea for a cookbook and that publishers would say 'sign here', but no, not one publisher would take my call. I wasn't famous, I had no following, no culinary expertise, and at the time, it was all about Nigella, and Jamie Oliver, and intricate recipes like asparagus custard made with 15 ingredients. My ideas about simplicity in the kitchen were very contrarian.

I was devastated and bewildered by all the rejections, but I believed the whole world was busy, that this cookbook would revolutionise people's lives by saving them money, time and anxiety in the kitchen. So, I googled 'What does self-publishing involve?' Looking back, I'm so bloody thankful no one signed me because I've kept the IP and the lion's share of the profits.

How did you begin?

I had a degree in international finance, so I sat down and ran the numbers. With no distribution network, I knew I needed to invest in a website, as well as pay for strategic advice from accountants and solicitors, as I didn't want someone choking on my chicken pie and suing me! In the end I worked out it would be $26,000 to get all that done, as well as to produce and print 2,000 copies. The numbers showed I needed to recoup $36,000 gross to cover it all. My husband said, 'go for it', and so I pulled the money from our mortgage. Having the mortgage hanging over me motivated me no end to make the book a success, and I became a marketing machine overnight.

In 2007, *4 Ingredients* was the biggest selling book in Australia, and every publisher started knocking on my door, but by then I knew the financial pie chart and understood the cost to create, print, market and warehouse the books. Even their best deals came nowhere close to making it worth my while. As my brand expanded with new titles, I became a publishing force in my own right.

In 2009 though, we were starting to get international enquiries, and I realised I couldn't replicate my marketing and distribution in the northern hemisphere and needed to align with an international publisher. I went to the Australian ones I liked the most and said, 'I'm tendering for an opportunity to work with you because I want eyeballs from overseas'. I did a joint-venture deal (not a traditional publishing deal) with Simon & Schuster Australia, and signed a seven-book deal with Simon and Schuster USA in 2011. What I learned is that if you can attract sales here, it will be noticed elsewhere, but I also learned that you don't need to give up your IP to have a mutually beneficial relationship with the industry.

What are some strategies that have worked for you?

Turning up. In 2007 and 2008 I could have earned an entry in *Guinness World Records* for the greatest number of live book signings. We were doing them during the week and up to two or three on a Saturday. I would always cook beforehand, bringing in a *4 Ingredient* cake or slice, because I knew as soon as someone tasted it, the book sale was a done deal.

Listening to people. The signings were great research, and *4 Ingredients Gluten Free*, another big seller, came about because of customer requests. It's also how I learned to align myself with companies and organisations far bigger than mine. For example, an endorsement from Coeliac Australia, Diabetes Australia, or Thermomix means newsletter exposure, access to expos and sudden access with a huge megaphone to various target audiences.

A focus on my ideal reader. I always ask myself: what will resonate with my target market? How will they receive it? Will they love it?

Rights retention. I've retained 100% ownership of every image, recipe, video, blog and asset. Even when I've sold recipes and images to publications and grocery chains, it's never outright or exclusive. I can still use the recipe or image for other purposes, just not for direct competitors.

What are some of your top tips for other self-publishers?

Social media. Before you write another word of your manuscript, go and create your social media sites. Immediately start sharing your story, a picture of you and where you're writing and what you're drawing inspiration from. That's the journey, the trust people will buy into. Then, when your product comes into being, your following already knows, loves and trusts you. By building your own following, you'll have an immediate market.

Nothing comes from inertia. Even on down days when no one's taking your call, dust yourself off. Keep sending out emails and media releases, keep reminding people of the benefits, and why your story's good. Create momentum.

No one knows your product better than you. It's easy to hire a PR, marketing, or digital agency, but the more you can learn to do and control yourself, the better. We didn't have the funds to outsource marketing at the start, and so had to learn about it from scratch, and it became the greatest gift. Now we have a brand manager and also hire younger, smarter people who teach us their skillsets. Upskilling makes you more knowledgeable and useful; you need to be constantly looking to improve.

If you find a great team, stick with them. I've had two photographers shoot all my 36 colour titles; familiarity makes for speed and fluidity. I work with a designer based in Auckland over Skype, so if you find a great talent, it doesn't matter where they are in Australia or across the world, technology makes it possible.

What are you most proud of?

Being able to build a brand and products that are trusted and loved, working with my family. I also love that the books are becoming intergenerational, so that the 12 year old girl who learned to cook from my children's cookbook in 2008 is now a mum with her own child buying the latest edition of that book for her daughter or the new *Keto Air Fryer Cookbook* that back then, we couldn't even have imagined would be a thing! That book, which was published in 2021 was my biggest first print run ever; 70,000 copies just for starters!

What's the best piece of advice you received from another writer?

I wrote my fourth book with Deepak Chopra. When we met at the Hyatt in Sydney, he said 'The fastest way to happiness, Kim, is to make others happy.' Since then, I've always tried to help others whenever I can. Give, and it will come back to you.

2

WHAT TO WRITE

W hat ingredients will you use to create your masterpiece? You might already know exactly what to write, or have even written your first draft, but if you haven't begun, are second-guessing your original idea or struggling with momentum, let's run through some basics to help you get cooking!

TYPES OF NON-FICTION

Begin with a visit to your local library, or a real-world or virtual bookshop. Walk the non-fiction aisles with your eyes, allowing your pupils to be the pupils as you take in the diversity of works. You'll see that most non-fiction books fall into one of the following categories:

- how-to: instructive books such as how to build a chicken coop, how to invest in real estate, how to plan a wake, etc.
- biography and memoir: my year or life as a monk/influencer/child of hobbits/politician/sex worker/death doula/actress/refugee/plastic surgeon to the stars/country kid/activist/anarchist/canteen coordinator, etc.
- lifestyle: books on cooking, travel, diet, health, gardening, home décor, etc.
- self-help: to do with relationships, parenting, dating, careers, etc.

- business/professional: thought leadership, business principles, entrepreneurship and more
- true crime: from missing persons to murderers, corrupt police to the inner thoughts of inmates
- sport: Australia's greatest captains, the history of female surfers, community sporting sagas and fallen sports heroes
- pop culture: from behind-the-scenes books linked to TV to analysing the politics of reality TV series through to music or movie genres
- religion and spirituality: insights into faith, atheism, agnosticism, world religions and all sorts of spirituality
- observant/analytical: books on current events, history, politics, social and psychological commentary, etc.
- humour: satire, joke books and anything that makes us laugh
- reference and text: historical to scientific, dinosaurs to digestion and everything in between, written for adults and/or children
- art: coffee-table books on subjects ranging from photography and design to coastlines and country homes
- gift: tiny, odd-shaped, cheeky, gimmicky, witty books.

These books can be written in a variety of styles.

- Plain English: The dog was a pug.
- Scientific: The Canis familiaris, of the family Canidae, exhibited typical brachycephalic features.
- Literary/creative non-fiction: Its muzzle, accordioned like a horizontal pancake stack, leaked bubbling syrup onto the plush pile.
- Humorous: What do you get when you cross a pug with a hyena–rottweiler–dingo cross? I have no idea, but if it starts to laugh, I'm joining in.

What makes a book unique is not just the subject you choose, but how you choose to write about it, the angles you take and the voice you use. More on that later!

WHERE TO GET YOUR IDEAS

Some writers struggle with too many ideas, others with not enough. Ways to generate ideas include:

- Tap into yourself. Listen to the questions your brain churns over each day. What are you curious about, challenged by, or want to champion? It might be something you're an expert in, or want to become an expert in. It might be something that makes you laugh, or something that changed your life.
- Read, read, read. Whether it's reading books that leave you wanting more, social media posts that intrigue, conference papers, or magazines, you're sure to find a topic that needs more exploration or a different take.
- Listen. Great podcasts present all sorts of new information in compelling ways and often feature cutting-edge ideas and insights. Something you hear might trigger your book idea. Also, listen to people around you—what concerns are they expressing, what is that couple arguing about in the coffee shop, what is your nephew really into right now, what thoughts keep recurring in your own head?
- Walk your way to your big idea. Walking helps clear the mind so fresh thoughts and insights can enter.
- Make notes. We're all living through history, and we're all living through unique day-to-day personal experiences. Keeping a journal is not only great for exercising your writing muscles, but it can capture colour and insights you can make use of in the future.

Whatever way you come to your idea, you'll ideally be absolutely absorbed by your topic to increase the odds of finishing your book ... even after writer's block strikes and the realities of daily life start to bite. Why? Because if you're not driven by and in love with the topic, you may not be able to muster or sustain the effort needed for the marketing push that self-published titles require to get (and stay!) airborne.

Your next challenge then becomes the creation of your own niche around the idea you are fired up about.

Ready for lift off?

Try not to copy others. Find something interesting and original to say and say it well. We should not be chopping down trees, or using endless gigawatts of energy to power vast warehouses of servers, in order to pump out more mediocrity into the world.

— ROD MORRISON, PUBLISHER/EDITOR

FIND YOUR NICHE

If you can find your niche, readers will be able to find you. Here are just a fraction of the non-fiction titles published about Shakespeare: 12 books, each with a completely different take on, or niche built around, the same subject matter.

- *Shakespeare: A Beginner's Guide*
- *Shakespeare's Little Book of Wisdom*
- *A Year in the Life of William Shakespeare: 1599*
- *Playing Shakespeare: An Actor's Guide*
- *Shakespeare's Restless World: A Portrait of an Era in Twenty Objects*
- *As She Likes It: Shakespeare's Unruly Women*
- *A Travel Guide to: Shakespeare's London*
- *Reduced Shakespeare: The Attention-Impaired Reader's Guide to the World's Best Playwright*
- *Will and Me: How Shakespeare Took Over My Life*
- *Shakesqueer: A Queer Companion to the Complete Works of Shakespeare*
- *A Thousand Times More Fair: What Shakespeare's Plays Teach Us About Justice*
- *A Feminist Companion to Shakespeare*

There's some choice there for sure! When thinking about your topic, drill down through the crust and on past the mantle, right to the inner core of what your potential reader is interested in.

I called my book *Small Farm Success Australia* because I wasn't trying to teach the big guys of agriculture how to make hay.

Similarly, this book doesn't try to solve the problems of fiction writers because it's targeting the specific pain points and opportunities for non-fiction writers. And even then, I'm not targeting all non-fiction writers, just those who might self-publish.

> Aspiring non-fiction authors: when you think you have found your niche, think some more. How can you refine the scope of your book to make it irresistible to your ideal reader?

— VIRGINIA LLOYD, PUBLISHING MENTOR AND AUTHOR

If you've found your category, delve deeper. For example:

- advice for victims of defamation ... which occurred in a group chat
- gluten-free meals ... for vegans
- make-up tips ... to create the perfect zombie look
- macrame ... for men
- crafting ... with cat hair (this is a real book!)
- styling ... your toilet ... with succulents
- housewives of ... wildlife rescue
- knitting ... your dog's face on a jumper (this is a real book—my sister bought it to immortalise the family pooch in wool).

RIGHTS

At this stage, before you dive head-on into the writing, consider the issue of legal rights. If you're primarily writing about someone else, you might need to officially secure the rights to your subject's story to obtain their cooperation and also protect you from being sued.

If you are writing your memoir, you won't need rights to your own story, but you will need to understand the personal and legal ramifications of revealing personal information about yourself and others. Seek legal advice even if you plan to tell the story as fiction.

No matter what you decide to write, or how specific it is, bring something fresh to your reader. How do you do that? Start with a plan. That's what the next chapter is all about.

3

CREATE A PLAN

If your aim is to deliver a fantastic book, do what every agent and publisher expects from every not-yet-an-author hoping for publication: create a book proposal. Why? It will become the blueprint from which you centre, plan, write, and market your book.

Think of your proposal as a plan to the who, what, where, how, but most importantly, why of your book.

- Why does your book deserve to exist?
- For whom is it written?
- What problems will it solve for your readers?
- Why are you the right person to write it?

A proposal document will help you to focus and create clarity. It forces you to decide on the content and angle of your book, now, and creates space for you to think about how to make your book 'evergreen', so that it continues to sell well into the future. That is, what approach can you take so that your book won't become out-of-date too fast, or so that it can easily be updated with the release of a new edition? I've had to think a fair bit about that with this book, balancing what information will still be relevant in a few years and so is valuable in print, versus what material would be better updated fresh on my website.

I always recommend authors limit references to contemporary musicians, celebrities or social media memes, because they date very quickly and will make your book seem dated too.

— VIRGINIA LLOYD, PUBLISHING MENTOR AND AUTHOR

Your plan is like a guidebook to your book, something you can pull out and refer to on your journey whenever you feel stuck. Being forced to think deeply about your subject matter before you begin, right down to the nitty-gritty of chapters and their content, gives you a roadmap for your book.

Doing this work upfront saves you from false starts and off-topic forays. Oh, and it is way better to research and write a 3,000-word book proposal than jump headfirst into writing 33,000 words of a book that doesn't deliver what readers want, and so isn't likely to sell.

 Get across other books on the same subject, especially current ones to make sure yours is different. I go and buy every book on my intended subject as I'd prefer to know what's out there rather than plagiarise by accident. It helps you avoid trotting out the same tired ideas and quotes other writers have already used.

— ANDREW GRIFFITHS, BOOK WRITING COACH, AUTHOR
AND SPEAKER

Your book plan becomes a living document, one that you can adapt as you go. However, the bones of it give you the structure and focus needed to complete your book, and complete it well.

Here's the basic structure for your plan, with explanations to follow:

- introduction/overview
- target audience
- about you/the author
- comparison titles
- format and length
- synopsis
- chapter outline and titles
- deadline.

INTRODUCTION/OVERVIEW

Nail the core essence of your book in a summary containing a couple of succinct, punchy paragraphs.

- What's your book about?
- Who does it matter to?
- Why are you the right person to write it?
- How will it achieve its goals?

TARGET AUDIENCE

Often, when authors are asked who their book is aimed at, the reply is 'Everyone'. But since when has 'everyone' been interested in the same thing or liked being spoken to in the same way?

> If you don't want to add to the already bloated world of useless content, ensure your book adds value to your chosen target audience. Understanding their challenges, interests and motivations will significantly impact what you write, how you write it and how much you write.
>
> — JAQUI LANE, THE BOOK ADVISER

Writing your book for everyone might mean you appeal to no one. And you don't want that! So, who might your audience be? The more specific you are, the better. For example:

- Men 65+ ... living with a partner with dementia ... who are feeling hopeless.
- Single women ... with a love of 50s fashion ... who want to make their own clothes ... from recycled fabric.
- Family and friends interested in reminiscing ... about 20 years of annual get-togethers ... at the Crazy Camper Coastal Caravan Park.
- Potential online start-up companies facing a challenge in retaining Gen Z employees working from home ... that they need to fix fast and creatively ... on a small budget.

Military Historians. Snapshot of the start a success of a small military Academy. Stories about the pupils.

- Roller derby participants ... who want to build a bad-ass brand ... and get a sponsor.
- Survivors of bullying ... from a work colleague ... seeking legal and life advice.
- First-year university students ... studying online ... and hating it.
- Australians ... of Sri Lankan heritage ... planning a wedding ... that's cross-cultural.
- Readers interested in Australian true crime ... and the psychological impact on police investigators.

Researching your target audience also helps you quantify the size of the market for your book, and where they currently get their information from, which, in turn, will help with your eventual marketing strategy. In the *Look—It's Your Book! Companion Workbook*, I include an example of the target market I originally prepared for *Small Farm Success Australia*, it might give you some ideas as to how to research your own book's audience potential.

ABOUT YOU/THE AUTHOR

In the end, it's all about the reader, but it's also very much about you. After all, you're the one who must deliver the goods. So, of all the people who could write this book, why you? Of all the books you could write, why this one? And, why are you writing it now?

You can answer the questions above by delving into those below.

- What's your background and expertise?
- What have you written before, if anything?
- What awards have you won? What associations are you a member of?
- What's your unique take? What can you bring to this book that no one else can?
- Why on earth do you want to spend all this time, money and energy writing, and then promoting, this book?
- What are you truly passionate about?
- What platforms do you already have (e.g., a social media presence, a blog, a YouTube channel, etc.)?
- Do you have access to facts, experts and interviewees who will make this book better?

- Do you have any media contacts and experience? What is your level of marketing expertise?

COMPETING TITLES

Now it's time to research your competitors. Competitors are good to have because it proves there's a market for your topic! But there's also such a thing as too much of a good thing if you're not bringing something new to the table.

- What books have been published on the subject in the last 5 years? (See further on for how to find this information.)
- Who wrote them?
- How many have they sold? What is the potential market size? (Yes, a lot of this will depend on topic, size of audience, marketing budget, the zeitgeist and execution at the time.)
- How will your book be different? What new angles or topics will it cover?
- How will it add value for the reader?

There are various ways to research competing titles.

- Check your local library and bookstore and search categories and titles at online bookstores. Read the reviews too, especially the bad ones to see what people felt the book missed.
- Nielsen Bookscan reveals the size of the market for specific categories and titles. You may be able to access it through someone in the industry (such as a distributor) or you will need to pay for each specific book you want data for. Keep in mind this data focuses on bookstore sales only and does not capture direct sales, which makes up the bulk of many self-publishers' sales.
- Keep an eye on the media for articles about the latest sales figures. For example, in a story by Melanie Kembrey in *The Sydney Morning Herald* on 13 April 2021 titled, 'Brittany Higgins signs major book deal after three-way auction', it was revealed that up until that time Julia Gillard's *My Story* (2015) had sold 77,000 copies, Rosie Batty's *A Mother's Story* (2016) had sold close to 50,000 copies (not including ebooks or audiobooks) and Bri Lee's *Eggshell Skull* (2018) had sold 35,000 copies.

FORMAT AND LENGTH

Aim for as many words as it takes to get your information across in an interesting, effective, and entertaining way.

So, are you writing a handy, waterproof, pocket guide to frog identification or an in-depth exposé of academic culture at an elite university? Do your readers want a concise leadership tip, accompanied by a brief case study they can enjoy each day over coffee? Or do they want to be taken on a two-volume, un-put-downable journey into your escape from a downed plane via camel across the outback into the face of a Category 5 cyclone?

25,000 or 125,000 words? Deciding on the approximate length of your book before you begin writing is important for a few reasons.

- It gives you a sensible word count to aim for. There's simply no reason to write 80,000 words if the audience's expectations based on similar books is only 40,000 words.
- The more words you write, the longer it will take and the more expensive your book will be to edit, proofread, print, bind and ship (case in point, this book! But it took a lot of words to do the subject justice.). I really should have cut a few pages from *Small Farm Success Australia* because it came in at 322 pages and weighed 508 g, pushing it over Australia Post's 500 g threshold and substantially increasing the cost of postage. *Honey Farm Dreaming* came in at 272 pages and 385 g, which allowed me to package it well while remaining below the 500 g threshold.
- If you overwrite, your key messages may be lost in the word jungle.
- However, it has often been said that 'no writing is ever wasted'. A lot of it could be considered research and sometimes you've just got to 'write it all out of your system'. I did that with this book, hitting a peak of 112,000 words before going at it with a chainsaw. I've also made some of the cut-but-useful material available online and in the workbook.

To find out the average length of a book in your category, count the average number of words per page and multiply by the number of pages. Books vary in terms of page and font size, margins and spacing (between lines and letters), so by checking a few books and coming up with an average, you'll get a good idea of what's currently popular in the industry. Overall, though, your word count needs to be driven by what will work best for your target audience.

Also, note whether other books in your category include graphs, tables, illustrations, cartoons or photos. That might be a signal that the expectation is there. Check how many are included so you can decide how closely you want to follow suit. For example, is there one illustration per chapter, or one on every second page?

SYNOPSIS

The synopsis is a more detailed take on your overview. It is more common for fiction manuscripts and really only needed if you're trying to attract a traditional publisher. However, going through the process is a good opportunity to check that you're crystal clear on the essence of your book, and it might be seen as the start of formulating your 'elevator pitch'—that 10-second response to the question 'What's your book about?'—that you're going to need at some point when the marketing begins.

CHAPTER OUTLINE

What information are you going to share and in what order?

By outlining chapters now, you establish the building blocks for your book and since you're doing the thinking upfront you won't waste energy trying to 'write your way' to solutions.

Sure, once you get into writing the book more ideas will pop up and you can add them in, but having a solid outline at the beginning makes your job so much easier. It's like a novice artist joining the dots versus trying to draw freehand—the end result will be closer to the intended outcome if you have a rough outline to follow and only need to fill in the gaps.

~

INSIDE ADVICE: JAQUI LANE, THE BOOK ADVISER
SIX STEPS TO A DETAILED CONTENT OUTLINE

1. List the key elements of what you want to say in dot-point form. You might end up with 10 dot points or 100, but the important

thing is to get what's in your head out of your head and onto a sheet of paper or a computer screen.

2. Keep working on this until you feel you've captured everything you want to cover.

3. Once you have your ideas and concepts down, create a logical order for these thoughts and group them together. These groupings then become chapters.

4. Rework this until you're happy with the order of the chapters and the order of the key ideas within each chapter.

5. Give the chapters headings, and then create sub-headings for the ideas within the chapter. (If this is your first book, especially if it's a business book, try to keep your chapter numbers to around 7 to 10 and work towards a final count of around 30,000 words. You can always flesh it out later with additional case studies and stories.)

6. It might take several attempts to get an outline you're happy with. If you aren't sure, ask a friend or colleague who is familiar with the topic you're writing about.

~

CHAPTER HEADINGS

It's strange that even though we can knock out 45,000 words, when it comes to writing a four- or five-word heading, many writers freeze. However, it's important to get your chapter headings right because prospective readers will scan the Table of Contents (TOC) of your book to help them decide whether to buy it or not. Then, if they buy it, they use your headings to browse, navigate and orientate themselves.

Good chapter headings are accurate about the information that follows, are written in the same voice as the chapter and are similar to your other chapter headings. For example, in a book on natural pet care, you wouldn't have one chapter headed 'Furry Toys to Help Fido Feel Fine' and the next chapter heading 'Canine Thoracic Therapy'.

In this book, I decided to opt for simple headings, whereas in *Honey Farm Dreaming* they were funnier and more evocative, but in keeping with the style of the memoir (e.g., 'Fat Max and the Forty Thieves', 'Farmerceuticals', and 'Reboot Gumboot').

You don't have to come up with the final headings right now—the process of writing might provide inspiration later on—but if you can direct some of your energy towards crafting your headings now, it will also help you to write suitable content under them.

BOOK TITLE AND SUBTITLE SELECTION

Whereas some people know exactly what they want to call their book from the moment they start writing, others (me!) lie awake at night, multiple choices scrolling across scrunched, tired eyeballs.

Great titles sell books. They jump out at readers in bookshops, help readers discover your masterpiece through search engines, are memorable and can be the beginning of a powerful brand. Here are some tips for yours:

- Make it compelling. The title needs to sum up the book's topic in a memorable, punchy way. The subtitle then rounds it out by delivering a promise of what's inside.
- Combine words to evoke emotions in your target audience such as curiosity, compassion, humour, surprise, or desire.
- Keep the title as short as possible so it can easily be read on a book cover on a shelf, or as a thumbnail on a screen.
- Make it relevant to the topic.
- Promise solutions, not just problems.
- Be original. Even though you can't copyright book titles, it doesn't make sense to use a title that's already in the marketplace.
- Find the X factor, something catchy and memorable.
- Create a unique yet adaptable title. This is especially important if you're planning a series of books and want each one to build on your brand. For example, *The Barefoot Investor: The Only Money Guide You Will Ever Need* was followed by *The Barefoot Investor for Families: How to Teach Your Kids the Value of a Buck*.
- Incorporate keywords that customers are actually searching for (more on this below).

Selecting the best of the best

- Don't let ideas get away. Set up a folder, and whenever you come up with a new title idea, add it to your list of possible choices.
- Use a tool like Publisher Rocket to discover the most popular

keywords shoppers are typing into Amazon's search area, how many books are being identified by those keywords, and how much money those books are making. This is a great way to research your international competitors and use the keyword learnings to shape your titles.

- Once you're well into writing your book, brainstorm a list of 5 to 10 possible titles and share them with your first readers and editor for their feedback. My editor Geoff Whyte landed the title for this book very early on!
- Pick the three best choices for title and subtitle and re-run them through a tool like Publisher Rocket.
- Discuss your final three options with your editor, local bookstore owner and librarians to get their input too.

Check if the title is already in use

Do your research. Find out if your preferred title is already in use.

- Run searches on book sites and the internet in general.
- Run the name through ASIC's company name register to ensure it's not the registered business name for someone's company.
- Check trademarks, too, using IP Australia's Australian Trade Mark Search.
- If part of your strategy is to build a brand and other income streams around your book, register the title as a URL.

SET A DEADLINE

Without a deadline, you'll be without a book. Goals give us something to aim for and boost flagging motivation.

Small Farm Success Australia and *Honey Farm Dreaming* both took me about a year from concept to book launch. For this book, I set myself a goal of completing the final draft within 12 months. Just made it!

 Set a deadline and at least two sessions of two hours per week to work on it. More and longer is better, but this is a workable minimum. By doing this you can finish a 30,000-word book in 2 to 3 months. Writing though, like most ventures, takes commitment, consistency and self-discipline, so realistically, it will take most people 4 to 6 months to write a book of about 30,000 words.

— JAQUI LANE, THE BOOK ADVISER

❧

With your plan in hand, you're ready to write. Let's get to it!

4

WRITING TOOLS

You're ready to write or have already started. Fantastic. But what's the best way for you to get those words down? Whatever way you're comfortable, because wrangling new software and going on a steep learning curve takes a huge amount of effort and brainpower and can kill your flow.

If you're happy with pens, paper, sticky notes and manila folders, no problem. If you're familiar with Microsoft Word or Google Docs and don't want to try anything else, that's fine. If you're not much of a writer, but more than happy to talk, perhaps dictation is the way to go.

That said, just like a blender can whip up a smoothie quicker and easier than a potato masher, the right tools in the right hands may dramatically lift your productivity.

DICTATION AND TRANSCRIPTION

No time or desire to write, but happy to talk to yourself? This can be a fantastic way to get words down without a worry about spelling, typing or grammar. Just talk your thoughts through. There are plenty of apps and software for dictation and transcription, including Otter, Rev.com and Temi. You can also use your phone's voice recorder, buy a software package for your computer (such as Dragon), or use the simple *talk to text* function in Microsoft Word or Google Docs' *Voice Dictation*.

INTERVIEW TOOLS

Another great way to get thoughts down on your topic is to have a conversation or question and answer session with a friend, colleague or expert. You can do this in person, on a tool like Zoom, or using apps such as Tape-ACall, or for iPhone users, Just Press Record.

RESEARCH AND ORGANISATIONAL TOOLS

Traditional paper and virtual index cards allow you to lay out pieces of your book such as chapter headings and move them around to see where they best fit. You also won't get bored with a whiteboard or corkboard, but if you don't have room for one, there are virtual alternatives too. Other tools assist with organising bibliographies, citations, research and keeping your research together. Some tools and services to look into include Evernote, Trello, Zotero, ZoteroBib and Trove. The latter is an online resource that allows you to explore a wide variety of Australian archives.

DEDICATED WRITING TOOLS

Want to concentrate on writing? Perhaps stick with a word processing program you already know, such as Microsoft Word or Google Docs. Or, if you have the capacity to learn new software, love the thought of bells and whistles, are not easily overwhelmed and may potentially write a number of books over time, it's worth investigating Atticus and Scrivener. Both these programs offer many useful tools for writers.

> Keep your software simple. Some people buy writing software but don't invest in the time it takes to learn how to use it the right way.
>
> — KELLY IRVING, BOOK COACH AND EDITOR

PRODUCTIVITY TOOLS

Writing productivity suffers every time a text, email, phone call, instant message, social media post or headline interrupts your train of thought.

> It's a myth that you can rebound quickly from distractions. The fact is, it can take up to 15 minutes to restore concentration following a distraction, due to a refractory period in the brain. A temporary shift in attention from one task to another—when an email alert pings, or when someone stops at your desk—increases the amount of time necessary to finish the primary task by as much as 25%. This phenomenon, known as 'switching time', drains our mental energy and makes it harder to get back to the task at hand.
>
> — DR PAIGE WILLIAMS, *BECOMING ANTIFRAGILE*

You can stop distractions by turning off your phone and alerts, and by setting your word processing screen to 'full screen' so you're not tempted by other programs. If your willpower wanes, turn off your WiFi too. There are a number of productivity apps you can trial too including Cold Turkey, FocusMate, Written Kitten and Rescue Time.

Momentum is everything when writing, so track your achievements too as nothing spurs us on more than having wins. Things you can measure include the number of interview requests you've made through to how many hours you worked on the project that week.

Calendar management and appointment scheduling

Plan ahead by blocking out writing time in your diary, and if setting up multiple research interviews, make it easy for people to book appointments with apps such as Calendly, Booklikeaboss, Accuity Scheduling and others.

Virtual Assistants

Don't have the time, head, or heart to wade into admin, research, or marketing tasks? A virtual assistant might be able to help. You can hire a local or international virtual assistant at sites such as Airtasker, Upwork, Fiverr, Guru, Virtualify and FlatPlanet.com.au.

ARTIFICIAL INTELLIGENCE

It sounds like science fiction, but yes, artificial intelligence (AI) is being used to create books and assist with translations. This doesn't mean you can press a button and AI will deliver you a perfectly written book, but it is a fast-moving area that may be of assistance to some authors, though also perhaps a threat. The Alliance of Independent Authors (ALLi) offers current information on AI and indie author champion Joanna Penn often covers it on the Creative Penn podcast.

GHOSTWRITERS

Perhaps you don't have the hours, energy, or skill to craft a book to your desired level of quality or deliver it in the right timeframe. This is where contracting a ghostwriter might help. However, quality ghostwriting does not come cheap. Depending on the subject, degree of complexity and their level of experience, ghostwriters can charge from as little as 25c per word through to $2 per word, plus costs. That means a ghostwritten manuscript of 50,000 words would cost between $12,500 and $100,000+. To find a ghostwriter, ask your network and look at books written by celebrities, politicians and sportspeople (who often thank their ghostwriter in their acknowledgements).

Alternatively, Life Stories Australia is an incorporated association of 'experienced professionals who help individuals, families, communities, organisations and businesses to record and document personal and collective histories'.

~

In this chapter we've looked at some tools and services to assist with your writing, but the trick to completing a book is to actually START writing it. Let's get to that now.

5

WRITE YOUR BOOK

The secret to writing a book is no secret: sit down, or stand tall at your upright desk, and just write. That's right, getting the words down, whether on paper, through dictation, or tapping away on your keyboard, is the only way it will get done. But there are some ways to make the process of writing easier and we'll cover those now.

MAKE TIME TO WRITE

Books don't write themselves, so set aside time to work on yours. Ideally, find decent chunks of time (2 hours or more), 2 to 3 times a week. And, if you can snaffle a half-day or more on a weekend, or a week away in a bungalow, fantastic! But last time I checked, we don't live in a perfect world, and free hours don't grow on trees, so it might mean you need to:

- Get up before everyone else or work on your book when everyone else has gone to bed.
- Grab snatches of time while you're doing other things, such as on your commute, while the kids are participating in their sport, or while you're in the waiting room at the doctor's surgery.
- Give up your favourite TV shows. Binge write your book, rather than binge watch other people's creations. You can always catch

up on what you've missed once you've written your own 'The End'.

- Learn how to use dictation programs, or record on your phone whenever you're out driving. Hands-free, of course.
- Take a few days of annual leave so you can double down on the project and build up some steam.
- Set a deadline for each chapter and post it on the fridge. Goals are a strong motivational tool for many people, and when you commit to them, magic happens.
- Build a regular writing habit and keep at it. But also, be kind to yourself. Sometimes your planned writing time will be nuked by a sick child or a colleague's cry for help. Just make up the time as soon as you can.

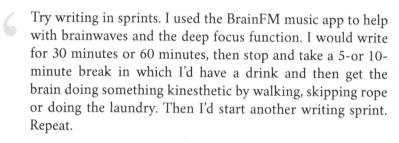

Try writing in sprints. I used the BrainFM music app to help with brainwaves and the deep focus function. I would write for 30 minutes or 60 minutes, then stop and take a 5-or 10-minute break in which I'd have a drink and then get the brain doing something kinesthetic by walking, skipping rope or doing the laundry. Then I'd start another writing sprint. Repeat.

— DR PAIGE WILLIAMS, *BECOMING ANTIFRAGILE*

MOMENTUM MAKES WRITING EASIER

Besides your regular planned writing time, take one step each day toward making your book happen. You could:

- locate experts and send out emails for interview requests
- edit an interview you've already done
- research a key subject
- read or re-read a chapter of this book or another resource for self-publishers
- spend a set amount of time on social media devoted to engaging and learning from others within your specialty
- brainstorm your title.

BACK UP YOUR WORK

Writing is an effort, and you don't want to end up crying into your quinoa or sobbing into your sausage due to technical blunders or IT failures. Avoid them by backing up your work, frequently, regularly, and fastidiously.

As part of this process, settle on a file-naming system so you can keep track of your latest draft. As an example, *Book Draft March 18 2024* is better than simply *Book Draft 3*.

SACRED WRITING SPACE

Sometimes we tell ourselves lies. Big. Fat. Lies. Lies such as, 'If only I had the perfect computer, the perfect chair, the perfect desk, a quiet corner, no job, no bills, a separate office, a quiet family ... then I'd be able to write.' The truth is, even though any of these scenarios would be amazing, you might have all of them and still not write. What you really need to do is just write.

So, where to get those words down? Though it might be ideal, you don't need a perfect space to write.

I've written this book with my laptop plonked on top of scattered pieces of my mum's 1,000 piece work-in-progress jigsaw puzzle; sitting in a chair at the local library (exposed to everyone visiting the biography aisle with a librarian leading a children's sing-along in the background); and on a picnic rug under a eucalyptus tree on the grounds of the Koala Hospital.

I've written it sitting on a shaded park bench overlooking the Pacific Ocean while buffeted by 50 km/h gusts; with my laptop propped up against the steering wheel while waiting at school pickup; and in bed (in fact, I typed these words into my phone when I woke at 2 am one morning and couldn't get back to sleep until they were out of my head).

Ideal? No. Do-able? Absolutely.

Not one perfect space did I have, and you might not have access to one either. But don't let that stop you. Don't let everything not being perfect serve as an excuse.

Make a space in your head, wherever you are, and work from there.

REFER TO YOUR OUTLINE

All that time you spent planning your outline, chapter headings and key points when you were writing your book proposal will pay off big time now. Regularly refer to your outline to keep you moving forward. What?!

You didn't bother? Believe me, it's not worth missing this step. Head back to Chapter 3 right now and get that proposal written—the words come much easier when you're merely adding flesh to an existing skeleton.

SET YOUR WORD COUNT GOALS ... OR NOT

Some people love to hold themselves accountable and get good results from setting word count goals for each writing session. They're super-motivated by seeing their word count rise. However, relying on an ever-rising word count can also be a trap, as most good books are good not because of how many words they contain, but because of the quality of those words.

Your message needs to be succinct, clear and waffle-free. Start lean; you can always add content later, as there are interesting ways of adding stories and supplementary material to a book, but you don't want to dilute the message in the book just so you have a higher word count.

SET YOUR DICTIONARY

Set your dictionary for the audience you're writing for. In Microsoft Word it's easy to do, click on *Review: Language*.

If you're writing primarily for an Australian audience, click on and select *UK* or *AUS* as your default. If you're targeting mostly US readers and don't want your colors to be colours and your organized to be improperly organised, click on *US*.

If you didn't select the correct default when you began writing, just *Select All* of the text in your document, go to *Review: Language* and click on the one you want. Note: This won't magically change the spelling, but you can then run the spellcheck to fix things.

WRITE, DON'T EDIT

Self-editing as you write is like yanking the handbrake on when you're driving up a steep hill: it's not going to get you anywhere fast.

In your first draft, not every sentence needs to be perfect, nor every comma conventional, and finding a better (more advantageous, superior, suitable, effective, worthier) word using a thesaurus can come later.

What you're looking for in your first draft is 'flow'. You want your brain and heart to be free to unleash and unload onto the page.

Leave the editing till later; for now, just write.

FIND YOUR VOICE

The way you write, also known as your 'voice', is as unique to you as your fingerprint. Sometimes it may take a few chapters before you find your natural style and then it will come much easier.

Write from an authentic place, not thinking about how others will react or what you think they think of you.

 One of the qualities of great writing: the author feels like they are inside your (the reader's) head. How can you achieve that most connecting of qualities in the words you write? It's about empathy and honesty. Being willing to share what is close to your heart and the knowledge of what troubles we humans share.

— KATH WALTERS, BOOK COACH

WRITER'S BLOCK

Words don't always come easy, and you may have to force them at first, but if you keep at it, you'll eventually unplug the dam. 'Writer's block' can also just be another name for fear, which leads to procrastination and blockages in all walks of life.

When you truly can't bear to write, use your normal writing time to work on other aspects of your book, such as research or your marketing plan. Don't let those precious hours go to waste.

Whenever you can, though, always aim for momentum. Even 15 minutes a day spent on your book is better than nothing.

One sentence will lead to another, and those sentences will ultimately lead to your finished book.

 Procrastination and self-doubt lead us to playing small. To give yourself the freedom to be who you are as you write, instead of comparing yourself to others who have gone before you, write out this sentence and place it on your wall or on your computer, in plain sight: 'This book is about the world of <theme or topic> according to <your name>'.

— BEV RYAN, BOOK COACH, SMART WOMEN PUBLISH

MINDSET

In Dr Paige Williams' self-published book *Becoming AntiFragile*, she wasn't specifically writing for authors, but I found three areas that resonated with me as a writer.

Hope: 'Researchers have found that hope plays a central role in driving persistence, motivation, goal setting, and innovation. In fact, a meta-analysis has found that, all other things being equal, hope leads to a 14% increase in productivity by making people feel more engaged and enthusiastic about work.'

Intention: 'Intentionally set and focus on your goals. When you do, your brain will filter and focus incoming information in such a way as to help you achieve them—almost without trying!'

Courage: 'You need courage. Take a bigger, braver view on the impact you could have in your world and the world at large.'

Hope. Intention. Courage. Give yourself the gift of all three!

> Make all decisions about your book from the mindset of the capable, accomplished person you want to be seen as (and have been in the past, many times), then step into that mindset when you work on your book.
>
> — BEV RYAN, BOOK COACH, SMART WOMEN PUBLISH

I've found my books really get off the ground and I commit to them when I've put enough research and thought into the book proposal—and still have the energy and desire to write it. I then verbalise what I'm doing, and tell my husband, kids, and sister, 'I'm going to write a book about ...'

Next, I focus on achieving small things, like putting subheadings under different chapter headings, jotting down research and adding a paragraph here and there. I bring my focus right down to the small things I can achieve, rather than being overwhelmed by how massive and crazy the project is. (With this book, at about the halfway mark, I had to really fight not to be overwhelmed by the scope of it, and the fact that I was writing for writers.)

I know I'm really on my way when I start reaching out to people for interviews, because I certainly don't want to waste anyone else's time and energy. Once those interviews start, there's no turning back. I feel compelled to deliver because I owe it to other people. I feel accountable, and feeling accountable keeps me moving forward.

~

INSIDE ADVICE: JAQUI LANE, THE BOOK ADVISER
THE MINDSET THAT WILL GET YOU TO THE FINISH LINE

Purpose

You have a clear purpose in writing your book and can clearly articulate it.

Focus

You know or are willing to take a deep dive into discovering precisely who your target audience is, what their challenges are and how your specific knowledge/insight will help them with their challenges.

Discipline

You are committed to allocating the time needed to plan, write, learn and action (or delegate) the critical tasks to take your writing through the production and marketing stages.

Commitment

You understand that this is a long game and that your book is a key tool you can use to share and leverage your knowledge over time with hundreds or thousands of people.

Energy

Your book will require a consistent and persistent application of your energy. This energy needs to see you through the writing, production, and marketing of your book over two years (or more) … it's about stamina.

Passion

Your book is the manifestation of your knowledge and insights, probably built up over many years, if not decades. Be honest with yourself. Do you like playing with the idea of writing a book much like a puppy plays with a slipper, or are you serious about sharing your passion and knowledge?

Accountability

You take action, rather than continually finding reasons why it's not the right time. Research from the US has found that over 80% of business leaders want to write a book, yet only 1% get around to it. Which group are you in?

~

But you know what? You don't have to write this book all alone. So much collaboration goes into bringing a book to market, and it starts with finding experts to interview who will enrich both you and your book.

6

INTERVIEW EXPERTS

U nless you're writing a memoir, you'll likely need to interview, use research by, or quote other experts. Even if you're writing a business book based on your own experiences, or you're a photographer or artist showcasing your works and creative process, there'll be someone who can add further value to your readers.

Why interview experts for your book?

Experts are mega-interesting and likely know more than you, or at least enhance how you frame things. They can be incredibly generous with their time and knowledge, and it's not only your readers who will benefit from that (through interesting insights, facts and angles that will help them understand the topic better)—the expert will likely also benefit in some way, such as through exposure.

It also means you won't need to come up with the entire 60,000 words yourself, hooray! I mean, imagine trying to write or read this book without all the great contributions from others? Thank you, experts!

How to approach experts

Send a short email with a polite interview request. Briefly mention what your book is about, why you are writing it, why you want to interview them, and on what specific topic.

Include an example of the questions you'd like to ask and let them know you're happy for them to either email their responses or set up a time for a phone, Zoom, or in-person interview. Include a deadline in the email so they know how long they have to get back to you.

What if they say 'no'?

Thank them for their time and, depending on their response, perhaps ask if they could recommend an alternative expert. If not, just get on with it—research an alternative expert and reach out afresh.

How do I prepare for the interview?

Start by reading up on the Media Arts and Entertainment Alliance's (MEAA) Code of Ethics. Even if you're not a journalist, use these principles to guide your interviews and the writing up of them.

Next, read up on your interviewee so you are well prepared and then draft the interview questions to elicit responses to enhance your content.

Be clear on the information you are seeking; however, when interviewing (if not via email), leave plenty of silence so they can add extra colour to their answer. It's often in an interviewee's afterthoughts that you get the gems. Also, plan how you will record the interview using your phone, an app, Zoom or other method.

 With research, it's easy to go down never-ending rabbit holes. Determine your research goals at the start and then discipline yourself to stop when you've found the information you need.

— VALERIE KHOO, THE AUSTRALIAN WRITERS' CENTRE

How do I to find experts?

The task of finding experts is a common challenge for non-fiction writers and also a hurdle regularly faced by journalists who often have even tighter deadlines. Thanks to Rachel Smith of Rachel's List for granting permission to reprint *The Ultimate Writer's Guide to Finding Expert Sources* here.

~

INSIDE ADVICE: RACHEL SMITH
FOUNDER, RACHEL'S LIST

Ask your own network

If you don't have a file of useful network contacts to call on, you need to create one. My own database is a treasure trove of decades' worth of medical experts, psychologists, public relations contacts who have sizeable client lists, media contacts at major industry organisations, businesspeople, authors, chefs ... and more. It is essentially a freelancer's little black book, and it can be a massive time-saver if you write on the same topics or need to tap into an expert source quickly.

Universities

Most universities have great media departments that can put you in touch with academics. Either browse through the university's website to find the expert you need, or email the media department and ask them to facilitate an interview with a relevant academic.

Facebook

Facebook can be good for finding experts, but I find it better for tracking down random case studies. I have used Facebook to find female tradies, puppy owners, fans of blue-light glasses, psychologists who treat tweens, mental health sufferers in high-stress industries, and many more. Your personal networks will often share if they know the right people. Facebook is also a bottomless pit of specialty groups on everything from disgruntled corgi owners to parents dealing with fussy eating. Always ask the group admins if it's okay to post a request for experts or case studies before you proceed, though.

Google News

Typing 'mushroom experts' or 'addiction experts' into Google's main browser may bring up experts to contact, but Google News can help you find recent articles about the topic and the types of experts and case studies that have been used by other writers. While I'm not suggesting you reach out to exactly the same experts, it can give you some ideas about where you might locate similar types of experts to target for your book.

Google Scholar

If your book involves scientific or health/medical writing, this can be a great source for finding high-level experts or academics, or recent papers published on the topic you're writing about. You can then track down the authors of those papers at their academic institutions to see if they could be potential expert sources for you.

Help a Reporter Out (HARO)

You register here as a journalist and do a call-out for a specific source. Once you get approved by the HARO team, sources come straight to your inbox. I haven't used HARO myself, as my work is mainly for Australian clients, but I imagine this would be very useful if you need to source any US-based experts.

LinkedIn

LinkedIn is crammed with experts of all kinds, many desperate for media mentions—what better place to tap into them? You can pop a post out via your profile or trawl industry groups to see if you can find someone specific to target.

Industry associations

Sometimes finding good industry sources requires a little legwork with industry associations. There are associations for every interest imaginable, from astronomy to zoology, podiatry to project management. If you often write on similar topics or in the same niches, it's a good idea to take note of the media contacts at the organisations you'll use regularly.

Media Diversity Australia

This is a nationwide, not-for-profit directory compiled to help writers access diverse multicultural talent and voices for interviews.

Media Stable

Here you'll find a directory of media-friendly Australian experts, ranging from engineers to nutritionists, dating to leadership.

Gage

Formerly known as Request A Woman Scientist and founded by 500 Women Scientists, this is a global search platform for finding women and gender minorities in STEMM. It is committed to fostering greater diversity and inclusivity in terms of the STEMM voices featured in news stories and on conference panels and boards. They also have a great resources section packed with links to various databases and platforms that will help you get in touch with women scientists and scientists from under-represented backgrounds.

SourceBottle

This useful tool was started by veteran PR professional Bec Derrington many years ago and can be invaluable for finding experts and case studies FAST. Be warned, though, since this site pairs writers with sources who are seeking publicity, call-outs on some topics can also result in your inbox being clogged with irrelevant responses and offers from people suggesting new story leads that may not be at all relevant to your book. If you can find the gold amongst all of this, you'll be one big step closer to finding your expert.

Telum Media Alert

Use this service to reach thousands of sources across the Asia Pacific region.

TravMedia

If your book is about travel or hospitality, you can send out an alert on TravMedia to be contacted by PRs around the globe with clients in the places you plan to cover.

Twitter

Twitter can be brilliant for finding sources—you simply tweet out the type of expert you're after and how potential sources can contact you. Including the right hashtags (basically the subject matter with a '#' in front of it) and encouraging other writers and journos to retweet you by asking for their assistance can help extend the reach of your tweet and get you closer to finding your expert. It's also a great place to build relationships with experts in your niche.

~

What do I do with their answers?

I loved interviewing people for this book and found it difficult (because it felt disloyal) to edit some hour-long interviews down to just one or two sentences. But as the book took shape, I just had to do what I thought was best for readers. It's about finding the nuggets of wisdom and information in responses to enhance the book. Once you are close to final draft stage, you then seek permission to use the quotes in their final format and Chapter 16 details how to do this.

~

But want to know who else besides your interviewees can help you get this party started? And who you might need to turn your fears into fearlessness and your lack of knowledge into confident competence? There are plenty of leads in the next chapter.

7

HELPING HANDS

T here's a myth about writers only achieving something if they're locked away in a garret with no external assistance, stimulation, or distractions. And seriously, how yawningly boring. The truth is, throughout the process of writing and publishing a book, we writers need all the helping hands we can get.

 I wish I'd known the value of a mentor. Though the value of working alone is you can develop without group think, and many of us introverts aren't used to consulting others, getting someone to look at your work early is important. My books would have been better minus thousands of words, and I should have written in essay form rather than newspapery-reportage, but I never asked, and no one told me.

— PAUL DAFFEY, JOURNALIST, TRAD AND INDIE AUTHOR

Here are some organisations, communities and specialists that may give you the heads up and hands up you need.

ALLIANCE OF INDEPENDENT AUTHORS (ALLi)

ALLi's annual membership offers great value. It's a not-for-profit virtual treasure trove of information, resources and advice. You'll find everything from podcasts, guidebooks, and discounts on publishing services to online access to a worldwide community of indie authors happy to share their knowledge. If you want to find your self-publishing tribe, ALLi is the place! It has an active online community full of answers and ideas, and the only downside is that due to the amount of information, it can sometimes feel a bit like floating under the floodgates at Warragamba Dam with your mouth open.

There are so many benefits to being part of an online community including the connection it provides with other writers who are going through similar experiences to yourself. If you're having a tough day or have a burning question that you need to ask, an answer can just be an online post away. It's a support network at your fingertips.

AUSTRALIAN ORGANISATIONS

The following organisations offer a range of services, from FAQs on publishing to links to legal advice, networking events to courses on writing craft, advocacy and industry discounts for members: the Australian Society of Authors (ASA), Australian Writers' Guild, Writing NSW, Writing WA, Northern Territory Writers' Centre, Queensland Writers' Centre, Writers SA, Writers Victoria and TasWriters. There is also the Australian Writers' Guild (AWG) and the Fellowship of Australian Writers (FAW).

On the publishing side, there is The Small Press Network (SPN) and the Australian Publishers Association (APA).

BOOKS, PODCASTS AND WEBSITES

Want to write a great book? Read great books. Want to know the latest on writing and publishing? Tune into podcasts. Podcasts can inform and inspire and are a fantastic way to learn about book marketing techniques. Find one that suits your needs and settle in. New ones are popping up all the time, so keep your ear out for recommendations from your writing network and I'll have an updated, recommended list online. We will cover using podcasts as a marketing tool and as a way to leverage your content in Part IV. It's an exciting area to explore!

TAKE A COURSE

Over the years, taking courses has benefitted my writing and self-publishing business immeasurably. It was the encouragement from co-students and Gloria Kempton, the teacher of an online memoir course, that motivated me to improve, finish and publish *Honey Farm Dreaming*. I also built my skills and confidence and made useful writerly connections thanks to the Australian Writers' Centre Freelance Writing Course, easily earning the price of the course back from commissions by publications *The Guardian* and *The Sydney Morning Herald*.

 How do face-to-face and online writing courses compare? Well, some people love hanging out in real life. Others love the convenience of online. In our courses, the same course materials are covered regardless of delivery, but I think the benefit of online is that you can revisit the materials in case you need to revise a particular topic or writing technique.

— VALERIE KHOO, AUSTRALIAN WRITERS' CENTRE

Personally, I really like doing courses that mix theory with practical writing assignments, especially ones that offer teacher and peer feedback. I like them because I leave with words on the page. And those words turn into opportunities.

My very first traditionally published book came about because of a course too. I was living and working on Heron Island, doing a writing course by correspondence at night, and the very last assignment was to produce a book proposal for a real publisher. I sent it away and the timing must have been just right because a month later the helicopter dropped back the mail and in it was a book contract and an offer of an advance for *How to Get a Job in Hotels and Resorts*. It went on to sell thousands of copies! So, thumbs up to courses.

I've listed some course providers on my site, let me know your favourites too so I can add them.

GRANTS, FELLOWSHIPS AND RESIDENCIES

Yes, there is funding out there for writers. It may enable you to hire an editor, sequester yourself at Varuna (The National Writers' House), or be a paid 'writer in residence'. You can even get export grant assistance for marketing your works overseas. Unfortunately, there is lots of competition and the art of applying for and fulfilling the requirements requires more writing—in the form of form-filling, justifying and meeting milestones. But for the right book, and the right author, it can be the break you need. If nothing else, the application process makes you think more deeply about what you are doing and why, and the unique talents you bring.

GET EARLY FEEDBACK WITH A MANUSCRIPT ASSESSMENT

Though you can certainly seek early advice on your manuscript from your writing community—and it's a great idea to do so—it might also be wise to get a professional to look at your first or second draft.

A manuscript assessment, also known as an appraisal, is by no means a necessity, but it can focus your thinking and help you take your early draft to the next level. You can also use the process to get 'unstuck'.

Manuscript assessors (who might also be editors) are entirely objective. They don't need to stay in your 'good books' or see you the next night at a party, so they can tell it like it is. Prepare for a nice slice of frank and fearless advice.

Manuscript appraisal services take a helicopter view of your work and are offered by a variety of individuals and organisations. They tend to focus on the strengths and weaknesses of your manuscript, including structure, voice, content, and any glaring errors.

I've had hits and misses with manuscript appraisal services. Some have offered incredibly detailed and useful feedback, while one sent back a few paragraphs along the lines of 'This is great, loved it', but offered no useful advice on ways to improve the manuscript.

I'd recommend anyone looking for a manuscript assessment confirm the prospective assessor's experience with your genre before proceeding. Someone who edits fantasy fiction will not be the best editor of your memoir. Similarly, clarify the level of detailed feedback you will receive on your manuscript. You will need a constructive response that will help you maximise the effectiveness of your message, make you think about how your material could be reorganised, or split up into shorter chapters; even suggest what might be missing that would increase the appeal of your work to your ideal reader.

— VIRGINIA LLOYD, PUBLISHING MENTOR AND AUTHOR

For a manuscript of between 20,000 and 80,000 words, your investment for an appraisal might range from $400 to $1,400 as you need to pay the reviewer for the time it takes them to read your manuscript, as well as the time they need to think about it, go back over it, pull out examples of where you can do better, and offer further suggestions for improvement.

You can avoid this step if you are a confident writer with access to some good free advice, but if you have the money, the process can help draw out the areas of your manuscript that need more work.

FRIENDS, FAMILY AND CHAMPIONS

It is a fantastic boost to be able to share your author dream and journey with someone who you know will encourage and support you, and perhaps keep you accountable too. This person, or people, may also come in handy when you need to share your manuscript with first readers (there will be more about that part of the editing process in Chapter 9).

We all need someone in our corner. Who might that person be for you?

KEEP WRITING

You've started writing and that's wonderful. But now you need to find it within yourself (perhaps with the external support of a writing buddy or coach) to keep writing. Why? Because in addition to all the reasons you decided to embark on this project in the beginning, you need to finish it to avoid the dreaded Zeigarnik effect.

∽

INSIDE ADVICE: KATH WALTERS
BOOK COACH

You may not have heard of Bluma Zeigarnik, but she knows what is in your head. What's in your head is this: unfinished tasks.

Zeigarnik was a Russian psychologist who noted our brain's obsession with unfinished tasks. They pop into our memory at inopportune times: in the shower is a common one. Mid-Downward Dog. And, sadly, 3am.

This is called the Zeigarnik effect. Unfinished tasks make you feel unsettled, slightly obsessed. But, when we do stuff, snap. We forget the tasks we have done in a jiffy.

It's because we evolved before we learned to write a to-do list. We had to remember.

What does that mean for all those authors who start, but do not finish, their book? It means misery. A life of your brain reminding you to get your book done.

Who else can help bring your manuscript to life? Read on.

8

BOOK DOCTORS AND COACHES

Just as a personal trainer can help you with your fitness program, a book doctor (sometimes also known as a book coach, book consultant, book whisperer, or book doula) can help guide you and your book to publication. Or, not to put too fine a point on it, whip you and your book into shape! Some editors can also fill this role if they are ready, able, and willing to bridge the gap between editing and mentoring.

 My book took about 15 months from concept through to publication. I spent about $18,000 getting it to publishing stage, but if I ever do a second book, I won't need to spend as much on advisers as I now understand the process and know I can do it.

— FIONA BLINCO, *ONLINE MARKETING FOR BABY BOOMERS*

If you struggle with motivation, or if you are highly motivated but find it difficult to get your thoughts organised and onto the page (or just want to do it in the quickest timeframe possible), a book doctor might be an expensive but invaluable guide. A mentor and taskmaster, they're able to hold you accountable and wave both the carrot and the stick to get you to the finish line.

~

INSIDE ADVICE: KELLY IRVING
BOOK COACH AND EDITOR

What kinds of services do you provide?

I help authors get their work to a publishable standard so it meets their business and personal objectives. Often this might involve helping them pitch it to publishers, or it might be getting their book to a stage where it can be self-published using a curated network of mine. My sweet spot is helping people understand and articulate what their book is really about, running it through a commercial lens, and then bringing strategy and structure to it.

How many books have you helped bring to life?

I've worked with hundreds of authors on hundreds of books. In one year alone, I had 24 of my authors from my community publish books, half of which were self-published, and half were picked up by traditional publishers.

What do you see authors struggle with most? Where do they go wrong?

- Being able to articulate what's in their head and get it down on paper. Yet it is easier to work with words when they are on a page, then when they are trapped inside your head.
- The emotional aspect: it's a cliché, but people who have written books talk about how the process of writing was the biggest transformational journey they have undertaken. Especially in non-fiction. This is your life's work, something that's deeply personal, and being able to share that with strangers take guts, and there's a lot of self-doubt involved. The upside of this work is that it will help you level up personally and professionally, but any kind of growth is hard emotionally.
- They don't want to be judged: we've all been on the receiving end of a self-published book that you open and just put straight to one side because it's poorly conceived, written, or produced.

Everyone is petrified of producing one of those books. The emotional turmoil and the inner critic and all the other stuff that comes up is huge. High achievers often struggle the most because they are fearful of getting their book wrong, or it not living up to expectations or standards.

- Fear, discomfort, and lonely writer syndrome: sometimes my coaching sessions are a bit like psychology sessions. People are trusting me by sharing their lives, and I'm a safety net. It's a very intimate process. You don't need to be a good writer to write a good book, but you do need the right systems, structures, and people around you who will kindly provide the brutal truth and help you address your psychological blocks.
- They focus on their needs, rather than their readers' needs: a lot of people talk about writing a non-fiction book to position themselves in their field so they can do things like charge more for speaking gigs. That, for me, is not why you write a book—that is the result of writing a good book. Writing is a thinking process. It helps you to crystallise your ideas and the message you are taking to market. Your book is an opportunity to connect with your audience in a truly authentic and genuine way. It's all about understanding who you serve and delivering something of value to them, not just increasing your speaking fees.

What are the traits of the successful authors you see?

They have good intentions and realistic expectations. Everything comes back to why you are writing the book. If you're going into it for book sales, then realistically you're trying to be a professional writer—that could take years and there are different strategies for that. Most of my clients aren't about making money from individual books—they're investing in something else much bigger and more valuable. What they do have, though, is internal motivation, specific and tangible goals, and more importantly, a service mindset. They also have skin in the game, usually some kind of financial commitment so that they do the work.

What are some tips you have for authors?

- Many readers are astute and time poor. They skim read and can smell bullshit a mile away. But they know when they see value. A great book is not just about what goes into it, but what you leave out. Really identify who your ONE reader is, their specific pain point, and what it is you want them to do or feel as a result of your book. Anything that doesn't relate to or move them on that journey should be left out.

- Define what success means to you. It's easy to say, 'I want to be a bestseller', as anyone can achieve that on Amazon because it's just about strategy and price points in a certain category. But it's a hollow victory. Be more specific about your objectives, such as 'By writing this book I will be able to create a particular course or a presentation.' If you then create that course or presentation, you have ticked off one of your goals AND you can look at selling that course, which will make you multiples back compared to individual book sales.
- Manage your energy, not your time. You will be way more productive after a walk and some fresh air, rather than punishing yourself at your desk for hours rewriting the same paragraph.

Final thoughts?

A book is a platform for your voice—so use it. You don't have to write a book to sell 50,000 copies or start a global movement. We don't all have to have big visions of serving millions of people. Change is really small and it starts with all of us. We need more voices who solve real issues for others: they're the people who should be writing books. Indie publishing is awesome in terms of providing a platform for ordinary people. They are the extraordinary ones.

∽

I hope you're finding this book useful and readable so far. If so, don't thank me, thank the editors and all the people who gave input along the way. Editing makes all the difference to a book, which is why it gets an entire chapter next.

9

EDITING

Wow! What a huge achievement—your first draft is finished. Congrats! Now you can take a breather from creating and move on to culling, rewriting and polishing.

> I'm wrestling with an edit and intend to never have another idea for as long as I live. Ideas are where the trouble begins! The absolute pits! Down with ideas!
>
> — EMILY GALE, AUTHOR

I had to laugh when I saw Emily's tweet, because when you're at the beginning of a rewrite, you sometimes wish you'd never begun writing the book in the first place.

It's easy to be overwhelmed when you realise your first draft still needs so much work, but by approaching it in bite-sized pieces, sentence by sentence, chapter by chapter, you'll get there.

If you're working with a book doctor or paying for assisted publishing, they will take care of some of these processes for you, but for a full self-publisher, you will need to organise and coordinate the process yourself, outsourcing as needed.

Here are some tips to get your second draft underway.

INITIAL SELF-EDIT

1. Take a break

Yes, you and your words have been joined at the hip for who knows how long. You need a break from each other.

> When you've finished, put the manuscript away for a month then come back to it afresh and pressure test it for flaws. There will be many.
>
> — ROD MORRISON, PUBLISHER/EDITOR

Time apart will help you see your words with fresh eyes. You'll be able to break up with them more easily and then knit them back together with better perspective.

And don't feel bad or lazy, you're not abandoning your work by putting it away for a while. You can use this non-writing time to work on all the pre-publishing and marketing activities you need to line up. Oh, yes! And celebrate! By finishing your first draft, you've already achieved so much more than many wannabee writers.

2. Fire up the printer

Something magic happens when we see our words in print rather than on a backlit screen: errors jump off the page, wordy sentences are exposed and new ideas spring forth. There's also something cathartic about using a pen to highlight, delete and add afresh.

3. Talk to yourself ... and listen

When we read aloud, our brain hears things our eyes can't see. You'll be amazed at the unnecessary waffle, the number of clangers needing the chop and how reordering and rewriting a word here or there makes your book so much better.

> I often suggest that writers read their draft out loud using a copy of the manuscript saved in a different typeface from the

one in which they wrote it. This simple change will help you
pay attention to every word you read.

— VIRGINIA LLOYD, PUBLISHING MENTOR AND AUTHOR

4. Go big and then go 'hone'

Read for the big picture and then zero in, thought by thought, line by line,
sentence by sentence to make your work shine. Once you've done this,
you're ready for the next stage of the editing process.

SPELLING AND PUNCTUATION

You'll soon be sharing your manuscript (with first readers, an assessor or
editor) and though you don't need to worry about spelling and punctuation
when getting your first draft onto the page, it's now time to search and
destroy any errors by using the powerful spellcheck and punctuation tools
inbuilt in programs like Word.

THESAURUS

Are there better (more compelling, effective, refined, optimal) words you
can use to bring interest and energy to your work?

A print or online thesaurus might strengthen your work and can alle-
viate your reliance on and repetition of the same old words. That said, clear
writing is always best.

GRAMMAR CHECK

Good grammar would make this sentence better; it would make it bolder,
stronger, fresher; it would improve style and consistency. Unfortunately,
good grammar doesn't come naturally to us all.

Thankfully, there are plenty of tools we can use to tidy things up before
we send our manuscript to a professional editor. Some of the things these
tools can pick up include:

- The use of active versus passive voice. Active language brings
  immediacy, clarity, and energy to the written word. Passive
  language, well, it brings zzz, snore, apathy.

- Tense consistency.
- Issues with singular vs plural.
- Dangling modifiers.

Some grammar tools like Microsoft Word's *Tools and Review/Spelling and Grammar* are free, while others require payment. Examples include Grammarly, ProWritingAid and Hemingway Editor.

I ran my second draft through ProWritingAid and was amazed at the errors it found (gazillions!) and the improvements it suggested for everything from sentence structure to punctuation. It's a powerful tool—a little like getting a full clean and polish at a carwash versus a hose-and-sponge job by a toddler. Using a software program like this also means that rather than getting bogged down fixing the small stuff, your editor can concentrate on adding even more value to your work.

SPACING CHECK

In Microsoft Word, turn on *Show/Hide formatting marks*. This lets you see the formatting (spaces, etc.) behind your manuscript. If you've used double spacing at the end of each sentence (it used to be mandatory, but not anymore), it's easy to fix using the *Edit/Find* and *Replace* tool.

Once you've done as much self-editing as you can, bring in either an editor or your first readers. You can do this in either order depending on what you're trying to achieve.

FIRST READERS/BETA READERS

It's common to feel insecure and nervous about putting your work out there, but feedback will improve it, even if your ego takes a battering.

First readers (also known as beta readers), though no match for a professional, can be a good early sounding board.

Source your beta readers from your professional and writing network, friends who are big readers, and family. However, to avoid useless and even potentially harmful feedback, avoid toxic and jealous types, and anyone so sweet they won't tell you the truth, even if you have lipstick on your teeth and toilet paper trailing from your shoe.

When asking someone to read your work, give them a short list of questions to elicit some useful feedback. Being told 'Yes, I liked it' won't help you improve your work, but honest answers to the following questions will:

- What did you like about the book?
- What did you think was missing?
- Where do you think I can improve?
- Did you want to skip through any parts? Why?

When you receive their feedback, you'll probably feel either elated or deflated, but neither feeling is an excuse to stop work. It's still early days, and there's always something that can be improved. You want this book to be the best it can be, right?!

QUALITY CONTROL

Quality editing leads to an all-round improved reader experience.

 No writer is a master of their craft. Some are more adept than others, but every writer has blind spots, unfortunate peccadilloes, lapses in judgement. The best often make the most heinous mistakes. Some key problems can be poor writing; poor research; sloppy expression; ill-considered ideas; being 'unfit for purpose'; being ignorant of the zeitgeist and the market ... the list goes on! An editor—like any creative producer—ensures that the work is the best it can possibly be so that the author shines on stage.

— ROD MORRISON, PUBLISHER/EDITOR

Successful self-published author Tim Heard puts it plainly: 'Get a good editor. You might think you're a good writer, like I did (after all, I had 30 years of writing experience!), but it's amazing what a good editor can do. There's a big difference between a good draft, a great draft and the final copy, and it's an editor who makes that difference.'

Tim still remembers smarting when his editor asked him not to send his draft manuscript as a single Word document, as it would cause her computer to crash as a result of all the changes she'd need to make using Word's *Track Changes* function. He replied, 'What do you mean? I've never had *Track Changes* crash a computer before', to which she replied, 'But I'll be making thousands of changes'.

He couldn't believe it, thinking there was no way she would be making that many changes. He'd sweated blood over it for months, thought it was in really good shape and that she'd just be tweaking it. 'But I'm glad I kept my mouth shut because when it came back to me, there were literally thousands of changes, and they were really good. It was a great learning experience, and humbling, too. You need a good editor. You need someone else who is skilled and detached.'

> Every piece of text can be improved by someone reading it who is not the writer. An editor brings a fresh eye to the work, and they represent the reader. They can identify and explain what is unclear, what is overwritten, where more information is needed, etc. Understand though that a close, careful edit can take time. The author shouldn't expect a professional edit to be done quickly.

— BERNADETTE FOLEY, PUBLISHER, BROADCAST BOOKS

EDITING SPECIALTIES

The key editor types (though many offer more than one service) are as follows:

- Commissioning editors: these are the gatekeepers at the traditional publishing houses who decide which authors to take on. By backing yourself, you don't need to worry about these!
- Developmental/structural editors: these editors work with you to shape your book, so it stands the best chance of success.
- Copy/line editors: these editors take on a more micro role to ensure that each sentence and word is the best it can be.
- Sensitivity readers: according to Reedsy, 'Sensitivity readers are a subset of beta readers with the express purpose of spotting cultural inaccuracies, representation issues, bias, stereotypes, or problematic language.'
- Proofreaders: proofreaders apply the magnifying glass, checking for everything from spelling errors to irregular spaces to unplanned font changes.

This book came about thanks to a first reader (my long-suffering friend Susie Jones), followed by an early assessment with an editor (Geoff Whyte) with a focus on structural advice. Then, more rewrites later, it headed back to Geoff. More rewrites and then off for a copyedit and proofread (Tina Morganella). But if you find any errors, don't blame them, it's my fault for playing with the text and design right up to the last minute (very naughty and I don't advise it).

~

INSIDE ADVICE: GEOFF WHYTE
FREELANCE EDITOR

Why do writers need editors?

We all reckon we can write, in the sense that we've been doing it since we first picked up a pencil in primary school, but there's a world of difference between writing reports at work, or emails to friends, and writing an entire book that conveys a lot of information in the clearest, most concise manner possible.

The main role of an editor is that of a discerning first reader providing honest, objective feedback in a diplomatic way. Editors can act as muse, mentor, and, sometimes, devil's advocate, working to pin down exactly what you're trying to achieve, identifying any problems, and offering solutions that will enable you to achieve your goals.

What are some things you wish authors knew about the editing process?

A good edit takes time, so if you're working to a deadline, ideally you need to leave your editor plenty of time to work their magic. And don't just assume that once you've sent the manuscript off to your editor, it will come straight back fully formed and ready to publish. There will almost inevitably be some discussion, negotiation, and further work for you to do (and your editor to check again) before everything is in good shape.

What is a common mistake you see non-fiction authors make?

Some people make a New Year's resolution that this is the year they're finally going to write that book and aim to get it done before they return to work after the summer holidays. That's to say, they rush things, and end up with a very patchy manuscript in which that core idea that they've been tinkering with for a while is quickly surrounded by a hastily constructed framework. Unfortunately, this often results in significant omissions, strange detours, or other fundamental problems in the structure of the manuscript, and while an editor can polish your manuscript until it sparkles, they can't spin gold out of thin air.

What other hints and tips do you have for writers?

Read a lot. The best way to learn to write well is to read widely and think about what makes the good books work; see if you can identify what isn't working in less successful books.

Be prepared to revise your work as many times as it takes. Don't think that any of that work is wasted though. It's all part of the process of clarifying your thoughts, and you'll often find that revisions reveal things that you knew were in the back of your mind but hadn't yet crystallised in your thinking. They might also provide the raw material for subsequent books.

~

INSIDE ADVICE: TRICIA DEARBORN
FREELANCE EDITOR

What are some things you wish authors knew about the editing process?

An editor will only make (or suggest) changes when they believe it will improve the quality of the work. That said, the final decision as to whether to make the change is always up to you.

They also won't read the whole manuscript in order to give a quote. (Reading a manuscript can take days, and an editor is not going to do this before they've been hired for the job.) They're more likely to cast an eye over it, to get a sense of the lay of the land, and of any factors that might influence how long the work will take.

What is a common mistake memoir authors make?

A common mistake memoir writers make is trying to cram everything in, without taking the time to consider which events are the most significant. Alternatively, some memoir authors skip over necessary detail, not realising that information in their own heads is filling in the gaps. Some fail to take a step back to consider what is likely to be of most interest to someone who doesn't know them personally.

How can authors make an editor's life easier?

When you contact an editor about your manuscript, let them know what kind of service you're after, if you know, but it's also fine to get the editor's opinion on what service they think might be most useful to you. Tell them your intended audience, your ideal timeline, how long the manuscript is (how many words) and a little bit about what it's about (there's no need to send long descriptions or synopses at this point, as part of an editor's job is assessing the manuscript as if they're a reader and knowing too much about it in advance can interfere with that).

Once you've agreed to work together (don't send a manuscript along for an editor to 'have a look at', with no clear brief or agreed-upon fee), send your manuscript through as a Word file with the font size set to 12 point. Don't use fancy or coloured fonts, or fiddly formatting, or place the text inside text boxes.

Accept that once the manuscript has gone to the editor, it is effectively in quarantine, and (unless there's some matter of urgency) it's best not to contact the editor while they're working on it. Also, resist the urge to tinker with your manuscript while it's being edited. No editor wants to receive a 'revised' version when they're partway through editing the version you sent them to work on.

Expect the editor to charge for their time. If you want to negotiate a payment plan (which many freelance editors will accommodate), do this upfront, rather than after the edited manuscript has been delivered. Pay promptly.

What other hints and tips do you have for writers/self-publishers?

Contact your editor with plenty of time to spare prior to going to print. Some editors will be booked up months in advance. And expect to pay appropriately for a skilled professional's time. The work an editor does can make an enormous difference to your manuscript's quality and readability.

∽

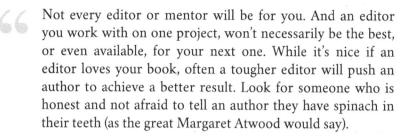

Not every editor or mentor will be for you. And an editor you work with on one project, won't necessarily be the best, or even available, for your next one. While it's nice if an editor loves your book, often a tougher editor will push an author to achieve a better result. Look for someone who is honest and not afraid to tell an author they have spinach in their teeth (as the great Margaret Atwood would say).

— ROD MORRISON, PUBLISHER/EDITOR

WHERE TO FIND AN EDITOR

Track down the right editor for you through the following.

- The Freelance Editors' Network (FEN) is a group of Australian-based editors who offer a range of services including manuscript development, structural editing, copy editing and proofreading.
- The Institute of Professional Editors (IPEd) is the professional association for Australian- and New Zealand-based editors. It has a database of editors that you can search based on your specific requirements.
- Flick to the back of your favourite non-fiction books and zero in on the name of the editor who the author thanks. It's possible they might be an in-house editor at a publishing house, but it's just as likely they're a freelancer. Track down their details and send them an enquiry.
- Reedsy has an international directory of editors that is searchable based on region plus area of specialisation.

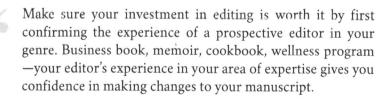

Make sure your investment in editing is worth it by first confirming the experience of a prospective editor in your genre. Business book, memoir, cookbook, wellness program —your editor's experience in your area of expertise gives you confidence in making changes to your manuscript.

— VIRGINIA LLOYD, PUBLISHING MENTOR AND AUTHOR

INSIDE ADVICE: SAMANTHA BRENNAN
SPECIALIST RECIPE EDITOR

What does a trained recipe editor do/look for?

Recipe editing requires a good understanding of cooking, an ability to translate sometimes technical and complex instructions into plain language, a methodical approach to editing and a passion for food.

A trained recipe editor makes sure that the instructions of a recipe are easy to follow, that the accompanying images mirror the ingredients and method of the recipe, that the recipe itself is achievable or aspirational (depending on the audience), and, most importantly, the recipe makes sense and is correct!

Alongside the technical editing, it's also important that a recipe editor work with the recipe developer—and that could be a home economist or a nutritionist, a celebrity chef or a lifestyle blogger, a brand ambassador or a food writer—to make sure the recipes, and the content that frames those recipes, are accurate and reflective of any messaging or creative intentions. We don't need summer salad recipes in books about winter comfort foods, for example!

∼

FILE HYGIENE

Implement some type of filing system so you know which is your latest draft and where it is. There's nothing worse than tidying up a draft only to realise you weren't editing the latest version. Or realising that you, or your editor, deleted something that you now want to reinstate. It's so easy to lose track of edits. So:

- name and date each version
- use the *Track Changes* function in Microsoft Word
- potentially use a shared document in Google Docs so you can view and/or add to each other's changes live
- if editing using two open documents at once, change the font colour in the non-master so you can easily see which one you're altering.

Those who have used similar tools in a corporate environment might already be familiar with tools such as Dropbox, Asana, or Slack that make sharing easy.

STYLE GUIDES

A style guide is a set of standards that set out how to write, format and design documents. It's like a rule book for writers and editors to achieve consistency in the final work. For example, how to treat numbers: written (twelve) or numeric (12); 10 000, 10,000 or ten thousand? How to treat names, including titles of books, such as whether to use *italics* or quotation marks.

Style guides also contain rules about punctuation, citations and end notes.

Following a style guide, or having your editor implement a style guide across your work, gives it consistency and cohesiveness, and improves readability.

Some of the major style guides include:

- Australian Manual of Style (AMOS) published by Biotext Pty Ltd and Macquarie University.
- The Australian Government's Style Manual online only now and the most widely used for Australian government documents.
- Oxford Guide to Style.
- The Chicago Manual of Style followed by many non-government publishers.
- The Australian Style Guide from the Plain English Foundation.

DATA CHECKS

You've checked spelling, spaces and grammar, but how about your data? Pull out your editorial nit comb and go through your information strand by strand. Are names spelled correctly? Are dates and figures spot on? Are the appropriate references cited?

CHECK ALL WEBSITE LINKS, AND FORMAT OR SHORTEN URLS

Triple check all the URLs you've included in your manuscript. Don't just side-eye them, click on each and every one of them to ensure they still lead to the right place. Do this as close as possible to publishing time so they are as current as possible.

Also, if you are planning to sign up for affiliate programs (see Chapter 55), start signing up now so you can include the correct affiliate links.

URLs in ebooks

Links are much easier to include in ebooks than in print books. In ebooks, you embed them behind words, names or phrases using functions such as *Insert link* in Microsoft Word. Readers will be able to click on a link and be taken straight to the appropriate website.

Do not, however, include shop links to Amazon in ebooks you upload to Apple and vice versa as they will be rejected due to linking to a competitor. Layout programs such as Vellum and Atticus, which we discuss in Chapter 19, allow you to set up different links depending on where you will be selling your book.

URLs in print books

URLs in print books look ugly on the page and interrupt the flow of the text. Lengthy URLs are also annoying, if not impossible, for readers to type into their browsers.

That leaves you with some choices to make regarding including URLs in print books. You could do what I have done for this book, which is to provide readers of the paperback with access to a file with all relevant links listed by chapter or subject matter. To do this, include a note at the front of your book about this system and how they can access it. It's not perfect, but does offer a work-around and keeps the paperback clean and easy to read.

Or you could include all the URLs in an Appendix or throughout the book, using a shortened link for each URL. A shortened URL makes it easier on the eye for the reader and saves space. Services that do this include Bitly, Capsulink, TinyURL, Geniuslink and Kutt, which is free and open source.

The only problem with using these services is that the free versions are inflexible, while the professional versions can set you back US$100+ annually for the lifetime of your book. You're also stuck with the same supplier (who could raise their prices over time) because if you change services, it renders the links in your printed book useless. This would create a terrible reader experience for anyone who has bought a copy of your book.

A final option, if you are super tech savvy (and not a mere mortal like me!), is to use a service such as YOURLS to set up and run your own link-shortening service. That may give you the best of both worlds.

In the end, it's not only about the reader's experience, but also about what is workable for you as an author and publisher.

PROOFREADING

Proofreading will be one of the last wands waved over your manuscript. You can use accredited humans for this, as well as paid tools such as PerfectIt, and the reasons why proofreading is so important are covered in this next slice of Inside Advice.

~

INSIDE ADVICE: TINA MORGANELLA
ACCREDITED EDITOR

What does a proofreader do?

A proofreader will read the final version of the copy to ensure a book is error-free and professional looking. It differs from copy editing in that a proofreader is just picking up obvious typos, layout problems and format/style errors, rather than finessing words, or checking punctuation, grammar and expression.

What makes a good proofreader?

Attention to detail, patience, being a stickler for rules and pedantic about the little things, and consistency. It's such a satisfying job. I've had people write it off as the most boring and soul-destroying job you could ever have, but I love it!

What do you wish authors knew about proofreading/what are the misconceptions?

I wish authors knew the difference between a proofread, copy edit and structural edit. All of those require different time commitments and skill levels. And the responsibility of the writer changes too—a document that has had a copy or structural edit will absolutely still need to be proofread. Authors are sometimes surprised by this and the budget required. Even though I proofread my own book, I still paid someone to do a final proofread for me, as you can never pick up all the errors in your own work.

What is the proofreading process like?

First up, the author would contact me and send me a sample of their work so I can provide a quote. Then, when they're ready, the author sends me their Word document so I can use *Track Changes* to record my corrections and changes and add comments and suggestions. It's then the author's responsibility to either accept or reject my changes and produce a clean document.

It's a good idea for a copy editor to read the manuscript twice—once to undertake the copy edit, and a second time to do the proofreading, checking that all the changes have been correctly implemented—but the reality is, people generally don't have the time or money to run this second check. Therefore, I ask authors to ensure they put plenty of time aside to go through all my changes very carefully, and to ask for clarification if needed.

What's the best way to find a proofreader?

Ask your writing community and go to a reputable source like IPEd.

You've conceived, written, rewritten, edited and proofread your book so it's polished and ready for the next stage … or at least you're well on your way. The next section is all about the different ways you can choose to publish your book.

PART II

PUBLISHING YOUR BOOK

10

TRADITIONAL PUBLISHING—THE GOOD AND THE BAD

Whether your manuscript is still an idea in your head or already written and edited, you're serious about its future success and want to find the optimal way to publish it. In this section we investigate the various publishing alternatives for your work, as well as the steps needed to take your manuscript through to a saleable product.

Let's begin by exploring why a traditional (trad) publishing deal remains the shiny object many writers covet, and why it may or may not be the right step for you. Then we'll move on to the alternatives.

TRADITIONAL PUBLISHING: THE POSITIVES

Validation/prestige

A trad publishing deal doesn't guarantee your book will be better or anywhere near as profitable as one you publish yourself, but signing on the dotted line with a well-regarded publisher has cachet. It means you can tell your family, colleagues, nay-saying friends, ex-English teachers and writing group sceptics that your words well and truly jumped the slush pile, acquisition meeting and contract negotiation hurdles, and proudly announce that 'I actually did it. Yeah! So there!' It also means you might be invited into the heady world of writers' festivals and expert panels and be treated with a degree of reverence and respect by the industry and media.

Distribution and bookstore visibility

Dream of seeing your book piled high in bookstore windows? Or, if not in the window, facing out on the shelf? Or, at the very least, sardined between a sea of other books? Big publishers and bookstores work together like oil companies and petrol stations: one controls the product, and the other has the direct outlet to customers. Access to a network like this makes life easy for authors, as your publisher's distribution network and the bookstore's head office do most of the work. You don't need to be involved in pricing, shipping, nor learn the art of merchandising. It also means your book will be available online and promoted in the bookstore's marketing material.

The advance

An advance is a forward payment of royalties based on how many copies your publisher thinks will sell and is meant to help fund you during the writing of the book. You might have heard the term bandied about when an enormous advance is paid to celebrities, politicians, or—about as often as a unicorn sighting—a debut author. You hear about these big advances for precisely that reason—they are few and far between.

An advance is often split into three equal payments: one when you sign the deal, another on delivery of the completed manuscript, and one when the book is launched. But please, temper your expectations. Firstly, according to a 2021 survey by the ASA, 'For the majority of authors, advances are not paid and, where they are paid, they continue to be low. Alarmingly, 58% of respondents indicated they received no advance for their work' and just 13% received an advance over $10,000. (The ASA's 2020 survey showed 23.89% received an advance of between $1 and $4,999).

Secondly, advances aren't earned on top of royalties. Royalties are payments made per book sold, and an advance is an advance payment (the hint is in the name) of those royalties, so you won't receive any additional royalties until your book has sold enough copies to cover the cost of any advance you received. This is called 'earning out'. The ASA's 2021 survey noted that a whopping 40% of respondents indicated that they did not earn out their advance, 'highlighting the high-risk nature of publishing and also the double-edged sword of advances, given that if you don't earn out your advance, you are often unlikely to attract a subsequent publishing offer.'

Income with few costs

Traditional publishers aren't charities. They must see commercial potential, or they won't take you and your book on. It's only through book sales that they can cover their operating costs (office space, salaries, freelancers, printing, distribution, marketing, legal fees, author liaison, admin costs, etc.). One benefit of working with a trad publisher is that they cover all these costs for you. You don't need to dip into your own pocket for image rights, cover design, editing and proofreading. The only investment you really need to make is the time devoted to the writing and marketing of the book. This makes it relatively risk free. After all, you're not a charity either!

Work with publishing professionals

Enjoy the benefit of dealing with people who inhale and exhale books, bibliographies, metaphors, market research, titles, fonts, and fact checks. Publishing houses are full of brilliant word wranglers, design divas, mojo motivators and all-round general publishing gurus. Yes, as a savvy self-publisher you can find the right people and end up with a product just as good or better than anything publishers churn out, but being 'in-house' means you can leave the bulk of the back end to them.

Focus and time

Sure, you'll still need to juggle family, friends, and core employment while you type away, but having a publisher behind you will free you to focus on the writing. Not having to invest headspace in becoming a publishing entrepreneur may give you the room you need to build a better book or even pen a second book in quick succession.

Visibility to international publishers

Depending on your subject and how successful your book is, a deal with an Australian publishing house may elevate your visibility with international agents and publishers. First stop Nobbys Beach, next stop New York!

Marketing and publicity

Publishers employ in-house and external marketing and media relations specialists. These guns know how to get books in front of social media influencers, book reviewers and journalists at major media outlets. They know how to spin a story, dangle the angle, and cut through the hundreds of media releases that cluster bomb journalists' desks each day. Once they get the cut-through, though, it will still be up to you to do the interviews and tell your story in a media-savvy way.

But traditional publishing is not all glossy hardcovers and cocktail party launches, and that's why more and more authors are choosing to self-publish.

TRADITIONAL PUBLISHING: THE NEGATIVES

Ah, the thought of all an all-expenses paid lunch at a luxe, hatted restaurant with the crème de la crème of publishing society toasting your signing success … is something you can dream about, while reheating last night's takeaway pizza for breakfast. That's because traditional publishing rarely lives up to the hype for the bulk of authors for a range of reasons.

First, you must break down the door

And it's not just any door, it's a door that would have kept Viking hordes at bay. It's a door that may no longer be oak-panelled, but may potentially be bulletproof glass atop a security building, accessible by limited edition key card only.

Getting that key might take years, sucking your focus and enthusiasm as you chase non-responsive publishers and literary agents, while worrying about how your little darling is doing at the bottom of the slush pile. And it will be a big pile, as confirmed on the *Words and Nerds* podcast when Dani Vee interviewed literary agent Fiona Inglis of Curtis Brown Australia. Fiona disclosed that their agency receives over 400 unsolicited submissions each month.

You may also need to get used to self-consolation after spending days reading submission guidelines (from one of the few publishers or agents open to new author queries), only to realise you just missed the annual submission window by three minutes.

Or you might score one of the coveted spots at a pitching event or meet-the-publisher golden hour at a writing festival—which you then spend weeks fretting about and preparing for, instead of doing the work of writing your book. Unfortunately, your literary speed dating hook-up is over in minutes, and so might be your opportunity if you and your pitch don't perform or if it's 'just not what we're looking for right now'.

Just trying to get in the door can collapse your confidence and if you do manage to nudge it open, next you'll need to hurdle the acquisition meeting where you might hear the gut-wrenching sound of the door being slammed shut for the final time when the editors, accountants and marketing team don't all agree to greenlight your book.

 The first publisher I sent my book to wanted to publish it, describing it as an 'inspiring and moving ... beautiful work'. But then it was knocked back at the acquisitions meeting because it wasn't 'commercial enough'. A second publisher described it as 'remarkable writing and a powerful story', and then went on to say, 'memoirs tend to work in the numbers we need them to only if authored by someone of big national recognition ... the numbers just wouldn't work for us.'

— TRICIA D. WALKER, AUTHOR, *GREENHOOD*

Oh, where did those three years of your life go while chasing the elusive trad deal, when you could have been out writing and self-publishing your second or third book?

Financial cost

What? Don't the publishers pay for everything? Not really.

First, the slush pile reader won't bother reading more than a paragraph or two if your work is not captivating. And, to get to captivating, unless you're the second coming of a Pulitzer prize-winning author, you will likely have had to pay some serious bucks for a book doctor or editor before submitting, anyway.

You will also need to carry the cost of writing the book, because, as the ASA notes, 'Given the number of authors not receiving an advance and the fact that the author is also the last person in the supply chain to be paid, and can wait more than two years from the delivery of their manuscript to their first royalty payment, it is evident that authors are increasingly self-funding while writing their books. This is a significant barrier to entry into publishing; being able to afford the time to write and manage the time-lag between labour and payment.'

Publishers will also charge you more than cost price to buy copies of your own book. That's right! You can't just pick up at-cost copies for your family and friends, and to sell at your author talks and seminars. You'll be paying whatever rate the publisher deems appropriate. Not just the printing cost, but enough for the publisher to make money, too. Sometimes, you might even have to agree to buy a certain number of copies up front, which means you end up becoming as much a profit centre for the publisher as a receiver of profits.

Low royalties

Royalties are the percentage of book sales paid to an author. Traditional publisher royalties might look a bit like this:

- 5% royalty for mass market paperback sales (softcover books sold in stores like Kmart)
- 7.5% royalty for trade paperback sales (softcover books sold in traditional bookshops)
- 10–15% royalty for hardcover sales (not many debut authors are released in hardback)
- 25% for ebook sales (but, they often sell ebooks at highly discounted prices compared to print books, and online retailers take a huge chunk too).

So, if your book's recommended retail price (RRP) is $25, the royalty you receive may be as low as $1.25 per copy if it's a mass market paperback or as *high* (emphasis all mine!) as a whopping $3.75 for a successful hardback title. Your ebook royalty might come in around $1.75.

Sure, your royalty rate might increase once you hit a certain number of sales (e.g., 5,000 copies), but only if your book is a mega success and you locked this into your original contract negotiations.

And for you to have done that, you are likely to have needed a literary agent's involvement, which means you can say goodbye to another 15% of your royalty earnings to pay for said agent.

Oh, and you only earn this income if you have sold enough copies to pay out your advance!

Slow royalty payments

Then there's the fact that your royalty payments won't hit your bank account until at least three months, but more likely six months, AFTER the month in which the books were sold. Your publisher may then pay you on an ongoing monthly or quarterly basis.

Invisibility

Yes, the big publishers can get your book into bookstores, but only if a bookseller agrees to stock it. And then, only strong sales of your book will keep it there. Your book will have just a few short weeks to compete with titles with bigger marketing budgets and bigger names, so while it might make it onto the shelf, there's no guarantee it will stay there. And though it would be wonderful to score a window display or see it on the front counter or attracting attention at the entry, books by new authors are rarely stacked high or placed face out on the shelf. This can lead to a speedy disappearing act for your book.

Returns

You only just got your book into bookstores, and now it's being returned?! Yes, after invisibility comes the dreaded returns, where bookstores exercise their right to return unsold or slightly damaged books to the publisher months later. These returns eat straight into your royalty earnings, and you can go from a high of lots of early book sales to a low as they all trickle back in.

Speed to market

Speed to market is another of the driving reasons people choose the indie publishing path.

There's no use writing a book on a hot topic, only to see it simmer, then sputter, on a traditional publisher's timetable. The process of getting your book from submission to acquisition meetings, to contracts to editing, to the end goal of launch and distribution can take years. That means serving your originally hot topic lukewarm at best. The delay might even mean the conversation has moved on.

My memoir received a positive response from one publisher, with the caveat that they could not offer it a place in the publishing schedule for another two years. That is not warp speed. That is not my speed. With the manuscript already written, I indie-launched and began selling it within three months.

 I think your energy as an author moves on, and quite possibly, so does the market if it takes too long to birth a book.

— DR PAIGE WILLIAMS, *BECOMING ANTIFRAGILE*

Speed also applies to updates and changes. When a book is traditionally published and an error or new information is discovered, it's highly unlikely (unless a legal threat is involved) that a publisher will pulp the books and reprint an error-free version. With print on demand (POD) publishing, you can update your text, upload it, and have new copies within days with minimal wastage. Perfectionists especially will enjoy that benefit.

It's also hard to stay relevant, and it's even harder to convince a publisher to bring out a new version every two to three years to ensure that you do, but if you're in charge you can do whatever makes sense to you.

Lack of control

Control freak anyone? Or just like to have a say? Traditional publishing can be like the annoying family member who's always saying, 'You'd look better in this', 'Why are you eating that?', 'I think it would be better if you did this', 'I'm not happy with the direction you're taking', or 'Sit down while I'm talking to you.'

 My book *Diva* felt like my life on a page and I didn't want to sell myself into slavery, I wanted to maintain creative control. I felt some editors tried to sanitise my style, and one in particular tried to remove every skerrick of my personality from the page; it felt like someone had gone through me with a dose of bleach. Being a self-publisher meant I could easily move on and find a better fit in an editor.

— KERRY HOWARD, *THE TROUBLE WITH TRAUMA*

When you sign over your rights, you sign over control of the end product. Though you'll be involved, you won't have final say over the title and cover, how it's edited, or the marketing strategy. You can be told to cut chapters or add new ones, pick different interviewees and more. That can be wonderful if you're happy to leave the professionals to do what they're being paid for, but if you enjoy a lot more collaboration and have your own creative ideas, perhaps steer clear of a trad deal.

You're an unpaid member of the marketing team

You signed with the same publishing house as the ex-Prime Minister? That is literally amazing! But do you think you're going to get the same level of support, or access to the same amount of time from the PR team? Of course not. If they do get media interest, the publisher will expect you to do a lot of the unpaid heavy lifting promo-wise, including fronting up for interviews, author talks and profile-raising activities. Some traditionally published authors even co-fund the publisher's campaign!

> Traditional publishers typically only focus on marketing your book for about three months before the next wave of books comes in. So, the more you can do in the first three months the better. Hiring your own publicist though might cost between $5,000 and $10,000 (yikes) with no guarantee of book sales. In any event, you should build your own content marketing campaign, build your book community early and have a pre-launch marketing and engagement campaign.
>
> — JAQUI LANE, THE BOOK ADVISER

Bye-bye to your rights

This can hurt. You poured your heart and soul into your book but, to get the publishing deal, you may also have to pour away your rights to it (even when you've written a memoir and it's the rights to your own life story). Those rights might include foreign, electronic, podcast, merchandise, and movie rights. You might not even be able to repurpose extracts of your own work without permission from your publisher.

What happens if, a year into selling the book, you realise you want to bring out a spin-off title? Are you able to use the same IP? Can you play off the original title however you choose? Or will you need to go back to the submission and negotiating table where there's a likelihood you'll be told 'No, you can't go ahead', or 'Only if you buy back the rights'.

Consult with a service like the ASA's Contract Assessment Service before signing any contract, but even then, you might still have to give up many rights to secure the deal.

Splitting of your lending rights and copyright payments

A traditional publishing deal likely makes your publisher eligible for 50% of any payment from the Australian Public Lending Rights Scheme (PLR and ELR) and Copyright (CAL) schemes. These schemes pay creators and publishers for books available in libraries and/or for part-copying and use by educational institutions, government departments and businesses. See Part IV: Leveraging Your Book for more information.

Your champions move on ... but you can't

The editor who championed your book, your only actual contact at the company, leaves before your book is due to be published. You and your book become instant orphans.

You might get some support from the marketing team, but with no one internally breathing fire or sparking energy on your behalf you may find yourself at the back of the line—not because you've done anything wrong, but because no one knows you. You were someone else's favourite, your book someone else's baby.

This can also happen when a publishing house buys out or merges with another. Suddenly the publisher that rejected your book must digest the fact that they ended up with it anyway. This doesn't always make for happy families.

You want to write for a new audience

Perhaps you're already a successful author and your publisher will happily take a carbon copy of your last book, but you now want to write something completely different. I interviewed the wonderful queen of Australian romance writing, Valerie Parv, shortly before her death in 2021 and even though she had traditionally published 90+ books and sold more than 34 million copies globally, she self-published *34 Million Books* in 2021, in which she shared stories from her life, alongside writing tips.

> Why did I self-publish? I'm always up for a new adventure and the restrictions of COVID-19 threw the publishing industry into chaos. Indie publishing was a challenge and a way to keep my writing on the boil. Being in charge of every step was exciting. You are the boss ... but also the buck stops here.
>
> — VALERIE PARV, TRAD AND INDIE AUTHOR

Let's hear from another traditionally published author who's struck out on his own as an indie.

〜

INSIDE ADVICE: ANDREW GRIFFITHS
TRAD AUTHOR GONE INDIE

Why self-publishing?

My first business book *101 Ways to Market Your Business* was published by Allen & Unwin in 2001 and became a bestseller virtually overnight. I worked with them on another 10 books, then published one with Simon & Schuster, and have self-published my last two books. My latest: *Someone Has to Be the Most Expensive, Why Not Make It You?*

When I first began writing, I wouldn't have self-published in a million years because of the technical complexity, but so much has changed in the publishing world. I like having control over editorial and design and I'm in a better position to drive sales through my own email list and networks.

Going forward, I may also do traditional deals, but only if I'm convinced it will add value—such as tapping into a new market or giving me global access.

What was the writing and publishing process like for your latest book?

When I write a book, I like to do it in two-week blocks, and this time I headed to Tasmania. In the first two weeks, I write the shell of the book, about 30,000 to 50,000 words. It's untidy, but I get it down. Then I do another two weeks trying to make it resemble the English language. The third two-week period I use to fine tune. I then outsourced the project, including editing, design and cover, to Publish Central and had the books printed by McPherson's Printing. For the first print run, I did 1,000 soft-cover copies and 1,000 hardcover copies to sell as a limited edition. I've never gone with a hardcover before, but I felt that the book and the book's message justified it. I'm expecting to sell about 50,000 copies across all formats over three years.

The RRP is approximately $50 for the hardcover and $35 for the soft-cover. The production costs for the 350-page book (67,000 words), including editing, layout, proofs, cover, project management and the initial print run of 2,000 copies, was about $25,000. Any extra copies after that will be about $5 for the softcover and $12.50 for the hardcover.

I'm really happy with the end result, with everything from being able to print the inside cover in red to the fact that it looks like it's been done by one of the big publishers.

What marketing strategies have worked for you?

- I go all-in on marketing. I've invested heavily in my website (my goal is to get speaking jobs and partner with big companies, so it has to look great) and it continues to pay off.
- My own database: I've built up an extensive customer list over the years.
- As an international speaker, conferences are a very big channel for me. Sometimes I've sold 2,000–4,000 books at an event, but more often it's around the 250–600 mark.
- I'm active on social media, and continually build my brand. I've written thousands of articles, which can be found online on sites like Flying Solo, Inc and others, and I repackage my book and blog material several times to earn additional money from it.
- I take my books with me everywhere I go, whether it's to the

coffee shop or to give to the person sitting next to me on the plane, and I even leave them with the GM of the hotels I stay in. By doing this, I've earned hundreds of thousands of dollars in extra revenue through booked talks and consulting.

What are your top tips?

- Be clear about what your book will do, what problem it will solve and what you want the outcome to be.
- In the business space, something that has changed in the last five years is that having a general book won't get you results. People want specifics, for example, 'Teach me how to use Facebook ads', not 'Teach me how to use social media'.
- Just because your books are in the bookshop doesn't mean people will buy them: you must always be selling.
- To leverage your book, you can't have a poverty mentality about it; be prepared to give books away to the media and potential clients. Every time I give away a book it's a seed, creating an opportunity. All the biggest opportunities in my life, such as working with the European Union, can be traced back to me giving someone a copy of my book. It makes marketing sense. If I give away a book that cost me $6–$7 and someone signs up for a $30,000 coaching program, that's a great return on investment.

Best piece of advice from another writer?

When I was starting to write, I was told to place a photograph of my ideal reader right next to my writing space. I found this a powerful way to stop me straying from my target reader. You really need to know whether you're writing for CEOs, undertakers, or cassowary farmers.

∼

Intrigued? Inspired? Let's get into the good and the bad of self-publishing.

11

CHOOSING SELF-PUBLISHING

T his chapter is all about the type of publishing where you get to be the boss! You choose to do the work you like, are good at—or want to learn to be good at—and you also get to choose to delegate the rest, and to who.

 Indie publishing is a great option for self-motivated, entrepreneurial people. You can achieve great success if you treat it like a business.

— VALERIE KHOO, AUSTRALIAN WRITERS CENTRE

SELF-PUBLISHING: THE POSITIVES

You can be a nobody

Hurrah! You don't need to be famous or have hundreds of thousands of fanatical followers on your socials. You don't need to have married a Hollywood film star or been her personal trainer, won gold at the Olympics, or invented the cure for cancer. All of those would be great, of course, but even if you had done all three, it still doesn't guarantee you a palatable book deal with a traditional publisher.

Introverts can self-publish. Extroverts can self-publish. We don't need to prostrate ourselves on the front doormat of agents, sidle shyly up to publishers at festivals or spend dog years perfecting the ultimate email pitch.

We can avoid the whole rigmarole and just give ourselves permission to publish.

You want permission? Permission granted!

Retain all rights

The self-publishing approach means keeping all rights to your work and enjoying the freedom of being able to repackage and repurpose the content, in any shape or form, for any outlet or medium you choose ... forever!

You can pull books from publication if you decide to take a different path, or you can launch offshoots or more books in the series.

You can sign deals with foreign agents for translations or bring out an audio version. You can slice and dice your content into podcast format, merchandise with key quotes on them, or turn the concept of your book into a thriving consulting business. You can do whatever you like because you, and only you, own the IP.

Keep all profits

Though you've had to back the venture financially from the start, you'll also benefit financially by retaining 100% of the profits till the end. That's right, you get 100% of the royalty, instead of just 5%.

Sell fewer books but make more money

Yes, this heading sounds all wrong but, because you don't need to split your book income with a publisher, it means your profit per book is way higher, so you don't need to sell as many! That's right, you might make $10–$20 profit on a $30 book sale instead of just $1–$3. For example, at the time of writing, *Small Farm Success Australia* has sold more than 2,000 paperback copies (and is still going strong) at $29.95 ex-GST (RRP is $33 including GST). With a traditional publisher, at an 8% royalty, this would equal a gross income of around $5,000, but by self-publishing the book I was able to increase that gross income close to tenfold, plus earn 70% commission on hundreds of more ebook sales, and parlay it into consulting opportunities too. I've also received 100% of the income from PLR, ELR and CAL.

Speed and relevance

I'm not much for sitting around waiting for people to make decisions about my future. How about you?

If you have an urgent or timely message or idea you want to get out, and you're not prepared to wait for the 1 to 3-year publishing cycle of a traditional publisher (which is on top of your writing time!), you can turn things around quickly and just get your book out to market ASAP.

It means your book will be timely and, thanks to the flexibility of POD, you'll be able to update it, as well as bring out new editions.

Brand and product extension

Publishing your book your own way allows you to create spin-offs, including workbooks and podcasts, stationery and seminars, limited editions, even lyrics and lectures. Create, control, and expand your brand and empire on your own terms.

Test the market

Self-publishing is a great way to test the market with your ideas and writing style. It may also help you get runs on the board to build your fan base for your next book.

You can do it from anywhere and over any length of time

Indie publishing is incredibly flexible. You can run your operation from anywhere in the world, calling the shots from your backyard, a sun-kissed beach, the local coffee shop, or a cheery co-working space. You can even do it on your commute to your regular job. You also get to set your own deadlines, whether that's leisurely or lightning fast.

Choose the experts you want to work with

Many of the same people who design and edit for the big publishers (or have) are also available to freelance for you. This means you can outsource all the things you're not good at or dread doing, whilst tapping into the same expertise used by the big guns of the publishing world.

Working with these freelancers can bring efficiency, expertise and great energy to your project.

> You need self-belief to start and sounding boards to finish. Seek help for your weak spots.
>
> — GARRY BROWNE, THE PERSONAL BRAND CATALYST AND AUTHOR, *BRAND NEW, BRAND YOU*

It might be your only option

Indie publishing might also be the only way to get your book into print.

For example, there's no way a traditional publisher would have signed me to publish this book on self-publishing! Many topics are also too niche or controversial, especially given that publishers assess the value of your book through their own lens, and that lens often has a heavy commercial filter. Sometimes it's only after you've achieved success on your own that they go and get their eyes checked.

> You do not need a book deal to be a valid writer. You do not need to wait to be chosen. You can choose yourself and not wait around for something that may never happen. Your book will be read and enjoyed by actual humans.
>
> — LISA EDWARDS, AUTHOR, EDITOR, FORMER PUBLISHER

However, being master of your own destiny can have its drawbacks, so let's look at them now.

INDIE PUBLISHING: NEGATIVES

I don't want to be a downer after all that wonderful news, but you're not reading a fantasy fiction book. It's important that you understand the key pitfalls of self-publishing so you can decide if it's truly right for you. It may well not be and if it's not, the money and time you've invested in this book will have been great value for illuminating that!

It's entrepreneurial

It's funny that in every other industry, entrepreneurs are feted for their freedom, seen as the pinnacle of success, guts and glory. And yet, when writers take on the system and innovate for themselves, there remains this hint of, 'Well it mustn't have been good enough to publish properly'. This isn't true, but it's a label you may have to work hard to overcome.

Having said that, if you don't have an entrepreneurial bone in your body, if you lack marketing nous and have no bold ambitions, maybe it isn't the right path for you.

Time

How much time do you really have? Self-publishing is the Dyson® of enterprises; it will vacuum up every second of your day if you let it. There's just so much to learn, so much to do and coordinate, and it all takes time. Your time.

Upfront investment

Outsourcing editing and design to professionals comes at a cost. How much you fork out is up to you, but publishing can be an expensive business, and there are some costs you just can't avoid.

In addition to your unpaid time spent writing, publishing and marketing the book, some of your potential upfront costs may include:

- writing classes and books on writing and publishing
- memberships of organisations such as the ASA, ALLi and SPN
- computer hardware and/or software
- research expenses
- manuscript appraisals
- book coach or adviser
- editing and proofreading
- interior and cover design (even if you do it yourself, you will still need to invest in the software)
- indexing (if needed for your book)
- ISBN costs
- printing costs
- shipping costs

- marketing and advertising costs (such as author photo, website build and online marketing)
- legal and/or accounting costs.

Costs can quickly escalate if you keep changing your mind, or if you make mistakes requiring you to recall or reprint your book. There are ways around these costs though, including crowdfunding solutions, which you can read more on in Chapter 34.

Your new job title

Do you like a finger in every pie? If so, you'll be in your element. If not, nothing will prepare you for the different types of pies there are when it comes to indie publishing and how many pieces of those pies you'll be responsible for. You'll essentially be running a small enterprise and managing everything that entails, from marketing to IT, design to debtors and, of course, you'll need to keep your star employee (you!) happy.

If you're not capable of or interested in being an all-rounder, you'll need to hand over more of your hard-earned cash to pay someone, such as an assisted publisher, to do it for you. Don't worry though, there are plenty of people to help, it's just that you'll need to find the right ones for you and your project to keep the costs down and the quality high.

Quality control

Quality control is all in your hands, and self-publishing requires immense attention to detail.

First, you must write a book worthy of multiple readers' time, money, and attention. You then need to produce your book to a high level of quality. If you're a big-picture thinker and just not sufficiently detail-orientated, you'll need to outsource to someone who can dot your i's and cross your t's. Even then, the responsibility of choosing the freelancers who can produce the required quality is in your hands.

It doesn't cost any more to print a quality book compared to a crappy book, so write and produce the best book you can.

— ANDREW GRIFFITHS, BOOK WRITING COACH, AUTHOR
AND SPEAKER

Decision-making

Perfectionists can struggle with self-publishing because it's hard to know when your baby is ready. Tweaking and last-minute changes will always be tempting, and indecision and procrastination are particularly hard to manage when you're going it alone.

Marketing and visibility

Don't kid yourself. This project is not just about writing, it's about marketing. When you finally finish your manuscript, that's when the next wave of work begins.

Though it's not impossible, you'll need to work hard and smart to obtain visibility, drive sales, and open up other avenues of income around the book.

It's hard to nail down the data, and many figures are bandied about, but it's common to hear that the average self-published book sells less than 200 copies. If you were 'average', would 200 copies make it worth your while?

Self-belief

What's your level of self-belief?

Too much and you might avoid or ignore the feedback that could make your book great. Too little, and your fears and insecurities—and potentially the negativity of people around you—could silence you before you begin.

 Imposter syndrome rears its head for every writer. It's normal. The only people who don't have imposter syndrome are the people who should.

— ANDREW GRIFFITHS, BOOK WRITING COACH, AUTHOR
AND SPEAKER

If you constantly second-guess yourself, asking yourself 'Is this good enough. Am I good enough? Am I kidding myself?', you might find yourself wavering dangerously at each sentence, chapter, or even at the eleventh hour when you are about to push 'print' or 'publicity'. If this is the case, you'll need to find your staying-power shovel and dig deep.

Scams

Wannabee authors are much-loved targets of scammers and spammers.

Fabulous-sounding companies (aka predatory publishers and vanity presses) will likely target you. Their agents will claim to 'really believe' in your book, think it has 'bestseller potential' and claim to be able to help you get it into 'the hands of adoring fans'. They may even offer higher royalties than trad publishers (up to 15%)—but only if you pay for assessments, competition entries, mentoring sessions, marketing support and more. They might even ask you to pay to be in an anthology or compilation book … of which they will eventually want you to buy copies so you can show friends and family you were 'accepted'.

Generally, if it sounds too good to be true (or even just slightly dodgy, like a third party claiming to be acting on behalf of a major publisher)—it usually is.

Basically, don't tell yourself stories, and don't fall for other people's stories.

Stamina

The journey you're embarking on is not like serving up a burger and fries to go, it's more like the planning and execution of a lengthy degustation dinner. It's not fast fashion, it's the knitted woollen jumper you craft after you have shorn the merino you raised yourself from birth, then carded, dyed and spun the fleece.

The journey from getting your book out of your head to getting it in front of your reader takes stamina. It takes energy and persistence over a long period, often in the face of many barriers.

Without stamina, you face paralysis, or you may even give up entirely. That's why so many people who 'want to write a book', never end up doing so.

Purposefully moving through blocks, whether it be a writing, publishing, or marketing block, is the only way to successfully write, launch and sell your book.

Even with this book I struggled to get to the half-way mark. At times the project seemed unachievable. But I just. Kept. Going.

 One of the biggest differences between traditionally published authors and self-publishers is that traditional authors have a legal contract with a defined deadline. There's no such deadline for indie authors, and so they're always chasing a better idea or a different way of saying something. As a consequence, they often don't finish their book because they keep trying out different things. Time just keeps moving on and their motivation wanes.

— KELLY IRVING, BOOK COACH AND EDITOR

Let's hear from another author who had the stamina to write, publish and market his book. I've known Tim for more than a decade and can confirm that he poured the enthusiasm, knowledge and professionalism he puts into his daily life directly into this title. It's paid off, not only proving the power of self-publishing when done well, but also the power of words to change the world, in this case people's skyrocketing awareness of and reverence for Australia's native bees.

~

INSIDE ADVICE: TIM HEARD
THE AUSTRALIAN NATIVE BEE BOOK

Why self-publishing?

Serendipity! A colleague of mine, Glenbo Craig, had experience in the publishing industry. After attending my native bee workshop he said, 'There's a book in this!'. He strongly advised me to self-publish to retain income and control, and to keep the quality high.

The manuscript was 105,000 words with 550 illustrations and colour photos. We went on to work shoulder to shoulder, night after night, looking at every bit of content, page by page. If the text and images weren't balanced, I'd either edit down the text, write more, or play with the images and illustrations so every page was instantly cohesive and engaging. There's no way I would have been given that level of quality control and freedom in the traditional publishing world.

What was your writing and publishing process like?

For three months I literally emptied my brain through my fingertips and onto the keyboard; it was stream of consciousness. Then it took another year of refining and three rounds with a professional editor. Lots of rewriting! And then more time finding images and getting permissions. I knew it would be a big job, but I didn't factor in how big.

I ordered 4,000 copies for the first print run, thinking it would take three or four years to sell them, but they sold out within four months! In 2022 I was up to my ninth print run, and sales don't show any sign of stopping. I originally thought I might sell about 8,000 copies in the book's lifetime, but I think I could even end up selling 50,000. It's exceeded my wildest expectations.

What marketing strategies have worked for you?

- The initial concept and execution. Booksellers tell me I published a book that people want to read and recommend.
- Early readers: I had a lot of people read the manuscript for accuracy, some just a paragraph, some a chapter. That raised awareness and buzz.
- For every image I used in the book, I offered the photographer an acknowledgement and a free copy of the book. That was a great promotion because the photographers helped share and promote it. I probably gave away 500 books to people I knew would talk about it.
- We didn't go with a distributor, but with the help of my wife Katina I successfully targeted independent bookstores and shops at places like museums, botanical gardens, nurseries and beekeeping supply companies.
- We tried with a major online bookstore, but it didn't work out; they were not prepared to pay a fair price.
- Targeting library author talks and workshops. The average sell-through at an author talk is about 50%, but I also give 40 workshops a year and offer the host a trade discount to package the cost of the book into the workshop, that way, it's a win–win.

What are your top tips for other self-publishers?

- When you think, 'I don't have any words today', just turn your computer on, read what you've already written and start editing. That will get your neurons firing and your adrenalin running, and it feeds back on itself. Eventually, you'll get hooked on the buzz of daily writing achievement.
- You need to distinguish between people who have valid points about your dreams for your book and those trying to bring you down due to envy or ignorance.

What are you most proud of about your book?

The book won the Australian Book Industry Awards (ABIA) 'Small Publishers' Adult Book of the Year', the Whitley Award for Australasian Zoological Literature, and Gold at the Apimondia World Beekeeping Awards. But even more special was getting feedback from people who are not big readers—hearing that they read it from cover to cover. That means I've written a book that hasn't just taught people to like bees, it's also taught them to like books.

Best piece of advice from another writer?

Don't just fill a gap with your book, make it the best possible book to fill that gap.

~

But what if you think there are too many gaps in your skillset and knowledge to venture forth totally on your own as a self-publisher? There is another model that might suit. But first, a warning about vanity publishers.

12

VANITY PUBLISHING

You know what? You're a busy person, so let's not waste even a sentence fluffing up the image of vanity publishing and pretending there are positives. Why? Because vanity publishing is a predatory business model whereby often naive, insecure, or hopeful authors are prey to exploitation, so let's just head straight to the negatives.

VANITY PUBLISHING: THE NEGATIVES

ALLi defines a vanity press as 'a publishing service that engages in misleading or, in the worst cases, outright deceptive practices, with the intention not of bringing books to readers but of extracting as much money as possible from the authors.' They say, 'This is a definition which firmly identifies vanity presses while excluding the true publishers and reputable service providers.'

Vanity publishers make their profit by squeezing as much money as they can from writers, while taking no responsibility for quality or successful distribution. They can charge exorbitant fees and may inflate the fees for every service, from coaching and 'stretching' you as an author, to the printing of your book and even press release preparation. They may also show you a price list based on a tiny word count and then charge extortionately for any word over that length.

If you have money to pay for their 'services', it won't matter to a vanity publisher if your book is the most boring book ever written, if the spelling errors and structure make the book impossible to read, or even if you include information in the book that makes you liable for legal proceedings. Basically, it doesn't matter because you don't matter, nor your book. The only thing that matters to vanity publishers is the amount of money you are willing to put on your credit card to get your ego stroked and your book published.

The great site Writer Beware lists general and current scams, as well as the names of companies known for dodgy practices. ALLi's Watchdog Desk monitors the self-publishing industry globally, including Australia, and provides a rating system from 'Excellent' right down to 'Watchdog Advisory' which is coloured in a very alarming shade of red. ALLi also has a directory and searchable database of approved services for members. Support from the ASA and ArtsLaw can also be invaluable in working through contracts and dodgy offers.

~

So, what is the option in-between going it totally alone and a vanity press? That would be assisted publishing.

13

ASSISTED/CUSTOM AND HYBRID PUBLISHING

These models of author-funded publishing have many aliases, including assisted, hybrid, co-operative, contributory, facilitated and subsidy publishing.

Hybrid publishers have extremely varied business models, methods of working with writers, and approaches to marketing and distribution.

— JANE FRIEDMAN, EDITOR OF *THE HOT SHEET*

Some assisted publishers are little more than vanity publishers with lip gloss on, while others are experienced publishing veterans who know how to get the best out of you and your book and are perfect for the busy person who is not able to or does not want to be so hands-on.

Assisted publishing can be a particularly good option for people who are used to outsourcing and getting the best from such arrangements, but the challenge can be working out who are the champions in the industry and who are the charlatans.

Whereas traditional publishers make their income solely from the number of books (and rights) they sell, assisted and hybrid publishers make their income primarily from the number of authors to whom they sell their services, along with (for some of them) profits from these book sales. Often, the financial risk lands squarely on the author, with the hybrid publisher having little to lose if your book is a dud; however, there are some more respectable hybrid publishers where the author underwrites a quantity of books, but the financial risk is then shared.

ASSISTED PUBLISHING: THE POSITIVES

The process of using an assisted publisher is a little like handing your car over to a hotel valet rather than trying to find a vacant spot yourself in an 8-storey underground carpark (from which you then need to lug your bags to reception!). You just need to deliver your car (aka manuscript) and let the valet sort out all the logistics, including giving it a wash (edit and layout) and bringing it back to you nice and shiny and with no dings (great cover and proofreading), ready to drive straight out into the world. They may even chauffeur you in style and organise distribution of your book to online and physical stores.

Dealing with a supplier who has a proven track record in bringing quality book projects to market might make your writing and publishing process not quite a breeze, but at least less difficult and will likely be a good option if you are any of the following:

- technically challenged
- planning a business book
- in a hurry and time poor
- need someone to hold your hand when you take on new experiences
- not overly concerned about money
- used to successfully outsourcing projects and finding the best providers
- physically or mentally challenged in a way that would make it difficult to proceed on your own.

You may also find outsourcing ALL aspects of your book—perhaps even using the services of a ghostwriter—more effective than putting the time and effort into doing it yourself.

Good companies working in this space can, for a price, significantly speed up the book creation and production process compared with you trying to find, vet and manage individual suppliers. Look for companies that employ publishing professionals, have held a lot of author hands before yours, and already know the boxes to tick regarding cover design, online store listings, editing and the nitty gritty of print and ebook options and distribution. What you want is quality.

There are a number of companies operating in Australia and internationally in this space, including PublishCentral, Brio Books (now owned by Booktopia), Fontaine Press, Fremantle Press, Busybird Publishing, Vivid Publishing, Forbes Books and Scribe Media. Again, do your research to see if they are recommended by people in your writing community and to work out if any are a fit for you and your project.

ASSISTED PUBLISHING: THE NEGATIVES

The most difficult part of assisted publishing is finding an operator who truly cares about what you are trying to achieve and takes into account your best interests when providing and charging services. Here are some things to be wary of.

Flattery

We all love to hear that our book is great, but what we really need to hear is the truth. If you get sucked in by the flattery, you'll get well and truly sucked into the funnel.

The Funnel

The funnel is a spinning, disorientating stream of offers, extra services you never knew you needed and urgency (always a pressing urgency!) with limited-time deals and once-only opportunities. You might receive communications from multiple sources representing the company, as well as affiliated companies. They'll offer upgrades, widgets, and the yellow brick road to success. For a price.

The factory

Ask yourself this: do you think the editors, proofreaders and cover designers working on your book enjoy life in a publishing factory, having to take on any book, no matter the quality of writing or the dubious nature of the content? What do you think their pride and enthusiasm in their work might be in this situation? And seeing that the company knows how to churn out books, how will yours be different? Or will it be a cookie cutter version of other titles they've previously put out?

The costs

Though many assisted publishing companies will offer an efficient and economical path to publication and save you from making newbie missteps, others will be thoroughly exploitative. You really need to do your research. Is the quality going to be equal to the price? And even if it is, will you be able to obtain a return on your investment? This is not so much of a problem for consultants, professionals and business authors who want to use their book to help them achieve other goals, but if you're relying on book sales to generate an income, the premium you pay for an all-in-one service might cancel out your potential profit.

The fine print

At first glance at a price list, you might think the cost is for your 50,000-word book ... but perhaps the fine print says the cost only covers a 16,000-word book. Or the final price will depend on editing time (and that is a very elastic piece of string!). Or on how many images you want inserted.

The quality

These companies need to make money, and that may come at the cost of them giving your book enough attention to ensure its brilliance. If you decide to go down this route, here's some research to do:

- Ask the company to send you samples of books they've produced so you can see the quality of the design, editing, paper, cover stock and printing first-hand.
- Email a few of their published authors (not the ones listed in the testimonial section on the company's website) to find out how their experience was.
- Find out who will own the ISBN. (It's easy to get your own, see Chapter 16). Your aim should be to retain direct ownership of your ISBNs, after all, you're the one taking on all the financial risk of publishing your book, and you don't want to risk losing control of the title to the publisher in the future.

- Ask what you will be charged per copy when ordering author copies, the minimum quantity you need to order and what shipping costs will be.

∼

Fully outsourcing everything to one company might be the right solution for you, a relief even (and you won't end up needing to pull multiple all-nighters, dragging every neuron in your brain kicking and screaming to the party like I needed to do to get this book finished). But whichever way you go, you'll still need to make all the key decisions for your publishing business. The following chapters outline some of the things to think about and that you (or the consultants and companies acting on your behalf) will need to act on.

14

NAME YOUR IMPRINT ... AND YOURSELF

Y ou want to write this book. You must write this book. But you're likely facing a block. Or a wall of blocks! The wall is likely caused by your realisation that you don't have all the answers. Yes, there's the thrill of having a great book idea, but understanding how to write and successfully bring that book to market is a whole other story. Don't worry though, bit by bit, in this section you'll learn how to scale that wall. At times it might seem too high to get over, too wide to get around, but if you keep at it, you'll come to see it's just a process. All you need to do is keep ticking off the steps and you'll eventually get to the top.

It all begins with a name. Sure, you've already named your book, but you also need a publishing or imprint name (unless you would prefer your book be brought out under your assisted publisher's imprint).

What's in a name?

The name you use for your publishing name will be permanently linked to your title through the ISBN, the number that identifies your book in book-selling and library systems around the world. Most indie authors tend to use the same name for their publisher and imprint name. In traditional publishing, the hierarchy goes like this:

- Publisher: Penguin Random House

- Publisher's imprint/s: Knopf Doubleday, Crown Publishing, Viking Press, Bantam, Rodale, etc. (Penguin Random House has nearly 300 imprints!)

What are the benefits of using a publisher name?

It's a little like a 'trading as' name and looks more professional than simply using your own name. It also makes your book and enterprise practically indistinguishable from that of a traditional publisher, so at first glance, readers, bloggers, booksellers and the media probably won't realise your book is self-published and might be more open to it.

It's especially worthwhile if you think you will go on to publish more than one book.

What makes a good publisher name?

One that is not already in use by another publisher and that reflects the market you're writing for. A good real-world example is *Boiling Billy Publications*, which publishes outdoor camping and 4WD books.

However, if you plan to write books for a variety of audiences (like I've ended up doing), a more generic name that is flexible enough to span different subjects might be more appropriate. I use *CapeAble Publishing*.

Why do I need to decide on this name now?

The name is forever linked to your book's ISBN. The only way to change the name at a later date is to unpublish and then republish your book, which is a tricky process and best avoided. Finally, setting the name up also helps you think about your book not just as words on a page, but as a publishing enterprise!

How to find out if the imprint name you want is taken

Research names through the Australian Securities and Investment Commission (ASIC), IP Australia, Amazon and social media. A check on GoDaddy will also show if the URL is in use or available.

Don't be upset if the name you want is already in use by, say, a restaurant, because if your business is operating in a completely different space, you may be able to add the word 'Publishing' at the end of the name to differentiate yourself.

It's a good idea to register your imprint name as a URL because even if you don't have any plans to create a website, it will stop someone else from moving in on the name and causing confusion. Going to the extent of applying for a trademark is likely overkill for a micro publishing venture, but it depends on your ultimate goals.

Choosing Your Author Name

Do you need to create a new author name, or can you run with your own name? It depends:

- Are you proud of what you've written, and want your name to be associated with your book/s?
- Are you already established, or becoming established, in the field you're writing about so that your name will add cachet or drive sales by the time the book hits the market?
- Are you already using your name in business and want to use the book to drive sales of your course, business coaching, etc.?
- Is your name relatively unique or memorable?
- Can you register your own name as a URL and claim it across social media, even if it needs the word 'Writer' or 'Author' added to it (e.g., JackSmithWriter?)

If you answered 'yes' to any of the above, it sounds like you get to be you! Working with your own name helps build your brand, avoids confusion and is normally the best choice for a non-fiction author.

However, we're not all so lucky. This may be the case if:

- Your name is already in use by another writer, celebrity, or person of interest.
- Your name is relatively common and therefore not memorable to readers and media.
- You don't want to use your name for security reasons or to protect your family's privacy.
- You're trying to distance yourself from your family name so you're not swept up in their particular legacy, fame, or notoriety.

- You write across multiple genres and want to vary your author name so as not to confuse readers.

If any of these reasons ring true for you, a nom de plume might be the answer. But before you dive in, although a pen name might sound cool, it can be a poor long-term strategy for a non-fiction author because:

- It calls into question your authenticity: why should people put their trust in you and your book if you're not prepared to attach your real name to it?
- It's easy to slip up and not answer to your pen name when you're being interviewed or at a reader event.
- It causes confusion: how do you answer your phone? How should people who know you introduce you? How do you keep all your email and social media accounts separate? Who are you at talks?
- It can be far more difficult to organise bank accounts, copyright payments and your marketing efforts.

Choosing a pen name

If you really think a pen name is your best option, you can choose one in a variety of ways, including:

- Make it a variation of your real name, for example, Elizabeth Black becomes Lizzie Black.
- Add the initial of your middle name, so Ben Smith becomes Ben Z Smith.
- Use your or your mother's birth rather than married name.
- Use your nickname.
- Make up a name to suit the style of book you're writing.
- Use your first name and a made-up surname.

Overall, though, you're writing non-fiction, so to use a fictitious name would likely be counterintuitive and counterproductive.

∼

Now you have your name sorted, let's get down to business.

15

THE BUSINESS OF YOUR BOOK

A re you writing and publishing your book for pure pleasure? Or profit?

Whatever the case, decide early.

 People spend money going to the gym because it makes them feel good. Others get that same great feeling by writing a book. Not everything in life has to make money, so if writing a book is going to make you feel good, do it.

— LORNA HENDRY, BOOK DESIGNER, EDITOR, WRITER

Business Or Hobby?

According to the Australian Tax Office (ATO), it's 'important to understand the differences between a hobby and a business for tax and other purposes'. If you treat your writing as a hobby, you will not have an ABN. This can be restrictive for self-publishers as:

- you can only deal with IngramSpark (a major player in POD printing and distribution) if you have an ABN
- without an ABN, selling books to libraries and retailers may be too much hassle for their purchasing system.

Business structure

If you have decided you're not a hobbyist and are, in fact, in business, Fair Trading NSW warn, 'The structure you choose for your business should fit comfortably. A poor choice of business structure can prove painful.' Ouch! The most common business structures are: sole trader, partnership, proprietary limited company (Pty Ltd), association and co-operative.

Each structure has advantages and disadvantages, so talk to your accountant or solicitor to work out your best option. For example, they might say it makes little sense for you to take on the establishment and running costs of a Pty Ltd company at present, since starting off as a sole trader means you can just use your individual tax file number, you can still apply for an ABN (a free process at Australian Business Register) and you are permitted to earn up to $75,000 per annum before having to register for GST.

You might also already be operating a company that you can run your publishing business under. Best advice, though: speak to a professional before deciding.

∼

INSIDE ADVICE: MATTHEW TUCKER, CPA/BBUS CREATIVE CRUNCHERS (ACCOUNTANTS)

What are some key areas writers need help with?

In the creative arts, there's a strong inclination for practitioners to put their heads in the sand on the topic of finance because it's numbers and spreadsheets and things they 'don't understand'. The cornerstone is getting professional advice early so writers can gradually build skills regarding this key part of their business operation.

What do you see self-publishers getting wrong with their finances/tax?

First up, it's not taking substantiation seriously. People think of tax as a 30 June thing, whereas the key is learning to think about it every single day of the year. This trains your brain to recognise anything business related when it happens and capture it.

Second, there can be a lot of confusion around the GST system, especially when the majority of the royalty income earned is coming from overseas. Many people think that, unless their income is coming in from domestic sources there is no GST to be concerned with but that's not true. The $75k turnover test for the GST system includes overseas income, even if that overseas income—technically—would still not have GST in it even when a person is registered for the tax. It's very counter-intuitive, which is exactly why so many get it wrong. There's no doubt a lot of self-published authors are running around with income above $75k and are without a GST registration when the system would expect they'd be registered.

Some clients can also get a bit confused with earning income from overseas, being paid in foreign currencies, and being unaware of whether any foreign taxes have already been withheld from that money.

What's something interesting you've learned about self-publishing from your clients?

I've learned that it's VERY possible to make a profitable career out of it, if you're willing to work and can write, write, write. If you can find a niche and start developing a following, there are true fans who might pick up your third or fourth book, and that's where they start. They then go back to your first and second books. Your original works can find ever-increasing sales. It's like your typical AC/DC fan—that band still sells enormous copies of their very first album because people are forever discovering the back catalogue. That said, it requires a lot of investment, of both time and money, before some income starts to trickle back in.

∽

BUDGETING

Be clear about your goals for your book and your writing career. Like any business or hobby, if you aren't clear on your goals, it's easy to under-invest and strangle your chances or, at the opposite end of the scale, blow way too much dough.

Some business authors might invest $50,000 to $140,000 to bring a quality book to market because they know it will bring them even more in return (not necessarily from book sales!), but for me, though I'm still aiming for quality, my budget to get to print stage (including editing, proofreading, cover and interior design, indexing, author photo and ISBNs) needed to be less than $5,000. I was able to achieve this, while still supporting Australian-based service providers (who can sometimes be more expensive than foreign providers), because of my writing experience (not having to pay for handholding, writing courses and consultants), and because I already owned Vellum which I was able to use for interior design. Full disclosure though, my website build was on top of this cost, but I see that as a long-term investment, not just for this one book. Here are some things you might like to try so you can stay on top of your book finances.

- Set up a budget.
- Seek competitive quotes for services.
- Be aware of the opportunity cost. For example, if you have the money and want to outsource everything, your initial expenses will be higher but you will have more time on your hands for your regular gig (and family and friends!). Alternatively, if you plan to DIY, such as interior design, you'll have some upfront costs for software, but less ongoing professional fees … but also, less time!
- Keep receipts for any expenses you incur and work with your accountant to meet all your tax obligations.
- Understand that some costs are about investing in yourself as a writer for the long term, while other costs are project specific.

How many books will I sell?

Uh oh. Not even traditional publishers know how many copies of a book they will sell! So much depends on the topic, size of the audience, marketing budget, execution, and zeitgeist. It can also depend on how many additional books you end up releasing, as each subsequent book may help propel sales of your backlist while building an audience for your next title.

In an article in the *New York Times* on 18 April 2021 by Alexandra Alter and Elizabeth A. Harris titled 'What Snoop Dog's Success Says About the Book Industry', they noted that '98 percent of the books that (traditional) publishers released in 2020 sold fewer than 5,000 copies.'

Think about it. Those statistics are from the USA, a country with a population well over ten times that of Australia! If you're tapping into the US market, wonderful! But if your target is primarily Australian readers, our pie is a whole lot smaller.

A publishing insider commenting anonymously on a different piece in

The Guardian UK brought a dose of reality in relation to the UK market too, noting that 'It's not really a trade secret to tell you the average book sells between 800 and 1,500 copies. And when you factor in that some authors (the tiniest minority conceivable) sell millions, that must mean there are tens of thousands of other authors selling fewer than 800 ...'.

But what about your book? How might it fare? You can get more of an inkling by using the following sources as research tools.

- Nielsen BookScan's *Australia Lifetime Sales Data Report* helps you (for a fee) research the sales of similar books in your category through bookstore outlets (it does not take into account direct sales though, which is where many self-publishers concentrate their efforts).
- Trove will give you some idea of how many books you might sell into Australian libraries based on a search of other books in your category, but their statistics do not list all libraries or copies.
- Publisher Rocket, a paid tool, reveals Amazon sales information for books in certain key words and categories (more on this in the next chapter).
- Amazon is another handy tool for researching similar authors and titles in your category. In *The Nonfiction Book Publishing Plan: The Professional Guide to Profitable Self-Publishing*, authors Stephanie Chandler and Karl W Palachuk share plenty of useful advice, as well as lift the lid on how Amazon Sales Rankings translate into real-world book sales. Reprinted with permission here, these figures help take the mystery out of Amazon Sales Rankings.

Amazon Sales Ranking vs. Number of Books Sold Per Day:

- A ranking of 50,000 to 100,000 = 1 or fewer books per day.
- A ranking of 10,000 to 50,000 = 2 to 10 books per day.
- A ranking of 3,000 to 10,000 = 10 to 100 books per day.
- A ranking of 500 to 3,000 = 100 to 200 books per day.
- A ranking of 200 to 500 = 200 to 500 books per day.
- A ranking of 35 to 200 = 500 to 1,000 books per day.
- A ranking of 20 to 35 = 1,000 to 2,000 books per day.
- A ranking of 10 to 20 = 2,000 to 3,000 books per day.
- A ranking of 1 to 10 = 3,000+ books per day.

LEGAL ADVICE

Do you need legal advice before publishing your book? Best talk to a lawyer about that or with Arts Law Centre of Australia, Australia's independent national community legal centre for the arts who can help with topics including copyright and trademark infringement, defamation and breach of contract.

COPYRIGHT

In Australia, you don't need to send your work to a copyright office to register it. Just the act of writing it means that it's deemed to be yours. However, you can and should:

- Include the copyright symbol © on your work's imprint page.
- Regularly send a work-in-progress copy of your work to your email address in case you ever need to prove the date on which you created the work. This also means you will always have a back-up copy!
- You can also register your work with the US Copyright office if you specifically need or want a US copyright registration certificate (some online sites require this proof you own the copyright before you can upload your title).
- Keep in mind that although titles can't be copyrighted, if they are sufficiently distinct, they can be trademarked. Depending on your business expansion goals, you might want to consider speaking with a trademark specialist to help you decide whether the expense is justified.

INSURANCE

If you're running workshops related to your book or selling your book at events, insurance is often required. You might need to investigate overarching insurance for things like public and product liability, professional indemnity and property in care, custody and control. Certain organisations cater for the insurance needs of writers including Duck for Cover and Flying Arts Alliance Inc.

YOUR ESTATE

You are about to give birth to a book, but first let's discuss death. That's right, your book royalties and your copyright will become part of your estate when you die, so if you need to take that into consideration regarding your will, mention it to your solicitor.

US TAX FORMS

And what a great segue, from death to taxes! Australian-based authors selling books in the US through companies such as Amazon and Ingram-Spark need to fill out Internal Revenue Service (IRS) tax forms (and often multiple state-based tax forms) to avoid being double-taxed. The IRS is like Australia's ATO and filling out the forms prevents the US from withholding the full 30% tax from your sales. The forms are valid for three years and there are some handy, up to date tips at annafeatherstone.com regarding how to fill them out. NB: If you're receiving payments from overseas that can't be direct deposited, you can use services including PayPal, Wise and Payoneer.

You now understand a little about the back end of your book, and maybe have some of it underway, so let's run through the next steps necessary to take your final manuscript through to book form.

Settle in, there are a few! But take heart, all you need to do to see your book in print is to tick them off one at a time.

The scientific formula is: 1 small step x as many small steps as it takes = your book!

16

SEVEN KEY STEPS IN PREPARING FOR PUBLICATION

> Producing a book is a lot like doing a home renovation, it will take twice as long and cost twice as much as you think.

— MARK JONES, *BELIEFONOMICS*

The following 7 steps (not including all the marketing you need to be on top of, but we'll get to that later so you don't totally freak out), are crucial to your book's publication. They won't cost you much money, but they will likely tax your time, will and brainpower! You need to:

1. finalise permissions
2. commit to your cover blurb
3. write your author bio
4. seek testimonials, endorsements and advance praise
5. choose your trim size
6. finalise your metadata
7. secure your ISBNs.

Let's walk through them.

STEP 1: FINALISE PERMISSIONS

Permissions are an ethical, and often legal, obligation whereby you seek permission to quote or reuse the works of others.

Can I quote from publications and songs?

- Most media and publishing companies have an area on their website called 'Permissions' or 'Rights'. Check and act on their guidelines.
- In many cases, you can quote a line directly from a newspaper or book so long as you correctly attribute it with the name of the publication and the author and date. This is known as 'fair use'.
- In certain circumstances, you can quote a song lyric, but it can be a murky area. You would likely infringe on copyright if you include more than a line or two, so you need to seek permission from the copyright owner to avoid any claims. Song lyrics rights are notoriously costly to obtain.

Do I need permission from the people and organisations I've interviewed and quoted?

It's a good idea to ask them to review your use of their words prior to publication. Apart from being good manners, it helps avoid litigation and needless errors, and their feedback can improve your work. For example, a lot can change in the six months between conducting interviews and publishing your book, so if you're able to update key details, it makes for a better book.

Giving interviewees and organisations the option to check their contribution also catapults your book back into front-of-mind for them, which helps raise awareness for your impending book release. You can even politely ask them for a testimonial for the book at the same time (for more about how to ask for reviews, see Chapter 40). I've included a sample of my own permission request email in the *Look—It's Your Book! Workbook* that you can use as a template for yours.

What do I do with the permissions once I receive them?

Act on the responses by making any necessary edits, or briefly discuss why you won't be actioning them. Then file all the permissions somewhere safe so you can quickly and easily refer to them as needed. Add their postal address details to your launch list.

~

STEP 2: COMMIT TO YOUR COVER BLURB

If the cover and title catch a reader's attention, the very next thing they typically do is read the 'blurb', which is the compelling description written on the back cover. It is also used, perhaps in a slightly modified or expanded way, to describe your book in bookselling systems.

You will need to work on the blurb before you begin the back cover design, as the designer will need to know how many words it includes and which words to emphasise using graphic design techniques.

The blurb cements the reader's decision to purchase your book.

What makes a great blurb?

A great blurb:

- is compelling and irresistible to your target audience
- provides solutions and possibilities
- uses active language and short sentences
- is peppered with subtitles that reveal how readers will benefit.

How long should it be?

There are no set rules, but potential readers will often only give you a few seconds or sentences to grab their imagination.

Who can help me with my blurb?

- Your editor may be able to offer some insights.

- Marketing and sales specialists in your network, especially copywriters, can be helpful.
- Blurb specialists exist. They can be found on the internet and through author groups.
- Research by reading the back of all the latest releases and bestsellers.
- You. You know your book well, so go and research the back of other books to see how they do it. Draft up some possibilities and get feedback on your efforts from booksellers and librarians too.

~

STEP 3: WRITE YOUR AUTHOR BIO

Why do I need a bio?

An author bio is required for the metadata (the descriptive information about your book) that sits behind your book in bookselling systems around the world. It introduces you, establishes credibility and can be a great hook for media. It can also be used in shortened form on your back cover (or interior) in a way that turns browsers into buyers.

How long should it be?

A main bio works well when it is between 60 and 150 words. However, you will also need a shorter one of just one or two sentences for the cover and author talk posters.

How do I write a good one?

- Learn best practice by reading author bios from recently published non-fiction works. Which ones stand out?
- Write in the third person (your name), rather than the first person (I).
- Be interesting. Use active language. Edit out the waffle.
- Establish your credentials in relation to the book's subject: include relevant qualifications, awards, previous publications, achievements and experience.

- If a well-known person has said something positive about you, slip it in.
- Don't be annoying: no bragging, hyping or overselling.
- Avoid sounding like a cardboard cut-out: reveal an interesting or unusual thing about yourself to make you relatable.
- Include a link to your author website at the bottom so people can find out more.

If you find it hard to write your bio ...

Ask a friend, colleague or writing professional to draft it for you, or use another author's bio as inspiration, swapping in relevant details in your own unique style.

What do I do with it once I have it?

- Save it on your desktop, as you'll be using it a lot!
- Copy and paste it into metadata fields as required by sites such as MyIdentifiers and IngramSpark. (More on metadata soon.)
- Put it on your website, in the *About* section.
- Design it onto an A4 page, along with your author photo, to include in your media kit. Send it out with media releases and author talks too.
- Include a shortened version on your book's back cover or inner pages.
- Upload it to relevant online author sites (see Chapter 42 for how and where to do this).
- When things change, update it to keep it fresh.

∼

STEP 4: SEEK TESTIMONIALS, ENDORSEMENTS AND ADVANCE PRAISE

Famous authors are often asked to give debut authors within the same publishing house a snippet of praise to put on the cover. Readers, seeing a big name endorsing a new book, take this as important social proof. It convinces potential readers to trust the big name and buy your book.

But we're not in a publishing house, we're in our own house (perhaps with a cat, toddler or bowl of dessert on our laps). So, what do we self-publishers do?

We reach out ourselves!

When do I reach out for endorsements?

As soon as you have a professionally edited manuscript ready to go. If you ask before then, you're more likely to get a poor response because your manuscript isn't yet polished enough to be worthy of endorsement.

Who should I reach out to?

Research a list of 10 people relevant to your topic. For example: celebrities, academics and community, business and opinion leaders. Also, try other authors, people in your business network, social media influencers, book bloggers and professional reviewers. (There is more on seeking reviews using Advance Readers Copies (ARCs) in Chapter 40.)

 It can be difficult to get endorsements from people you don't know and high-profile people might often ask for payment. Authors are way better off identifying and engaging with key people in their area early on in their writing journey (and on social media platforms, especially LinkedIn). For example, authors could seek an interview with such people in research for their book and then engage them later on as part of building their book community. Of course, this has to be genuine.

— JAQUI LANE, THE BOOK ADVISER

How do I get endorsements?

Politely. First up, do your research so you can incorporate a personal message in your request. Include a brief explanation: the who, what, and why of your book and why you would like an endorsement from them. Ask if they'd prefer to see a full copy of the manuscript or just a chapter.

You could even note that you understand how busy they are, and mention that if they don't have time to prepare a testimonial, you have a few samples they might be able to choose from. Write these phrases in their style, reflecting their key messages and tone.

Include a suggested deadline in the email: 10 days is reasonable.

How NOT to get endorsements

By being demanding, rude, or responding angrily when someone doesn't respond quickly enough or declines your request. Also, by asking someone who has no relevance to your work. For example, you wouldn't ask a Kardashian to provide an endorsement for a book on bilbies.

What to do with an endorsement once you receive it?

Thank the provider, let them know you will send a copy of the book upon publication and immediately add them to your book launch list so you remember to send it. If you're successful in seeking endorsements, you may have too many to include on your cover. Decide which ones are the most compelling, and use them, the rest can appear inside your book and/or on your website and in your marketing materials.

What if the endorsement comes in after the book has gone to print?

Include it on your website and in your marketing materials. If the endorsement is from a very influential person, perhaps consider redesigning your cover, though this is only easy and cost-effective if you're using POD, not if you already have an entire print run in your garage!

I'm too nervous to reach out for endorsements. What should I do?

Just be brave and ask. It's better to have them say 'no' to you than for you to say 'no' to yourself by not even giving them the opportunity.

To give you hope, here's an endorsement I received for *Honeycomb Kids*, even though I had no personal or business connections with the endorser.

'One world. One humanity. One destiny. *Honeycomb Kids* gives you the ideas and tools you need to parent with the future in mind,' Professor Tim Flannery.

STEP 5: CHOOSE YOUR TRIM SIZE

Books come in all shapes and sizes, but what size is right for your book? Trim size is the term publishers use to describe the chosen height and width of each book.

If you're only producing an ebook you can skip this section, but if you're going to print your book, decisions about your trim size need to be made before you move forward with cover and interior design, as the size of your book impacts how the book will be laid out.

So, how do you decide, and what factors need to be considered?

Common Sizes

The best size for your book is one that suits your topic and market, so get down to your bookshop and check the sizes publishers are currently using for bestsellers within your category. You can also research this data online as the number of pages and dimensions of the book are often included in the product details section.

If investigating online, the first measurement given is normally for width and the second is for height. If you mix them up, you may end up with a landscape shaped book when you wanted it portrait!

I produce my books in 6" (15.2cm) x 9" (22.9cm) because I really like the size and, for the number of words I write (60,000+), it means the books are neither too thick nor too thin. However, I'm also in the planning stage of writing a picture book about how to self-publish a picture book, so that will obviously require a completely different trim size.

Other factors that play a part in your trim-size decision include:

- The cost to print and ship: the format of your book can affect postage and packaging prices and whether it is seen as a letter or a parcel. This depends on length, thickness and if it weighs more or less than 500 gm.
- The look of the book on the shelf: while larger trim sizes fit more words per page, they can also reduce the thickness of your book. Conversely, the smaller your trim size, the thicker your book will be, and therefore the text on the spine will stand out better.

∼

STEP 6: ORGANISE YOUR METADATA

What is metadata and where does it appear?

'Metadata' sounds like the name of a dating app for robots, but no, it's basically data about data. In the context of publishing, it is the descriptive information about your book that is shared across the internet and within the systems of the global book trade. Metadata filters across the internet, into search engines, book catalogues, and online and traditional bookstores.

Why do I need to care about metadata?

Metadata matters. I know my liberal use of exclamation marks annoys my editors, but you need to know this!!! When you do metadata well (ie:, thoughtfully, completely, and identically across the outlets mentioned further below), it will make your book easy to find.

According to the NielsenIQ team speaking at SPN's Independent Publishing Conference 2021 (fyi: these conferences are a wellspring of knowledge and inspiration for small publishers), books with all five additional 'descriptive' metadata elements filled in (keywords, short description, long description, author biography and reviews), on average sold three times more copies than books with none. And books with a cover image in their metadata sold approximately 94% more copies than those without. (Source: *Nielsen Book UK report: The Importance of Metadata for Discoverability and Sales*).

What does metadata include?

- Title and subtitle.
- Author name.
- Author bio.
- Book description: long (approximately 250 words) and short (350 characters).
- Book details (including trim size, page count and format).
- Publication date.
- ISBN.
- Keywords and categories and target audience.

What places will I need to supply my metadata to?

- My Identifiers service. Include it in the data associated with your ISBN. This will then feed into Bowker's *Books In Print*.
- The Nielsen Title Editor Service. This database is accessed by the global book trade. As an indie publisher, you can also use it to set up the metadata for your title (it takes about 5 to 10 working days to be approved).
- Your POD printer (such as IngramSpark and Amazon).
- Online retailers who you list your book with directly, for example Apple Books and Kobo.
- Your Goodreads, Amazon Author Central and Copper profiles.
- The National Library of Australia (Prepublication Data Service).
- Wholesalers and library distributors if you are using them.
- Anywhere you have an online presence, such as your main website, your socials, if you are guest blogging, etc.
- Any media kit information you send out.

Can metadata be updated once it's gone live?

Yes, it can be, however, you need to make sure you update it across all the places it appears. Try to do the research, thinking and work up front to make your metadata the best it can be from the get-go, but do improve it as you go.

What do I need to get right about metadata?

The keywords you use in your book description, title and subtitle need to be relevant to your book, so it will rank well in searches. You also need to spell each word correctly and ensure the numerical information is correct. I keep all the information in one document so I can easily cut and paste it, and so that it always matches, especially as it needs to be used across multiple formats and sites.

Why are the key words I use in my metadata important?

Key words help readers, booksellers and librarians search for and find your book amongst the millions of others available around the world.

What are the best ways to go about researching the keywords and categories to include in my metadata?

Look up the metadata for bestselling books in your category and/or use online tools to save oodles of time and so you can dig deeper into the results. Online tools include: Publisher Rocket (my personal favourite) and KDSpy.

Why might Publisher Rocket be useful to me?

It helps you discover the key words and phrases people type into Amazon, shows how many books are competing for those keywords, reveals book sale information and makes it easy to find niche categories that your book may do well in. It also shows you how many books you will need to sell to get a #1 bestseller ranking in your category. It will reveal the keywords that can do the heavy marketing lifting for your book; for example, there's no point using words in a subtitle or book description if no one is searching for them.

What do categories look like?

Let's say you've written a book about new dog ownership for young people. It might be categorised as Children's/Teenage general interest: Pets and pet care: Dogs. Whereas if you have written a book about working cattle dogs for farmers, it might be categorised as: Lifestyle, Hobbies & Leisure: Nature and the Natural World general interest: Farm and working animals.

Why is choosing my book categories important?

In libraries, bookstores and online catalogues we browse our way to the right book thanks to its placement in categories ranging from biography to history, gardening to art. Categories help readers narrow down interests and find books on subjects, without needing to know the exact name of the book or author, and they are especially important for self-publishers as you don't have to be a household name to be placed next to one!

How do I choose a category for my book?

Your research through Publisher Rocket might reveal a niche category where your book may get improved visibility but there are also two key subject category schemes operating that will help you discover the right category for you and that you will need to use in your metadata. Both are free services: the Book Industry Study Group's Book Industry Standards and Communications (BISAC) and EDItEUR's Thema. Visit their lists and drill down until you find the category your book best sits within.

Graham Bell, Executive Director, EDItEUR, recommends Australian self-publishers use both systems. 'Thema for the domestic and global market, but with the addition of BISAC specifically for US-based retailers where that market is important to the self-publisher.'

He notes that 'the above applies to both conventional print and ebooks, and that specifically for Amazon and its 'browse by subject' hierarchy, Thema is generally the preferred scheme for its storefronts outside of the US and Canada, while BISAC is preferred within the US and Canada.'

～

STEP 7: SECURE YOUR ISBNS

What is an ISBN?

ISBN stands for International Standard Book Number. An ISBN is used to identify, locate, and purchase your book across the global book industry. It is a unique identifier that links the book's publisher, format and edition details.

Do I need an ISBN?

Yes! It aids the discovery of your book in systems and increases a retailer's ability to find and order it in. The only times you wouldn't need to use an ISBN are if you are producing a book just for your family and friends, only selling direct, or if you are producing a Kindle-only book that will be distributed on Amazon. In the latter case, Amazon will assign your book an ASIN (Amazon Standard Identification Number). However, it's still a good idea to have your own ISBN.

Do I need a different ISBN for different formats and retailers?

You need a different ISBN for each format you produce (paperback, hardback, audiobook, ebook, Mobi, etc.). But it is just one ISBN per format, not per retailer. It creates huge problems if you assign different ISBNs to different retailers for the same format.

Why are some ISBNs 10 digits and others 13 digits long?

According to the International ISBN Agency, ISBNs were 10 digits up to the end of December 2006, but since 2007 they've been 13 digits.

Do I allow my publisher or printer to obtain the ISBNs on my behalf

Preferably not. It's important that you own your ISBNs. If you allow someone else to buy and allocate them, it means they will own your ISBN and have control of it in relation to that publication. You might choose to allow it though if the assisted publisher you are using has an excellent reputation in the trade and you want your book to come under their brand rather than your own.

Where do I buy ISBNs?

If you're writing in Australia and your business is located in Australia, purchase your ISBNs from Thorpe-Bowker's My Identifiers Service.

If you're Australian but living and running your writing business overseas, you need to buy your ISBNs through that country's outlet. For a complete list of international agencies, visit the International ISBN Agency.

How many ISBNs should I buy?

Buy a block of 10 as it's much better value. If you have not purchased ISBNs before, you will be charged an extra account set-up fee.

What do I do with it once I have it?

Once you have assigned the ISBN for your book, you can use it to access your cataloguing statement from the Prepublication Data Service (see Chapter 20) so you can include the statement on the imprint/copyright page of your book. You can also begin sharing information about your upcoming book with wholesalers and distributors.

What is an ISBN barcode and what does it do?

Grab any book from your bookshelf, turn to the back cover and you will see a barcode. This is the graphic representation of the ISBN that is attached to that book.

It provides retailers with a quick way to scan and obtain information about your book, such as the RRP and where more copies can be ordered from. The barcode links with their computerised sales and inventory system.

Do I need the barcode?

If your book will be sold by retail sale, a barcode is required by most retailing systems. It also makes your printed book look more professional. However, if you're only producing an ebook or publishing a print book that will only be sold through online channels, you won't need one.

How do I convert my ISBN into a barcode?

Your cover designer can handle this process for you, or use the ISBN.org converter or free barcode generator offered at Kindlepreneur.com. If publishing with IngramSpark, they have a tool that generates the barcode for you.

Do I include the price within the barcode?

It is not a good idea because if you decide to change the price, your existing copies will then be incorrectly priced. The price will also not be relevant in foreign territories and some stores like to be able to set the price of the book themselves.

Books without the price in the barcode have a special numeric code (90000) that tells a cash register to 'look up the price in your system', so for flexibility, I suggest using the 90000 code.

Phew, that was a lot. But remember, book writing and publishing is just a process.

It takes a lot to make a great cup of coffee too ... the seedling being nurtured, the tree being fertilised and pruned, the fruit being harvested so the beans can be extracted and dried, and then the process goes on and on to packaging, distribution and marketing. Finally, the coffee meets a spoon, machine or barista and you end up with a cup of coffee.

When you attend to all the processes, just like with a great cup of coffee (or mug of tea if that's more your style), you'll end up with a perfectly brewed book for you and others to savour and enjoy. And readers, booksellers and librarians will enjoy it even more when you top it off with a great cover. Let's cover that now.

17

YOUR BOOK COVER

People do judge books by their cover, so yours needs to be great! Don't save, don't skimp and please don't DIY. There are lots of areas where you can save costs when producing a book, but cover design is not one of them.

It was my professionally designed book covers that saw my books picked up, pretty much on sight, by readers, bookstores, libraries, and the media. I'm so, so glad I binned my initial DIY designs. Sure, I thought my initial concepts were okay, but I was kidding myself. My decision to invest in proper cover design was the best decision I made.

 Your 12 year old nephew who can use Publisher and Photoshop is not the person to design your book cover.

— ANDREW GRIFFTHS, AUTHOR AND COACH

A well-designed book cover sells your book for you. It will also make you proud.

WHAT MAKES A GOOD BOOK COVER?

It's been created with your target market firmly in mind

Who are you trying to reach? Imagine you're targeting businesspeople – are they just getting started in their careers, changing careers or at the end of their career? Are they trying to improve their skills in sales, human resource management, or to woo investors? Are they working from home, doing an MBA at night, or are they a job-sharing, child-sharing parent?

If publishing books in different countries, a different cover might be needed for each. I was mesmerised by the cockatoo on the Australian cover of UK photographer Tim Flach's book *Birds*, and then wowed when I saw the locally-relevant birds he featured on the cover in other countries.

 Please don't put an 'Amazon Bestseller' logo on the front of your book if you want independent bookstores to sell it. It may be worth doing separate print runs and leaving it off books you want to distribute through bookstores.

— CATHY BAYES HUNT, BOOKSTORE MANAGER

The colour palette, font and imagery target the ideal reader for the book

Let's say you have written a book about the Eromanga Natural History Museum's excavation of the 'Australotitan' fossil. The cover design would be completely different if you were targeting primary school students, academics, foreign dinosaur tourists, or Australian over-50s with a love of palaeontology.

It looks similar to other top-selling books in the same genre

Yes, it's great to swim against the tide and break new ground, but the time to do that is not with your book cover. If it's too different it will just confuse your audience.

It conveys the essence of the inner material at a glance

Give the viewer a clear idea of the subject matter and tone. For example, a memoir about a marriage gone wrong needs the cover design to convey whether it's a tragedy succumbed to or successfully overcome, or if it's a hilarious take on modern coupledom.

It's easily read, even when only displayed as a thumbnail

With so many people browsing for books from phone screens, the key text on your cover needs to stand out even when displayed as a thumbnail-sized image.

It's attractive in its own right

Some topics lend themselves to gorgeous covers, especially categories such as travel, cooking, gardening, art and wellness. In this case, people will buy a book not just for the content but for its cover, and the aesthetic it adds to their home décor.

 Being able to commission artwork is one of the reasons I'm self-publishing. A traditional publisher is very unlikely to spend money on a detailed original artwork for a first-time author.

— TRICIA D. WALKER, AUTHOR, GREENHOOD

PREPARE A DESIGN BRIEF

If you were building a house, you wouldn't just say to the builder, 'Go at it'. You would advise them of your preferences and set parameters so your dreamed-of reclaimed-timber tiny house doesn't end up as a three-storey homage to concrete, or vice versa. The same goes with book design, and the communication format is called a design brief.

For example, designer Gayna Murphy asks her clients to provide a brief that includes the following information:

- Format: what is the book's trim size? Is it portrait or landscape?
- Deadline: when does the book need to go to the printer?

- Image budget: can we only work with royalty free images, or can we commission a photographer or illustrator?
- Target market: who will want to read this book?
- Book synopsis: what is the subject matter, and what is its tone?
- Your preferences: what fonts and colours do you gravitate towards?
- Text: what text needs to appear on the cover?
- Author photo: do you want an author photo included on the back? If so, has the photo already been taken or can we plan your photo background and clothes to work with the cover design?

FINDING A COVER DESIGNER

If working with an assisted publisher they will arrange this with your input, but for the rest of us, thanks to freelancers, we now have access to the same cover designers as those used by big time publishers and bestselling authors. It's so exciting to have this type of talent work on your project! But how do you find them?

Visit a bookstore, note the covers that stand out. Flick a few pages in, to the imprint/copyright page. Listed toward the bottom will be the cover designer's name and you can then track them down via the internet.

Another great place to find a cover designer is through The Australian Book Designers Association (ABDA). In addition to a member directory, ABDA archives past winners of its annual design awards. View these and the SPN's *Book of the Year Awards* to see the best of the best.

The ASA's Style File also lists Australian illustrators while Reedsy has listings and reviews for designers from all over the world.

Freelance-type websites like Fiverr, Freelancer, 99designs and Upwork all boast creatives who might be up to the task, but find out upfront if they really know how to design compatible covers for your printer's specific needs. You may save money hiring this way, but will your book cover be able to go toe-to-toe with the best in your category?

WHAT DO COVER DESIGNS COST?

Fees vary widely from a few hundred dollars to closer to $2,000, depending on the designer and if you commission original art.

CHOOSING A GLOSS OR MATTE FINISH FOR YOUR COVER

Be guided by what's currently in bookshops in your category. What does your target audience expect and want, what does your designer suggest and what do you personally like?

The benefits of gloss include that it helps colours pop and can be eye-catching due to its shiny, reflective nature. Gloss is less likely to accumulate dust and it's easy to clean and wipe off spills. On the negative side though, it can look showy and won't suit all target audiences (such as the eco-minded), and dents and scratches are more obvious.

The benefits of matte include that it may be easier to read in a certain light because it's not as reflective, and it won't show up fingerprints and scratches as easily. It's also a bit more mature and elegant looking and feels nice to the touch. If yours is a poolside read though, steer clear, because it's easily water-damaged.

Still not sure about it? If you decide to go with POD printing, you can order one of each so you can see them side-by-side!

~

INSIDE ADVICE: TESS MCCABE
BOOK DESIGNER, FOUNDER: CREATIVE MINDS PUBLISHING

What design process do you go through with authors?

Once we've decided to work together and about the time the author has a close-to-finished manuscript, I love to see a collection of visual images they like—not just cover designs, but colour palettes, artworks, signage and the like, that speaks to them. We start with a questionnaire, which helps to get the creative brief in place, and if there aren't many visual references to help me ascertain the aesthetic direction of the book, some mood boards might also be developed. Then, I design a variety of covers and we work collaboratively to narrow down the options. The internal design (if it's quite a simple non-fiction book), the back cover and the spine are completed later in the process, usually towards the end of the book design.

How long does the process take?

Anywhere from a week for just a front cover, to several months for the full book design and layout process (with rounds of edits included). That's not me working full-time on one book: I work on projects for multiple clients at the same time and am often unable to begin something new for at least a few weeks after the client has approved my proposal. All this is to say: the more time you have for the design phase the better.

What do you wish authors knew about book design?

- That the process isn't just about putting the author's images and words into a file format that is acceptable for a printer. So much of the graphic design process is about understanding the author, the book's content, and the target market, and doing research and trying out ideas to see what works in practice. Plus, there is our intimate understanding of the power of typefaces (and which ones will/won't give your readers a headache after the first chapter).
- It's not only customers but also book retailers who will judge a self-published book by its cover. In a retail environment, you're competing with established publishers who invest a lot of time and effort to make a beautiful book, so less-professional designs stand out. When you're flying solo, a book's design can be the thing that makes or breaks your entry into traditional retail.
- The book title and subtitle aren't just words on a page, but oftentimes can be an intrinsic detail of the book cover's design, so to change the title or subtitle after the book cover design has started (or is nearly complete) can have a domino effect resulting in a less-impactful cover.

Be open to advice. There are some really bad, insipid book covers out there, so although you can't take on everyone's advice, if a librarian is saying 'this might not work', believe them.

— LEANNE WRIGHT, LIBRARIAN

GET FEEDBACK ON YOUR COVER

Once you have some initial design ideas, run them past your local book-sellers, librarians and people in your target market. I did for this book and am glad I did! They directed me away from my initial favourite to one they 'could see on the shelves'.

You can also use the cover design stage as a pre-marketing tool for your book. After seeking permission from your cover designer (and putting a DRAFT watermark over them), upload early sample covers to your socials or email list and ask which cover they prefer. As well as providing valuable feedback, it's a good way to engage with your target market and get them excited about your upcoming release.

SECURE THE SOURCE FILES/PURCHASE COPYRIGHT

When negotiating with a book cover designer, ask if they are happy to supply you with the source files. Having the source files in your possession can be important down the track if your designer is ever unavailable, uncontactable or leaves the industry. The source files mean you can have someone else update or make small changes rather than having to redesign or recreate everything from scratch.

Purchasing copyright in the finished design means you own it, and you can create other books that look similar but are designed by someone else, or make accompanying products like workbooks, or even make merchandise or a business logo out of the book title. Request for copyright assignment be included in the designer's initial quote. Designers gener-ally hate being asked to hand over source files (we are control freaks after all!), but proper remuneration makes it easier, plus you'll be covered legally.

— TESS MCCABE, BOOK DESIGNER

COVER FORMAT FLEXIBILITY

If planning different versions of your book, such as audio, let your designer know in advance so they can plan an adaptable design (audiobooks are square in shape) and so an element/text can be easily added (such as within an oval or stamp-like shape).

ENSURE YOUR COVER IS 'PRINT-READY'

There is no use creating a cover design in a format that your printer or ebook distributor can't or won't accept. Each has their own requirements for how they need files saved and delivered, so find out what this is before any design work begins.

LEVERAGING YOUR COVER DESIGN

Look professional, build your brand, and bring cohesion to your marketing material by having your cover designer also create and/or provide you with elements from the cover design that you can use as a template for your marketing materials and items such as workshop handouts. You will need to negotiate this, but knowledge of what fonts and colours were used, and getting access to particular design elements makes creating everything from social media banners to advance information sheets (see Part IV Marketing) so much easier and better.

That's covered off the basics about covers. Now let's add some colour with images and illustrations.

18

IMAGES AND ILLUSTRATIONS

L ush photography, cute cartoons, ancient maps, graphite drawings, pie charts, watercolour paintings … although not all books require illustrations or images, they can certainly enhance a book, and in some categories they're vital to meeting reader expectations.

Imagine a travel book without a view, or an illustrated history without, well, the illustrations. Drawing a blank? And have you ever read a memoir and been disappointed by the omission of photos of the people written about? Or enjoyed the memoir even more because snapshots enriched the centre pages of the book?

Yes, the right images will certainly enhance a book, and for some, such as coffee table and art books, they are the absolute selling point. But, including them will increase the cost of producing your book.

How to source images

You can take or make your own, commission a photographer or illustrator, or source them from image libraries where you can browse thousands of options. (Do be aware that if the image you choose is openly available, another author may have already used it and this might cause complications, such as Amazon not listing your book because the image is already on the front cover of another author's title).

What permissions do I need?

If using images other than your own work, you will need to get permission or pay for usage as it's unethical and illegal to reprint other people's images without permission. You can access images from royalty-free libraries, or, if using images from online photo services such as Shutterstock or iStock, double check that the rights you purchase include both print and ebook rights (if you plan to publish both versions).

If you engage a photographer or an artist, be very clear upfront about what rights you are paying for. For example, do you have the right to reproduce the image in a certain number of copies only, or is your use unlimited? Are you able to use the image in media, advertising, or merchandise? And is the image exclusive to you?

Images will add to the cost of your book

Commissioning a photographer/artist, purchasing rights and the increased design time required to integrate and lay them out (and convert screen-optimised JPEGs to four-colour CMYK files) will add to the cost of your book. There will also be much higher print costs if using colour and you might need to choose a more expensive, heavier paper to avoid the darkness of the image interfering with the printed text on the reverse side of the page.

Additional costs are incurred at ebook delivery stage too, with Amazon charging publishers an additional fee based on the file size.

~

INSIDE ADVICE: GUY DOWNES
ILLUSTRATOR AND CARTOONIST

What is the core role of an illustrator?

To find the human truth, the emotional connection, the nugget in what has been written: and then to illustrate it.

How do illustrations and cartoons add value to a non-fiction book?

- They support, amplify and reinforce what the author is trying to say.
- When done well, an illustration can help make sense of complex ideas.
- They catch attention by breaking up the page and making it look visually attractive.
- They give an extra dynamic to a book, so that, in my experience, if someone is browsing in a bookstore, diagrams and infographics tend to get people to linger on a page a little longer.
- We're all looking for escape, and illustrations can bring humour, a twist and light relief for the reader.
- A cartoon might not necessarily be a silver bullet, but it can be the spark for a reader and get them thinking afresh about a topic.
- An illustration or cartoon is like a chapter heading. It's the tip of the iceberg, the idea, that the writing helps explore in depth.
- Illustrations can be inspirational, not just informational.

Why do some authors not use them?

It might be because they've never considered them, haven't the budget for them or they might think their topic is 'too serious' for visual representation and that it might trivialise their work. I think it has the opposite effect, and an example of that is all the big newspapers using cartoonists to speak to the biggest issues of the day.

At what stage in the book-writing process is it best for an author to contact you?

Make initial contact once you're getting close to the final draft. This is a good time to ask if the illustrator has upcoming availability and to establish if you're a good fit.

How long can the process take?

It depends on how much work the artist has on, and the number of cartoons needed, so it could be as little as a week through to two or three months. I only start work once the author has a fully approved final draft, when all the ideas are baked in. It's much more efficient, as no redrafts are needed and the editor has already helped the author crystalise the main messages, which I then draw from.

What should authors look for in an illustrator and/or cartoonist? And what questions should they ask?

- First up, do you like the illustrator's style? I'm not for everybody. I stick to what I like and know, so you need to find someone whose style you love and will resonate with your target audience.
- Ask what other books they've worked on and view samples.
- Ask about costs. Be very upfront; for example, will it be an hourly rate or a package deal, and will the size of the print run matter? Will the illustrator be given an ad or any extra exposure in the book?
- Know approximately how many illustrations you want: is it one or more per chapter?
- Discuss the contract including IP and © usage. This should be covered in a *statement of work* so you understand what rights you have when it comes to reproducing the work in or outside of the book.
- In your initial discussions, do you feel like you have a good rapport, and is the work a good fit for both parties? Is there good chemistry? Will the relationship be workable?

What is the best way to find an illustrator and/or cartoonist?

- Ask within your networks and through author sites.
- Visit bookstores and look up the artists illustrating your favourite books.
- The *Australian Cartoonists Association* and *Illustrators Australia* both offer lists of current member contacts with sample art.
- View the ASA's Style File.
- You can also visit sites such as Freelancer, Airtasker, Fiverr, etc., that can be quite competitive with prices.

What do you wish authors knew about illustrators?

That we can get up to speed quickly on a topic. One of the misconceptions is that artists are just artists, but we also have a lot of expertise we bring to the process through life and business experience. Artists also have specialisations. For me, they are leadership, change, people and performance, whereas for someone else it might be botany. Finally, some of us offer bespoke work, some license our existing creations and some of us offer both options. My final tip to authors is to be open to the idea that illustrations can really enhance your book.

Your final book, how it reads, looks, how long it takes to deliver and how it is received by readers will be the sum of so many decisions you make along the way, including whether or not to use illustrations. Don't let paralysis by analysis stop you from moving forward though.

Research options and then make decisions on those options, one chunk at a time. That's all you really need to do to bring your project to life.

In the next chapter we explore your interior design options. And yes, that means a few more decisions for you to make, so have a stretch, grab your favourite beverage and see you over the page.

19

INTERIOR DESIGN/TYPESETTING

W hen it comes to houses, thoughtful interior design makes a home easy to enjoy. Similarly, interior book design makes it easy for readers to enjoy the content of a book. In this chapter, we'll cover outsourcing as well as DIY interior design options. If you're using an assisted publisher, you can just skip on ahead.

 For many business authors, a book is the new business card. It's an opportunity for branding. You're selling yourself as being at the top of your game, so your book's design needs to convey that.

— LORNA HENDRY, BOOK DESIGNER, EDITOR, WRITER

OUTSOURCING DESIGN

If you can afford to, bid farewell to the frustration, lose the learning curve, say sayonara to the stress and get a unique and gorgeous book design by handing the interior design over to a pro.

By working with a professional, you can not only achieve a bespoke design with a technically correct file, but you won't need to concern yourself with alignments, technical details and terms you never knew existed, such as widows, orphans and rags (widows being when a tiny last line, or just one word of a paragraph appears at the top of the page, orphans when just one line of a paragraph appears at the very bottom of the page, and rags when the lines look ragged on the right-hand side of the page because the text has not been justified). You want to avoid all of these so your book is easy on the eye and flows for the reader.

Where to find interior book designers

In addition to reading the imprint page of books you've enjoyed in order to discover the designer, try recommendations from your network, ABDA and sites including Reedsy, 99designs, Freelancer, and Upwork.

 Most designers allow for two rounds of author's corrections in their quote, but in my experience, most authors need four. Ask for these extra rounds to be included in the initial quote.

— JAQUI LANE, THE BOOK ADVISER

DIY INTERIOR DESIGN

I DIY'd the interior for this book. Yes, it's super simple and definitely not perfection, but it meant I could achieve my budget goals while also having visual control over what words to edit to bring the page count down. I also like tinkering with words, so having to go back and forth countless times with a designer doesn't suit me compared to being able to make a change and instantly see how it looks. But let's investigate the options for your book.

Reasons not to DIY interior design

- You want a gorgeous design, and a professional could do it way better.
- You don't know what you're doing ... you double space everything, think Garamond is the name of a French guy, and have no idea about the difference between 9, 11 and 13 pt font.
- It is another significant technical learning curve you can't or don't want to tackle.
- You can't justify the upfront cost of buying the program.

- You suspect you will spend too much time learning how to use the software (quite possible!) and finessing your design (more than likely!) rather than using that time to market your work or start on your next book.

Benefits of DIY interior design

- Save money on a designer. You can use free conversion programs for ebooks or hire or buy software. Buying software means you will be able to use it for future books too, thus spreading the cost out.
- Bring your print book vision to life by being able to experiment with different fonts and layouts.
- You can efficiently, economically and immediately make changes and update your ebooks and POD files when an error is spotted or as needed. This also comes in handy if you end up writing more than one book, as you can update the back matter in your earlier books to promote your latest release.
- If you are already a skilled artist or have a design background, cast your eyes over the book *The Crossroads of Should and Must: Find and Follow Your Passion*. Written and designed by Elle Luna, it shows how an author/artist can bring their own style to the occasion.

DIY INTERIOR LAYOUT SOFTWARE OPTIONS

This is a fast-moving space with each company regularly releasing new features.

Vellum

I've used Vellum to lay out all my print and ebooks except for *Honeycomb Kids* which a designer worked on. Overall, I love it for my type of books. The biggest difficulties I ran into were trying to include an index (which I had to create manually, and which didn't allow me to put the index in standard two-column format) and working out how to structure and format my Word file so Vellum could understand what I wanted for my headings and subtitles. Vellum has a guide for that. The software is user-friendly and quickly generates files for print and a variety of ebook formats. However, Vellum is only available for Mac (although you can use it in on a PC via the Cloud) and is not suitable for works involving too many illustrations or where you require a unique and intricate design.

Atticus

Atticus is the book formatting (and writing) tool for print and ebooks developed by Dave Chesson, a long-time book marketer and founder of Kindlepreneur. I would have loved to try out Atticus for the design of this book but in 2022, the software was still rolling out the features I needed. From the looks of it, though, Atticus could very well end up being a self-publisher's best friend and works for Mac and PC.

Adobe InDesign

InDesign is the software professionals use. It can help you design the most complex and beautiful books, but if you don't know how to use the program, it will be a learning curve of Mt Kosciuszko-like proportions. If you plan to produce many complex or particularly design-heavy books though, it may be worth it.

Affinity Publisher

A different model again, this design app offers all sorts of useful tools and templates, as well as lots of creative flexibility. It's worth a look as an alternative to Adobe InDesign if you're a designer-type or want to lay out a cookbook.

Reedsy Book Editor

Simple to use, the Reedsy book production tool offers limited book-size options. It does, however, let you import text and images and quickly prepare your book to the requirements of the key POD printers and ebook companies.

Microsoft Word

If you would prefer to use Word to format your ebook (it's not really suitable for print books), ALLi offers some useful advice. One tip is to set up *styles* for your chapter headings, titles, subtitles and paragraphs and then apply them throughout your document so everything is standardised. Note: if planning to publish with Amazon, you will need to meet the specifications in their current KDP formatting guidelines.

Ebooks are all about the simplicity of text, and Amazon, Apple, Kobo and IngramSpark all have a service that converts Word files to the files required for their ecosystem.

Draft2Digital (D2D)

If you will be using D2D as your sole ebook distributor to all the big sites, their book layout tool is simple and free.

 Understand that the last 20% of your book, whether it's the rewriting or attention to design, may take just as much effort as the first 80%. But it's that last 20% that adds the magic.

— KIM MCCOSKER, *4 INGREDIENTS*

FONT SELECTION

Dedicated book design programs offer a variety of fonts that work well for books. If you're using another type of program, steer clear of showy, gaudy fonts—you want the attention focused on the meaning of your words, not the look of them. In that vein, serif typefaces make for easier reading while large blocks of sans-serif fonts are difficult to read and best used for headings only.

Your font size needs to be large enough to be able to be read, but not so large that it looks weird or adds to your page count, as this increases the cost of printing your book. The most common-sized fonts for the main text of standard books are no smaller than 10 pt and no larger than 12 pt, with headers averaging 14 pt.

You can also adjust the spacing between lines of text (known as leading), as well as the space between individual letters (known as kerning) to get the right look for your book. Your margin settings will also affect your page count; a few millimetres can add up across the course of hundreds of pages.

COMMON INTERIOR DESIGN STANDARDS

Research books in your category, noting the approximate font size, margin spacing and other details.

- Nearly all books have the book title or author's name printed on the top of each left-hand (verso) page, with the title of the book or current chapter title appearing on the top of each right-hand (recto) page.
- New chapters have traditionally begun on right-hand pages, which might mean leaving a blank page if the previous chapter ended on a right-hand page. However, some recently published books by major publishers now start chapters on the left-hand side too. I've done this too as it's an eco-friendly and cost-saving move—these days, with all we know, why waste a perfectly good page?
- The first three words or the entire first phrase of the chapter are often presented in CAPITALS, but not always, or you might use *drop caps* (large, decorative capital letters) at the start of a chapter in a printed book. These look great in a print book, but depending on the program you use, might create issues in the layout of your ebook file. Just do a test to find out.
- Kindlepreneur's How to Format a Book is worth a look for more information, including how far down to start the text on a page and more.

~

INSIDE ADVICE: LORNA HENDRY
BOOK DESIGNER, EDITOR, WRITER

How do you describe what you do?

I guide people and organisations through the publishing process—from the point where they think they have a finished manuscript, right through to getting the printed book into their hands. I was a graphic designer for 20 years and then retrained as an editor, so it's quite a useful combination of skills for project managing books.

Why is book design important?

You write a book to communicate something. Writers and editors focus on words and sentences to ensure they're understandable and the message is being communicated, but a really important part of communicating a message is also visual. You can have a wonderful manuscript, but if the typesetting is clunky and the margins are wrong and the font is out of place, it can make it completely unreadable.

What do you like about book designing?

I've always loved print. I love the physicality of books. As a writer, when I first held my own book in my hand, it was the best day of my life. I love it when a client opens their box of books and gets that same feeling.

What makes a well-designed book?

When you read a well-designed book, the design doesn't intrude into your consciousness. In non-fiction, the different heading levels will lodge in your subconscious. You'll see Level 1, Level 2 and Level 3 headers and understand the hierarchy visually without having to think about it. Also, less is more. You don't need four fonts and colour inside, you just need to let the book be the book. The place for bells and whistles is on the cover, not the inside.

Where do people go wrong with book design?

If you are reading a book and you notice a font, there's a problem. Design should be completely in the background, unobtrusive, not showy. They also tend to want the whitest, brightest paper, and go too heavy with the stock. These books look and feel stiff and scream 'self-published vanity project'. Another problem can be when they use poor images. This is understandable if it's a family history and it's the only old photo you have of a family member, but in any other type of book a poor image just looks unprofessional.

What programs do you use?

InDesign for the bulk of the work, Illustrator for graphics, and Photoshop if images need manipulating.

What kind of paper stock do you like?

IngramSpark have a very nice cream/off-white lightweight paper. It looks like a real trade-published book. The only books that really need white paper are full-colour books. I like matte covers too, but if it's a photographic work sometimes gloss can lift the images slightly.

How long does it take to design a book and how much does it cost?

Depending on how busy the designer is with other projects, it can take approximately two weeks to deliver design concepts. Once the style is chosen, the layout process begins, and this can take another two to four weeks. Price will vary depending on the complexity of the design and the size of the book. Look for a designer who includes a reasonable number of author corrections in the initial quote, as you will always find something that needs changing.

How can authors communicate better with a designer?

When they're going over a design for the first time, instead of highlighting a problem, authors can tend to jump straight to what they think is the solution. They might think the text is a bit hard to read, so they say, 'Make the type bigger' rather than saying 'I find it hard to read.' If you convey the problem, we might realise it's the font that isn't working, not the size. Or perhaps it's the spacing between letters, or the line lengths. Rather than jumping straight to instruction, try to verify the actual problem and share that with the designer to get the best result.

Top tips

- It is much cheaper to ensure that your manuscript is thoroughly edited and error-free before you send it off for design, rather than to trying to fix problems once it has all been laid out.

- Decide on the trim size of your book early and don't change it once design work begins. It's like building a house—if you decide you want your walls thicker at the end of the build, there are going to be a lot of costs involved in renovating.
- Avoid A5 as a size: it needs to look like a real book, and you won't achieve that with A5.
- Throwing money at it won't magically create a great book. You have to do the work—the planning, the thinking, the writing—to create something you can be proud of and that readers will love. Ultimately, it's your book. An editor and designer can only do so much, so you really have to own the process.

And part of the process includes addressing all the extra bits that 'make' a book. Not just your manuscript, but the information that people see when they first open your book, and the last words read when they close it. Front and back matter is what we cover next.

20

FRONT AND BACK MATTER

Front and back matter includes all the elements of the book that are not the main manuscript. To see what this involves, flick through professionally published books to see what appears before the first and after the last chapter.

With front and back matter, you do have some flexibility as to what you position where, but there are also some common standards to adhere to. Here are the basics.

FRONT MATTER

The only pages that must appear in your front matter are the title page and table of contents (TOC). The imprint/copyright page typically appears here too.

Other pages you may like to include are half-title, advance praise, the dedication, acknowledgements (these usually appear in the back matter but can also be included upfront), foreword, introduction and 'how to use this book'.

What does the imprint/copyright page include?

The imprint/copyright page includes contact details for your self-publishing imprint, the copyright symbol © and author name, the year published, your disclaimer, ISBN number, names of the cover and interior designer and other contributors (such as illustrators, stylists and photographers), where and by who the book was printed and bound, and sometimes the paper type used. It is also where you place the cataloguing statement.

What is a cataloguing statement?

If you open a book that has been professionally published in Australia, you will normally see a cataloguing statement in the front matter on the imprint page. It will say: 'A catalogue record for this work is available from the National Library of Australia (NLA).' It sometimes appears with a graphic of the NLA building.

Once you have assigned your ISBN you can access your cataloguing statement from the Prepublication Data Service (formerly known as CIP, Catalogue in Print). It's a free service run by the NLA. You register with the service for exposure to libraries, but also for access to the cataloguing statement. According to the NLA, applications are processed instantly and your record will appear on Trove within 48 hours.

BACK MATTER

The back matter will most likely include:

- An Afterword. Use this to add a further understanding of your book or yourself or to talk about the journey you have been on since writing the book.
- Acknowledgements. Here is where you get to thank all the people who helped you on your journey with this book.

 I include extensive sales pages at the back of my book promoting everything from signing up for my programs to business coaching, bulk book buys and contact information for media to interview me.

— ANDREW GRIFFITHS, BOOK WRITING COACH, AUTHOR
AND SPEAKER

It may also include:

- Appendixes and resources. This is where you provide further useful information for readers (or you can include this material online).

> The value of an appendix is you can put the detail in there rather than it interrupting the flow of your story. But though appendixes do enhance books, they don't help sell them.

— PAUL DAFFEY, JOURNALIST, TRAD AND INDIE AUTHOR

- Endnotes/Footnotes/Bibliography/Further Reading. These provide readers with additional information and acknowledge the sources you drew on in the writing and research of your book.
- Glossary. Glossaries were once traditionally placed at the front of documents but many of the contemporary style manuals say that the glossary is usually part of the back matter (end matter) and precedes the bibliography. But if you think it will aid the understanding of your book, you can also place key terms in the front matter.
- Index. This is especially important for non-fiction titles to help readers quickly find key information. Index creation is covered in the next chapter.
- Additional/other titles by the author. This page creates an opportunity for readers to find out about your other works.
- Excerpts. You legend, you've already started working on a new book?! Include an excerpt or two here to whet the readers' appetites.
- Author services and promotions. A key benefit to being your own publisher is that you can advertise your other services right when the reader is thinking they would like to know more.
- A request for a review. A small mention that you would appreciate a review on online sites may prompt the reader to do just that. The more positive reviews your book gets, the better the social proof to other potential readers that your book is worth the time and money.

I'm not kidding when I say that writing the front and back matter can cause you almost as many sleepless nights as the actual manuscript. But you'll get there. And when you do, you are super close to the finish line! Next on your agenda will be the index. Read on to see if you need one for your book, and how to go about it if you do.

21

INDEXING

As a non-fiction book fanatic, I enjoy a great index. They are especially handy to quickly navigate back to specific ideas and mentions. An index can markedly enhance the usability of a printed book and is a feature held in esteem by librarians and readers. It's not crucial to include one, but it does show that you've taken the production of your book and your readers' needs seriously.

However, including an index in your book will require additional time and will add to production costs as either you or a professional indexer will need to create the index, and an index will add to the page count, thereby increasing your printing costs. It's also rare to see index creation included in assisted publishing packages. It's either not offered or offered only as a premium 'bolt-on' solution.

It could also be argued that there is an opportunity cost if you DIY the index, because that's time you could be using to market your book or undertake some form of paid work. Let's explore the issue—and opportunity—some more.

Do all non-fiction books need an index?

Look at similar books in your category to see what the norm is. If your book is relatively short and simple, or in a specific category, an index may not be necessary.

Regarding ebooks, it's not crucial to include an index because ebook search tools are powerful (even though not as comprehensive as an index which also helps locate and group concepts together). Also, there are no actual page numbers in an ebook to correlate to, so it's best to remove the print book index from your ebook file. If you would like to pursue a comprehensive index for an ebook, more information is available online at the Digital Publications Index.

When does work on the index start?

Only when your book is fully edited, proofread and laid out. It must be in its final form or you will end up with an index that doesn't correlate correctly with the pagination.

If preparing the index myself, what do I do?

You'll need to learn how to drive Microsoft Word's Index feature. You can access it by clicking on *References* then using *Insert Index* and *Mark Entry*. Many authors though find this very complicated so end up creating a separate Word or Excel file to list entries. InDesign has a similar tool. You can save a bit of time on your learning curve by reading up on ALLi's non-fiction index tips.

Guidance on indexing is also provided in style manuals such as the *Chicago Manual of Style*. There is also AS/NZS 999:1999, *Information and documentation: guidelines for the content, organisation and presentation of indexes*. It is identical with ISO 999:1999 and ANSI/NISO Z39.4-2021, *Criteria for Indexes*.

In the past I have used both approaches. For some of my books I paid for professional indexers, and for others I did my own indexing. The index in this book is a hybrid approach; professional indexer Sherrey Quinn indexed concepts while I indexed names and companies. But then, due to the limitations of the layout program I used (which doesn't allow for columns, shrinking of text and other formatting restrictions), I needed to do some workarounds and deleted some entries to keep the index manageable.

What is ANZSI?

ANZSI is a network of professional indexers with members in all Australian states and New Zealand. The Society recognises professional competence through accreditation of indexers. It maintains a list of indexers who are available to accept commissions. Their contact details can be found in Indexers Available.

~

INSIDE ADVICE:
THE AUSTRALIAN AND NEW ZEALAND SOCIETY OF INDEXERS (ANZSI)

A professionally compiled index:

- is clear, comprehensive and consistent in style
- is arranged in logical order
- includes headings for significant topics, concepts and names
- includes subheadings to help the reader locate specific aspects of topics without having to search through numerous pages
- connects all related headings in the index through the use of 'see' and 'see also' references
- includes explanatory notes to put headings into context
- may distinguish page references for illustrations, tables and footnotes from page references related to the main text.

How do I go about engaging an indexer?

To ensure your index is a good one, recognise that a good index takes time. Search the ANZSI database for a qualified indexer and advise the candidate indexers of the scope, content and target audience well in advance of your publication date.

~

So, now you have a good understanding of all the elements that go into creating the content for a book, next you get to decide in what medium/s to publish it. And don't worry, it's normal to feel a bit overwhelmed as you try to absorb all this information. Just take everything back to the core reason you're writing your book and let that initial motivation sustain you as you step through all the processes. You'll get there!

22

CHOOSING THE RIGHT MEDIUM/S FOR YOUR MANUSCRIPT

S ometimes we overwhelm ourselves thinking we need to be everything to everybody and that our book needs to be in every format to succeed. But it is at this pre-publishing stage that you can really weigh up which medium/s might be right for you and your work.

Depending on your circumstances and audience, consider releasing your work as one, some, or all of the following:

- ebook
- print book: softcover (paperback), hardcover, spiral bound, or large print (if your book's audience comprises the elderly, vision impaired or people with dyslexia)
- audiobook
- and other mediums, including apps, podcast, documentary, magazine or newspaper serial and courses.

The more mediums your subject matter is available through, the more opportunities you give your customers to buy and use it in a format that suits them. However, not every book should be in every format, so your decision needs to be underpinned by your strategy and ultimate goals. You can also always add additional formats at a later date or remove one from publication.

Ricardo Fayet from Reedsy offered interesting advice at the time he launched the hardback version of *How to Market a Book: Over Perform in a Crowded Market*. His advice on the reasons to release your book in multiple formats is abridged here with permission.

> The main reason behind releasing a hardback is simple: to keep Amazon happy. Why does it make Amazon happy if you have a hardcover edition on top of a paperback and an ebook (and potentially an audiobook)? Well, because it makes (certain) Amazon customers happy and Amazon search rewards multi-format availability. Also, higher-priced products get more search visibility from Amazon's search engine. Why is that? Another little-known fact about Amazon's search algorithm is that it rewards higher-priced products—provided they sell. So, in the case of audiobooks, they're expensive, high-margin products for Amazon. In other words, Amazon makes more money by selling one of these audiobooks or a hardback than by selling the corresponding ebook or paperback.
>
> — RICARDO FAYET, REEDSY

So, why, and how do you go about getting your manuscript into these formats? Let's run through that now.

23

EBOOK YOUR BOOK

Unless you are publishing something like a coffee table book, you will miss out on sales if you don't also release it as an ebook. Why? For many people in your potential target audience, ebooks are the main way they choose to read, these days. Some authors even choose to only publish in ebook form, not bothering with the extra work and costs required to be successful in print.

According to *Book Publishers Global Market Report 2021: COVID-19 Impact and Recovery to 2030*, ebook sales are growing rapidly in the US and European markets, and now generate a higher share of revenue than print books in markets such as the US and UK.

Why do people read ebooks?

- Price: ebooks are normally cheaper than print books.
- Convenience: ebooks are easy to carry and store.
- Immediacy: you can see a book of interest and begin reading immediately, even if it's 3 am and you are miles away from the nearest bookstore.
- Usability: it's easy to click through on the hyperlinks in ebooks, and other features such as the ability to highlight text and check definitions.

- Environmental sustainability: some people don't want trees cut down to print their books, even though there is obviously still a carbon footprint created by ereaders and server technologies.

Why publish an ebook?

- The audience is there! Ebooks continue to grow in popularity around the world, and they are a fast, efficient way for people to access your work.
- People who see your online marketing can buy and download your book instantly.
- There is no large upfront investment in a print run or interior design. It is also the cheapest and fastest way to launch a book locally or internationally and get it into the hands of readers.
- Ebooks allow you the flexibility to test the market, iron out bugs, make changes, learn as you go and experiment with pricing.
- Ebooks don't need to be 40,000+ words long to look good on a digital shelf.
- You can split your book and publish it as several ebooks, giving away the first one free to entice your audience to buy the remaining ones. Or give away the first chapter as a hook to get them to buy the whole book. You can even package small ebooks together to create a 'box set'.
- Unless your book is an exquisite art, travel, or coffee table book, or you are doing limited print editions, or want to keep the RRP at the higher end, there just aren't many reasons to leave sales on the table when an ebook is so easy to produce and deliver.

Downsides of an ebook-only approach

- Ebooks are not as prestigious as a print book.
- You can't hand a copy to someone or sign it with a personal note.
- Ebooks lack visibility on real-world bookshelves in stores, homes and offices.
- When giving author talks, ideally you want to display a stack of your books, which is great for visual interest and branding, as well as to sell afterwards, but you can't do that with ebooks.

- You can't hold a copy of your book for media photos and readers can't take great photos with it and upload them to their socials.

EBOOKS: TECHNICAL INFORMATION

If you are working with an assisted publisher, you can give this section a miss, they'll take care of the details for you. Phew! But for the rest of us, here are some of the basics you need to know. But remember, you don't spend days wondering how your fridge keeps things cold, so don't let not understanding how ebook technology works stop you from moving forward—you'll discover it's easy in the end.

What devices and apps do readers use to access ebooks?

Some of the main ways customers view ebooks include on their regular computers, tablet and mobile phones and through devices such as Amazon's Kindle, Rakuten's Kobo, Onyx's Boox, Barnes & Noble's NOOK devices, Apple's ebook reading app and Adobe Digital Editions ebook reader software and app. Interestingly, if your target market is Australian, Apple is the dominant phone used here, so if you are going to produce an ebook or audiobook it makes sense to publish with Apple (not just Amazon). There are also library-based services such as OverDrive and Indyreads, and new services and devices come along all the time.

What format does my file need to be in?

Different systems use different file types but programs and service providers (for example Vellum, Atticus, Scrivener, Amazon KDP, Ingram-Spark, Draft2Digital, Apple Books and others) can easily convert your Word file to suit. IngramSpark can also convert the PDF files you uploaded for your print book.

The key formats include:

- EPUB: this file type is used by more ebook readers than any other file format, although it is not compatible with Amazon Kindle devices. It is known as a 'reflowable' format, as the text and view changes depending on the device and user preference.
- KPF: Kindle Create is the format Amazon recommends for its Kindle book system and is reflowable.

- MOBI: this is a fixed-layout format.
- PDF: this is a fixed-layout format that many of us are used to, but it doesn't offer a great reading experience in comparison to reflowable formats.

File Size

The bigger and heavier your print book, the more it will cost, and that is also true of ebook files, especially as Amazon charges a delivery fee according to your ebook's file size. Lots of images can really add up, so if it makes sense, restrict your use of them and/or prior to adding them into your ebook, use software tools such as TinyPNG, ImageOptim and FileOptimizer to optimise and minimise their size. Always keep your original image safe though, and only apply changes and optimisation to a copy.

Digital Rights Management (DRM)

DRM is aimed at preventing certain types of digital files (such as your precious book!) from being shared or pirated. Each major player, such as Amazon, has their own version.

The challenge with DRM is that it means legitimate buyers of your work may not be able to access your book across their different devices (e.g., their laptop, phone, and ereader). Also, DRM can be hacked, so if someone really wanted to access and share your file, they could probably find a way to do it. If DRM is of interest or concern to you, consult ALLi or your digital distributor for the latest advice.

∽

I suppose I've taken a lot of words here to let you know that although producing an ebook uses technology, you don't really need to be tech-savvy to pull it off because there are plenty of programs and service providers to ease the way.

Hmmm ... but how does one go about bringing out a real-world paperback or hardcover? Let's cover that now.

24

PRINT YOUR BOOK

T his chapter is for people committed to seeing their words in print. Again, if you have a contract with an assisted publisher, they will take care of this for you, but just like a house you're outsourcing construction for, it's still good to know who, with what, and how your house is built, and what it actually costs. And if you're DIY through and through, hopefully these pages will get your through.

Why publish in print?

So many reasons!

- Many people prefer, if not solely read, print books.
- Print books make an impact.
- You can earn a good margin selling print books direct.
- Currently, only print books are eligible for PLR and ELR.
- Real-world retailers and libraries can stock them, giving them shelf space and visibility.
- You can sign books, adding a special note, and pile them up high at author talks.
- Read Jaqui Lane's quote below to seal the deal.

There's something about a printed book that conveys authority, credibility and stature. When books were first developed, they were rare, containing information and knowledge not readily available to the masses. This appreciation of the intrinsic value of books has stayed with us through to the present day. To be the author of a book delivers a level of authority and credibility (provided it is well-written and shares valued knowledge and insights) that an ebook simply does not.

— JAQUI LANE, THE BOOK ADVISER

Downsides of print books

They're more expensive and time-consuming to design, produce, make changes to, store and ship. Which makes them more expensive for customers too! They have limited interactivity and the options for the different ways to print can be confusing.

Hopefully though, the following information will solve the confusing part for you.

BOOK PRINTING OPTIONS

Let's start with an introduction to the two very different ways you can print your book: Print on Demand (POD) and/or a print run through a traditional offset printer.

POD printers use digital printing and can batch many titles by different authors together in one print run (i.e., the print line doesn't have to be set up just for your book). This leads to economies of scale and flexibility, even allowing you to economically order just one book at a time (such as for a proof), if that is all you need.

A traditional print run can offer higher-quality print and production, but you will need to order hundreds or thousands of books at the same time for this approach to be economical.

Let's take a closer look.

Benefits of POD

- You can test the waters for your book without a large upfront investment and can also make changes relatively easily and economically.
- You can print cost-effective proof copies and advance reader copies.
- You can order boxes of author copies as you need them to sell direct and at events.
- Both IngramSpark and Amazon offer POD, meaning you can reach a global audience.
- By applying pricing for distribution in the various currencies (AUD, GBP, USD and EURO, etc.), IngramSpark will distribute your title globally (which means retailers around the world can access it!). By going with Amazon, your book will be shown as 'Available/In Stock' on Amazon sites, and members of Amazon Prime may be more likely to buy it due to the free shipping offer. And the great news? You can go with both!
- You can place *Publisher Direct* orders through your IngramSpark account to be printed and shipped from one of Ingram's print facilities and delivered around the world to specific customers. Drop shipping like this and paying a handling fee means you don't need to get bogged down storing books or sending out orders. IngramSpark also gives you the opportunity to price your title for distribution in different markets: UK, AU, US, Canada, Europe and Global Connect. Check what similar titles sell for in those markets and price your title accordingly.

Negatives of POD

- It may mean selling through wholesalers into bookstores is unviable financially as the cost per copy is higher than with a traditional print run, meaning less profit margin for you.
- There are reduced options compared to specialist offset printers when it comes to customisation, papers, inks, sizes and shapes.
- Customer service will not be as fast or as personal, compared to when dealing with a printer directly.

- There is potential for lack of consistency and quality in the printing of images.

Benefits of an offset print run

- The price per copy (when ordering more than 500) is normally a lot cheaper which means you have more of a margin to play with and profit from. There really can be a huge difference in the price of an offset print run and POD and it adds up. For example, 500 copies @ $6ea in an offset run ($3,000) versus 500 copies @ $10ea via POD ($5,000) is a difference of $2000.
- The better price per copy may make it more workable to engage a distributor or offer outlets a better margin to stock your book.
- The quality of printing is better due to the technique of transferring/offsetting the inked image from a plate to a blanket, then onto the paper.
- Depending on how many you order, your price per copy will be cheaper than POD. If your book sells well, this option will put more profits in your pocket.
- You will have more choice when choosing environmentally friendly inks, papers, covers and processes.
- Experts at the printing company will be able to guide you through the process.
- The right printer can do bespoke work and help you create a book that really stands out from the crowd.

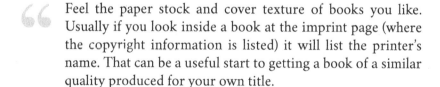

Feel the paper stock and cover texture of books you like. Usually if you look inside a book at the imprint page (where the copyright information is listed) it will list the printer's name. That can be a useful start to getting a book of a similar quality produced for your own title.

— TESS MCCABE, BOOK DESIGNER

Negatives of an offset print run

- It can be incredibly difficult to know how many books to print in your first run. If you order more, your price per book will be cheaper, but if you over-order, the economics won't work.

- How big is your garage? You will either need to find a vermin and damp-proof place to store a pallet (or more!) of cartons in your home or pay for them to be stored offsite.
- Though stacks of books may motivate you to get out there and sell, sell, sell, some people find facing a room full of unsold books daunting and deflating.

The book industry and book sales have shrunk over time but it is currently having a resurgence with people re-igniting their love of reading. That said, to sell 500 copies of a book in Australia these days is considered a bestseller, which means most books sell far fewer copies than this. Keep this in mind when planning your print run and expectations.

— CATHY BAYES HUNT, BOOKSTORE MANAGER

Benefits of doing POD and a Print Run concurrently

If you think the market will buy 500 or more copies, it might make sense to POD and offset at the same time. Why? A print run of 500 will give you a better price per copy (only if you're able to sell them all of course!), while POD gives you access to cheaper proof copies, loads of flexibility, access to international bookstore distribution through IngramSpark and drop shipping. I am planning on this model for this book.

CHOOSING A POD SERVICE

Plenty of Australian printers as well as services like Draft2Digital (for key overseas markets) offer short-run and POD printing options, but they may not deliver all the publishing benefits of the two POD behemoths in the Australian and global market: IngramSpark and Amazon KDP Print.

Both these companies have printing facilities in Australia and key locations around the world, and you don't need to choose one or the other. In fact, the advice from Orna Ross at ALLi is to POD with both IngramSpark AND Amazon ... even though Amazon can order your book through IngramSpark. That's right, in conjunction, it's the combination that optimises benefits and income. For example:

- Printing with Amazon will improve your book's visibility on Amazon as it will always appear as 'In stock'. This can encourage immediate consumer purchase (compared to it saying 'Out of stock, more on the way').
- Printing with Amazon means Amazon Prime Members have access to an enticing free shipping service.
- Though IngramSpark doesn't sell to consumers directly, it offers distribution to bookstores, libraries and retailers around the world.
- By not solely going with Amazon, it gets you around the awkward problem of bookstores disliking Amazon being listed as the printer and refusing to buy your book. (For similar competitive reasons, some independent Australian bookstores may be reticent about ordering books via Booktopia Publisher Services.)

The negatives of going with a dual POD approach include the time and effort needed to set up and maintain two services and the fact that the two companies do not offer all the same trim sizes, paper stock and added options. That means the two versions of your POD book may look and feel different depending on how you set them up and which company prints it.

If you do choose to use both services, set up accounts and your book with both companies using the same ISBN. Make sure that you set up with KDP first and DO NOT enable expanded distribution with them beforehand. You'll find plenty of online help on both their sites.

CHOOSING AN OFFSET PRINTER

Not just any old photocopy shop or printer will do for your book. Specialist book printers can really help your book stand out with features ranging from foil stamping to incorporating coloured ribbons which can be used as bookmarks.

You can find specialist book printers by looking at the imprint page of books (where the printer will be listed), speaking with your book designer and getting recommendations from your network. You can also check out the winners of the book category at Australia's National Print Awards.

Some experienced Australian book printers include Ligare, Ovato/Griffin Press, McPherson's Printing Group, Bright Print Group and SOS Print + Media. Even Kwik Kopy can assist with smaller publications.

A printer in your own state will likely achieve lower freight costs and you may even be able to visit the factory the day they print your book which could be great to capture for your social media!

Things to be aware of

Always ask for samples of books printed by the company before committing to go with them and be wary of sales pitches encouraging you to potentially over-order; after all, you can always do another print run if your book is a runaway success.

Freight costs can be significant, so find out what this will be to your area and ask the printer to give you an idea of the dimensions and number of boxes your order will arrive in so you can plan your storage solution.

If printing in bulk overseas, the quote may be significantly cheaper, but add on import costs, duties, and freight. And be aware that your book may be censored or pulled from the printing line if it breeches any laws of the country it is being printed in, even if you don't intend to sell it there.

 Everyone has a budget but don't scrimp, you'll end up with something that isn't just dirt cheap, but looks it too. Supporting Australian-based printers supports the Australian publishing industry as a whole.

— RICHARD CELARC, LIGARE

CHOOSING YOUR BOOK'S PHYSICAL FEATURES

If you have ever renovated or built a house, you know how many decisions need to be made! This tap or that one? What tile size looks best? What shade of white for the walls? With books, there are also plenty of choices.

Page colour

The options are usually various shades of cream or white. White will normally be used as the basis for coloured printing if that is part of your design.

Paper and binding type

Paper comes in various thicknesses/weights (rated using gsm), textures, and from various sources, including forests, sustainable plantations, or recycled.

POD publishers tend to offer fewer binding choices than commercial book printers. The key types of binding according to Ligare Printing are perfect bound, saddle-stitched, limp sewn and spiralbound.

> The smallest book we have self-published was approximately 32 pages and the largest 800 pages, though 256 pages is our most common size. No matter the size though, we work on multiples of 32-page sections as it works best for our production costs.
>
> — CRAIG LEWIS, BOILING BILLY PUBLICATIONS

Spine size

Spine size will change based on your book's page count and the gsm of the paper used, plus the cover type. Your cover designer will need this last detail to prepare your files for print. You can work this measurement out when finalising your book with your POD or offset printer.

FILE PREPARATION FOR POD AND/OR PRINT RUNS

A PDF ensures that your printed or viewed file retains the formatting that you intended for your book. Programs like Vellum and Atticus can do most of the work for you, but different printers will have different requirements and most require that fonts are embedded.

IngramSpark provide comprehensive checklists for PDFs and file creation, and commercial printers such as Ligare offer a Print Ready Guide. Have an understanding of how you will print your book, and with who, before you begin laying it out, so you don't end up bleeding tears that you didn't include a 5 mm bleed or whatever was required.

THE IMPORTANCE OF ORDERING PROOF COPIES

There's nothing worse than ordering 100 or 1,000 copies of your book to discover on arrival that they're poorly aligned or incorrectly formatted. So, before you go all in on a print run, order a proof copy to check that everything appears as it did in your original file. This also gives you a chance to see the book as your customers will see it … and it is quite possible you will find an error or typo you hadn't previously noticed.

With *Small Farm Success Australia*, I POD printed 10 proofs, distributing them to various people to scrutinise. And thank goodness! The early readers picked up errors including incorrect page numbers in the index, awkward spaces, and a missed letter here and there.

WHAT FACTORS GO INTO THE COST PER COPY?

These are the key elements (not including pre-publication services such as editing and cover design) that determine what your book will cost you to produce per copy:

- trim size (the width and height of your book)
- number of pages
- whether it is mono (black print) or colour
- number of illustrations or images
- cover type (soft or hard cover)
- binding
- whether you do a print run or POD, and what quantity price breaks you qualify for
- whether you do your print run in Australia or overseas
- the printing company you work with
- freight costs.

There can also be hidden costs, such as when IngramSpark charges you to upload revised files. The good news is that they do offer free codes for revisions and title uploads for members of industry groups. Check ALLi, the ASA and SPN's membership discount programs for any available offers, as it can well be worth the price of membership.

BEFORE YOU SET YOUR RRP

- Work out the actual cost to you of each copy. Include the printing cost, handling fees and freight per book. For ebooks, what are the charges for upload, e-delivery fees and commissions?

- Do your research. What are other authors charging and what are popular books in your genre being sold for? What might be the perceived value of your own work? This may vary by market as customers are used to paying a lot less for books in other regions of the world.
- Based on the numbers above, work out if you can afford to or want to use a distributor or offer wholesale prices to retailers.

THINGS TO TRY IF YOUR RRP ENDS UP TOO EXPENSIVE FOR THE MARKET

- Reduce the page count by cutting words or culling your resources section. (This can also be achieved by turning some interviews/case studies into download content on your website, which has the added benefit of creating a marketing hook to encourage website visitors to sign up for your newsletter.)
- Reduce the margins, font size, or the spacing between lines and/or letters as much as you can without negatively impacting reader experience.
- Ask the printing company for a better quote.
- For ebooks, remove some images and lighten your file size to minimise the delivery fee charged by Amazon.

WHEN YOUR FIRST BOOKS ARRIVE

You've finished your book, produced it and the first copies have arrived.

Take a moment. It's a monumental achievement. Seriously, congratulations! But when I say, take a moment, I really mean it. Don't open the box just yet. First, set your phone to record and capture the moment with an unboxing video. Why? Because seeing your book for the first time IS a special moment. It's worth capturing for posterity and you may even be able to use the video for promotion.

Go on, find someone to press *Record*, or press it yourself.

Now, open the box.

Wow. Hold that book in your hands, feel it's weight and texture. Turn it over, then over again. Let the pages flick through your fingertips. See your words, yes, your words, in print.

Fabulously done! Just fabulous!

HOW TO STORE YOUR BOOKS

Whether you have bought a truckload of copies or just a carton through POD, take great care in how you store them. They need a dry space as mould, humidity, damp and rain run-off will ruin them. Keep them protected from creepy crawlies and nibbling nomads. Once you've opened a box and taken some out, to prevent the remaining covers from curling, keep them neatly stacked and put a heavier book on top.

LEGAL DEPOSIT OF PRINT BOOKS AND NATIONAL EDEPOSIT (NED)

Now you have your print book in your hands, you have a legal obligation and one month to send a copy to your state library and the National Library of Australia. Legal deposit is a requirement under the Copyright Act 1968. The original purpose of the legislation was to ensure that 'a comprehensive collection of published material relating to Australia and its people is preserved for the community and future generations.' However, it also benefits publishers, as it gives your book greater searchability and visibility. I've popped a list of these library addresses on my site for you.

We now also have National edeposit (NED) which offers a similar service but for digital works. You can deposit your ebook through the NED portal, as well as 'nominate the level of public access allowed', including 'onsite only' which 'means the item can be viewed, but not downloaded or printed at any point in time'.

⌇

Let's hear it for you! You are so getting there, getting the knowledge to make your book a success and hopefully getting lots of fabulous words and ideas down to share with the world. And perhaps they'd like to hear it too, rather than read it. That's why the next chapter is all about audiobooks.

25

AUDIOBOOKS

I magine someone on the other side of the world going about their day, commuting in Chicago, dog walking in Dover or making lunch in Mumbai, while listening to your book. Or maybe your audience is closer to home and they have you in their ear as they plant bulbs in Balgowlah, bike through Bundoora or bop away in Brissie. Any of these can happen when you turn your manuscript into an audiobook for sites such as Audible, Apple and Spotify.

I get messages regularly from people who have listened to and enjoyed the audiobook version of *Honey Farm Dreaming*; people who would never have bought the paperback or ebook, but who embraced it because it was audio.

Australian presenter Rebecca Harper recorded and produced it for me. I met Bec through the local Firefly Book Club, loving the sound of her voice and sense of humour from the get-go. It was an ideal partnership. Unfortunately, even though it was a great learning experience, the audiobook hasn't been financially fabulous. The ensuing small royalties (less than $2,000 so far) are partly my fault (lack of marketing focus and budget), but it's also due to the fact that at the time of writing, Amazon's ACX service does not accept audiobooks directly from Australian authors for Audible. This means you need to do a work-around (I use a service called Author's Republic) and that means another finger in the pie between Amazon's hefty cut and that of the intermediary. But, depending on your book and your goals, it could certainly be worth your while. Let's see why.

Why do people listen to audiobooks?

- Convenience: to make use of time and enhance other activities, such as being educated or entertained while on the way to work, vacuuming, cooking or exercising.
- Vision problems: it might be easier to listen to a book than read it.
- Style of learning: they may be an audio rather than a visual learner.
- To relax and cocoon: being able to listen to an audiobook while commuting or waiting for an appointment allows people to 'escape'.
- Immediacy: people can hear about a book of interest and begin listening instantly.

Why create an audiobook?

- It's the only way some of your potential audience consumes books.
- The audiobook segment is the publishing industry's fastest growing area.
- Audio brings life and energy to your words.
- Having your book in multiple formats, including audio, gives your work better visibility on Amazon.

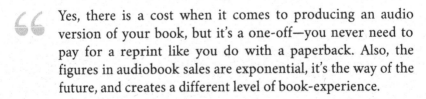 Yes, there is a cost when it comes to producing an audio version of your book, but it's a one-off—you never need to pay for a reprint like you do with a paperback. Also, the figures in audiobook sales are exponential, it's the way of the future, and creates a different level of book-experience.

— MARIA ISSARIS, AUDIOBOOKS@RADIO

Why avoid creating an audiobook?

- Your topic might not suit audio (for example, a recipe book) or your potential audience means it may not be economically sound. Or it may be in a format your particular audience doesn't embrace.
- If your book will need multiple updates over time, it's hard to do.
- You will need to record yourself or find a narrator. This is a costly exercise in terms of time, learning and money, with most audiobooks costing between $2,000 and $8,000 to produce depending on what level of service you require.
- ACX (Audible's audiobook marketplace) at the time of writing was not currently open to Australian authors. The workaround is to use a service such as Findaway Voices (owned by Spotify), Author's Republic or author2audio; however, the royalty that audiobook authors receive is only 70% of what those companies are paid by retailers, not 70% of the RRP.
- Even though audiobooks are growing in popularity, at this stage more money is still spent on print and ebooks.

What are the paths I can take to produce an audiobook?

You can:

- Fully outsource the narration and production. This is the easiest but most expensive path.
- Narrate the book but outsource the production of the audio files. This entails a moderate learning curve and time, but you contract someone else to handle the technical aspects.
- Narrate and produce the book yourself. This is time-consuming and difficult, but still doable for some.

If you're going to record your own audiobook, if it's, say, five-and-a-half hours long, it will probably take you triple that time to produce. There will be the inevitable stumbles over words, and my tip is to stop recording as soon as you make a mistake and re-do it on the spot. You will end up with lots of little files but it will save you wading through it all at the end trying to find all the parts you need to re-do.

— KERRY HOWARD, *THE TROUBLE WITH TRAUMA*

Should I record my own audiobook?

Perhaps, but you will need oodles of time, energy, an excellent speaking voice and diction. You'll also need to be patient as barking dogs, cantankerous cats and canaries, sirens and slight stumbles mean you'll need to do plenty of retakes.

You may also need to hire a recording studio (some libraries even offer them as a free service), or convert your loungeroom or walk-in wardrobe using blankets, to help deaden sounds and improve sound quality. A good quality microphone and being willing and able to scrupulously follow technical requirements are also essential.

Where can I find narrators and producers?

Of course, you could look in the mirror and find one right there! But there are many professionals ready to help, including Findaway Voices, and Australian services Author2Audio, Voices of Today, AussieNarrator.com and Spineless Wonders Audio.

NarratorList is the global version of AussieNarrator, so it includes narrators of any accent and location. You can also get recommendations through your writing community, or browse ACX.com for narrators, then try to contact them outside ACX by either Googling or searching for them on Facebook.

How do I choose an audiobook narrator?

They will need to have the right accent and tone for your audience and be someone who sounds like a person you can happily work with. You will need to know what they charge, and it's wise to research listener and author reviews of their work. Ask the frontrunners if they are happy to record a short sample of your book (either free or for a small payment) so you can make your decision.

Are there any set standards for audiobook files?

Yes, audiobook distributors set many technical requirements. These range from ensuring tracks must be free of noises such as mic pops, mouse clicks, excessive breathing and mouth sounds.

There are also requirements such as there needing to be between 0.5 and 1 second of 'silence' at the head of each track, and 1 to 5 seconds of 'silence' at the tail of each track. According to Amy Soakes of AussieNarrator, 'silence' in this case means not absolute silence, as in pressing 'delete' on your sound file and just leaving a blank silence. It means 'room tone silence', the quietest sound of your recording environment. 'If it is absolute silence,' says Amy, 'the book won't pass the requirements and will be rejected by the publisher, distributor or aggregator.'

Strictly adhere to your distributor's requirements to ensure acceptance of your audiobook. Amongst other things, your sound quality, tone and volume must be consistent throughout the recording.

Should I produce my own audiobook files?

It's one thing to record an audiobook, it's another thing to produce it to a publishable standard. You will need to be technically proficient, or your files will be rejected. To save yourself the hassle, especially for your first one, it might be worthwhile outsourcing the technical requirements for your files. But if you really want to do it, there are resources and courses on the internet to show you how.

~

INSIDE ADVICE: AMY SOAKES
AUSSIENARRATOR.COM

Where are we at with audiobooks currently in Australia?

Take-up for audiobooks in Australia is not yet as high as it is in, for instance, the US, but it is growing year-on-year. Since listening is technology based, it's often the younger adult audiences that are fastest to adopt consuming books via audio and they also fit with the younger audiences' fast consumption patterns—allowing for 'speed reading' (often sped up to double speed!). What about the older adult audience? At least part of their lower take-up is the stigma that 'listening' isn't the same as 'reading'. But as more people are introduced to the technology and realise audiobooks make tedious tasks more enjoyable, audiobooks will become a larger part of Australian book consumption. And audiobooks aren't going away. Multitasking to listen while attending to other tasks, is the way of the future.

How is audiobook production paid for?

Usually in one of four ways:

- Rate per finished audio hour (PFH): a set rate for each hour of finished audiobook, usually paid for with a deposit upfront and the balance upon completion. In Australia, typical PFH rates for fully finished, retail-ready audiobook files are between AUD$300 and AUD$400 PFH. The number of words per audio hour is usually estimated at 9,300 words, so a 50,000-word book should cost between AUD$1600 and AUD$2150, depending on the PFH rate and how many hours the audiobook ends up being. Why does the PFH cost seem so expensive? Audiobook production is labour-intensive, with each finished hour of audio taking 6 to 8 hours to produce.
- Royalty Share (RS): there's no upfront cost to the author, and the narrator receives nothing upfront for their labour or the cost of outsourcing any tasks such as editing, proofing and mastering. They then share the royalties, often with a 50/50 split.
- Royalty Share Plus (RS+), also known as a Hybrid Deal: a (modest) amount per finished audio hour is paid to the narrator, ostensibly to assist with editing, proofing and mastering costs, and the narrator and author then share the royalties 50/50. In Australia, typical PFH rates for the 'Plus' part of RS+ range from AUD$75 to AUD$200 PFH. There is also a version of this provided by one of the aggregators (Findaway Voices) where the price paid is half the PFH cost and the narrator receives 20% of the royalties.
- Royalty Deferred: once again, there's no upfront cost to the author, but the narrator is paid all of the sales proceeds until the amount they would have received under PFH is reached, after which the author receives all of the sales proceeds. (At the time of writing, this method was only offered by one aggregator, Audiobooks Unleashed Distribution.)

How much can I expect to make from audiobooks?

Ten years ago, the estimate was to expect one audiobook sale for every ten ebook sales. More recently, I've heard several authors state that their earnings from audiobooks were around 18 to 19% of their total book earnings (the rest being ebooks, with very minimal earnings from print books). Some genres do better in audio than others, but generally, if your ebook is selling well, your audiobook will also. If your ebook isn't selling well, then making an audiobook is unlikely to fix the problem—not without some other assistance, such as paid advertising. This ties in with another comment I've read multiple times: that the best way to sell an audiobook is with paid advertising for your ebook! This has been my experience as well. The royalty share books I've narrated that sell best are not necessarily those that are the best-written books, but rather those where the authors pay for Amazon ads for their ebooks or where the book has a BookBub promotion. For authors without a huge following, I think that is, unfortunately, the reality in the current cluttered book market.

 I recommend you don't try to bash out an audiobook in a few days. Instead, set aside two hours a day, day after day until you have finished the recording. Do it at the same time, in the same studio and under the same conditions.

— MARIA ISSARIS, AUDIOBOOKS@RADIO

There you have it. You now have the framework you need to produce your print book, ebook, or audiobook—all three if you're keen!

Now it's time to get them out into the world and into people's hands. That's the focus of the next two sections. First, we tackle distribution, and then we explore the ins and outs of marketing and how to maximise the return on your efforts.

PART III

DISTRIBUTION

26

AN INTRODUCTION TO DISTRIBUTION

The print version of your book is in your hands and looking great! Or perhaps it's in your computer as an ebook or audio file. Whatever the format, how do you get it to your readers? Through a process called distribution.

It's a little bit like being a farmer needing to sell a crop. You can sell it direct to customers from your farmgate stall, at farmers' markets and from your website, or you can drop it in to the local grocer for them to sell. You might also engage a wholesaler to take part of, or your entire crop to sell to the big supermarket chains, or at the wholesale markets to the browsing public, exporters, food processors and delis.

As a 'word farmer', you get to farm your book out in whatever way works best for you. You won't need to pursue every method, just the ones that support your goals.

What I've found works best for me (but it might be the opposite for you!), both financially and timewise, is a combination of distribution:

- Direct sales. I POD print by the box load and distribute them myself through my website, at workshops and presentations, and to local independent bookstores and retail outlets. In hindsight, for my earlier books, if I had known how many print copies I would end up selling, I would have done a combined offset print run, plus POD.

- IngramSpark's catalogue enables physical and online bookstores in Australia and around the world (including Amazon) to stock their shelves with my print books (if they choose) and order them in for customer requests. I offer a 40% wholesale discount and IngramSpark takes care of the printing, shipping and invoicing, sending me a monthly payment, minus printing and handling costs.
- Australian Library Distributors. My books are on library shelves and earning lending rights royalties thanks to these specialists.
- Amazon KDP. I made the ebook of *Small Farm Success Australia* available through Kindle. For this book though, I'm thinking of only making the ebook available direct from my website and perhaps through Apple Books, as I'm not keen on being forced onto Amazon's tiny 30% royalty if I want to price my book higher than the limit they set for 70% royalties (which at the time of writing was $11.99AUD). You can find Amazon's current royalty rate offers for different currencies by searching on the phrase *KDP list price requirements.*
- Amazon's Kindle Unlimited (KU) subscription program. The ebook of *Honey Farm Dreaming* is enrolled in the KDP Select program, which means it's automatically included in KU to help with discoverability by overseas readers.
- Author's Republic. This service distributes the audiobook of my memoir to more than 50 distribution channels (from Amazon's Audible to Apple Books).

∽

But what about you and your book/s? What methods of distribution will make sense for you? In the next few chapters we'll review wholesale, bookstore, library and POD distribution, as well as how you can run a DIY distribution program, even using affiliate networks and crowdfunding as ways to get your books to readers.

27

WHOLESALE DISTRIBUTORS

A question ... is your launch week goal to see your book flying off the shelves of multiple bookstores across Australia, and perhaps the world? If the answer is yes, you'll need to have written, produced and heavily promoted a fantastic book for a large target audience who are primed to buy it. And to pull it off, you'll need a deal with a distributor.

Why do bookstores prefer to deal with distributors not authors?

It's too much effort for retailers to deal one-on-one with thousands of enthusiastic authors when they can communicate with, order through, pay and schedule deliveries through just a couple of professional distribution networks.

The positives of working with a book wholesale distributor

- Access to knowledge and contacts. Their marketing material and salespeople can make retailers aware of your book, which is key to getting your book in bookshops. Once there, you'll enjoy a sense of pride as well as joy, bragging rights and hopefully lots of sales!

- They will store some of your print run in their warehouse, making bookstore fulfilment a breeze.
- They have established systems and procedures, so they can list your title on the major book databases (but remember, you can do this too if you decide not to use a distributor) and will handle all the paperwork, invoices, payments and returns.

The negatives of working with a wholesale distributor

- They are gatekeepers. Distributors may not even accept your book. It's their right to say no if their catalogue is already full, it's not of excellent quality, or they just can't foresee a big enough market for it.
- If profit from sales of individual books is your sole motive, an agreement with a book distributor may not be in your best interest. Why? A distributor will need to buy books from you at a discount of approximately 60–70% of RRP to pay themselves, as well as to be able to offer bookstores their expected 40–55% margin. After all, wholesalers and bookstores need to make money from your book too! On top of your printing and shipping costs, this arrangement could leave you with a tiny margin per book or might even throw you into deficit.
- Though bookstores may initially sell some copies of your book, just like with trad books, they have the right to return any they don't sell (or are slightly damaged) for a full refund, even months later. You will wear the costs of these returns.
- There are no guarantees. Distributors are not miracle workers—they can't force a bookstore to buy your book, nor a customer to buy it either.
- It can take many months for the proceeds of bookstore sales to trickle down from bookstores to the distributor to you.
- You will need to achieve a cost-effective, offset print run if the economics of wholesale distribution are to work. Since you can't know upfront how many books you will sell, this can be risky compared with POD printing.
- Distributors work to set promotional calendars. You will need to be well organised many months before your release date to be

able to coordinate bookstore availability with distribution, marketing and publicity.

- Be wary of distributors who make a profit by charging fees not related to the actual book sales achieved. This might be for random services including marketing, receiving/moving inventory and sending samples out to sales reps and clients.
- Distributors can and do go bust. Yes, this happens. In 2018, Australian distributor Dennis Jones & Associates went belly up just as the Christmas buying season was getting started. This left 1,300 creditors in the lurch, many of whom were indie authors and micro publishers.

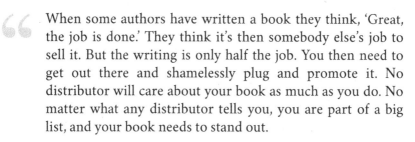

When some authors have written a book they think, 'Great, the job is done.' They think it's then somebody else's job to sell it. But the writing is only half the job. You then need to get out there and shamelessly plug and promote it. No distributor will care about your book as much as you do. No matter what any distributor tells you, you are part of a big list, and your book needs to stand out.

— JONATHAN SEIFMAN, BOOKTOPIA PUBLISHER SERVICES

Who are some Australian wholesale distributors?

There will be an up to date list on my website, but some (please do your due diligence on them and check with your writing community) include Peribo, Woodslane, Booktopia Publisher Services and John Reed Books. At the time of writing, John Reed Books had a sales and distribution agreement to distribute print books by ASA members.

What about international distribution?

You can achieve foreign bookstore access by printing your book with Ingram-Spark and making it available for distribution in markets around the world. However, if you, your book and your marketing budget transcend borders, you might consider doing a foreign print run and contracting a foreign distributor to handle book storage and in-country bookstore distribution.

One that is often mentioned in the US is Independent Publishers Group and its offshoot for publishers with fewer than 10 titles, Small Press United. Companies can change and new options emerge over time though, so tap into the knowledge and experience of ALLi and other successful authorpreneurs in your network.

ABOUT BOOKTOPIA

Let's take a closer look at Australian company Booktopia. Founded in 2004, it's listed on the Australian Stock Exchange and is an online bookstore and highly automated fulfilment company. It moved into distribution in 2017 and publishing in 2019 and continues to acquire other companies in the space. It both serves and competes with other bookstores and publishers. Here's why Booktopia is of interest to some self-publishers:

- You could have your book available and listed on their consumer website, either through a feed from your distributor, IngramSpark or through a deal with Booktopia.
- You could earn commissions as an affiliate (whereby you channel sales of your book and other books you promote, refer to, or blog about back to Booktopia and earn commissions—there is more about affiliates in Chapter 55).
- If accepted, you could use them to warehouse and distribute your title to bookstores. Be aware that some independent bookstores refuse or are reticent to order from Booktopia as they see the company as competition.
- Your book could be published by their publishing arm.

INSIDE ADVICE: JONATHAN SEIFMAN
BOOKTOPIA PUBLISHER SERVICES

Why would authors want their books listed on the Booktopia website?

We've had more than 31,000 5-star reviews for service on ProductReview.-com.au, have been voted Australia's No. 1 online bookstore, and our audience is large, loyal and buying lots of books.

What is the best way to get your title listed on Booktopia?

We can access your book if you have it available via POD on IngramSpark, or set it up with the ASA, who have an arrangement with a distributor. Or, if your book is of high quality and relevant to our audience, you can also approach us directly through our Publisher Services division about distributing your book.

Why do some indie books have success and not others?

Publicity is key. For example, a book written and published by 90-year-old Clarrie Briese, a former NSW chief magistrate, was tracking fairly slowly, and we thought it might sell 30 to 40 copies, until an article by *Sydney Morning Herald* crime reporter, Kate McClymont led to sales accelerating dramatically. More than 700 copies sold in the space of a few months and the story was also picked up by *The Australian* and ABC radio. Overall, that is a great example of how a book with modest expectations can overachieve through external press coverage. The same can happen for books with good social media coverage.

Another good example was Scott Pape's *The Barefoot Investor*. This wasn't one of our books, but the success was down to the fact that he had 100,000 very engaged people on his database. He did regular Q&As and there was no push marketing, as his audience were already eating out of his hands. He then directed the database to buy his book from particular retailers during a certain period, and this got picked up by the Nielsen book-sale charts. That got the book noticed by every bookstore in the country. It all started with an engaged audience.

How do you choose what books you take on through your distribution service?

We run a selection process whereby we work with authors who have realistic expectations of how many books they will sell. There's no magic formula, but it's authors who are out there plugging the book, trying to get it noticed and being tenacious that we tend to want to have a chat with.

What are your top tips?

- Sometimes really good books don't sell well and ordinary books sell like hotcakes. Often, the only difference is how they are marketed. A distributor's job is to amplify your efforts, but so much of this starts with the author getting the ball rolling. Get out there and publicise as much as you can. No distributor will advocate for a book as much as the author, and books are unlikely to get traction in the market if the author doesn't bang the drum hard to get the word out. Social media can be especially powerful in this regard.
- Bookselling is a crowded marketplace, and you need to do something to make your book stand out from the crowd. Find the audience, angles and story. Share your expertise and thought leadership, and engage. You can't just go out and say, 'Buy my book'. You need to earn the right to sell to them.

But what is another way for people to buy, and indeed, find your book? That would be through the distribution networks of the big POD printers.

28

POD DISTRIBUTION THROUGH INGRAMSPARK AND/OR AMAZON KDP PRINT

As a self-publisher, understanding POD distribution could be a key element in your venture's success. And even if you're doing an offset print run and using a wholesaler to distribute your books, it can also make sense to set your book up with IngramSpark and Amazon KDP Print in tandem. Why? You can use IngramSpark's drop shipping service as needed, and you also get access to both companies' overseas printing and distribution networks. Let's explore it all a little more.

Why use IngramSpark for distribution?

- Once listed with IngramSpark your titles will be available to more than 40,000 sellers around Australia and the world such as independent and chain bookstores including Amazon, Booktopia and Barnes & Noble, along with libraries, schools and universities. This doesn't mean they have actually 'bought' your book, just that they can access it if they want to purchase it.
- Bookstores are already plugged into the IngramSpark catalogue system and use it to access a wide range of titles and to save on freight, handling and admin costs by combining different books within the one purchase—yours as well as books by famous authors.

- Bookstores can't stock every title on their shelves, but if a customer wants to buy your book, the bookstore can quickly and easily check the IngramSpark catalogue to order it in. (This can also be a nifty marketing strategy! Get your friends to go into independent stores across the country to talk up and put a special order in for your book. This brings it to the attention of the bookseller, and, depending on your book—and how good a job your friends have done—may lead them to order more in).
- You get to choose and set the wholesale discount (I set mine at 40%) and specify whether you're prepared to accept returns (I don't, as return postage costs are a killer!).
- Many independent bookstores refuse to order from Amazon, which is why being with IngramSpark is so important to your distribution strategy.

What wholesale discount do I offer on IngramSpark?

You can offer a wholesale discount between 35% and 55%. Though a 55% trade discount is preferred by retailers, if your book is compelling and generating demand from their customers, they may still order it in without the full 55% discount. I have been able to sell thousands of books by offering 40%.

Should I accept returns with IngramSpark?

Returns are books sent back from bookstores when they either don't sell or are damaged in some way. IngramSpark does not accept any kind of returns in Australia, but when I'm selling in their overseas territories, I check the 'No Returns' option. Why? Even if it means some retailers won't take a chance on my book, if I agree to accept returns, I'm then liable for return postage costs. The returned books may also be damaged and unsellable by the time they make it back to me. Sure, choosing not to accept returns may mean I've lost some sales, but it's sure kept me safe from a tsunami of return costs.

Do I use Amazon KDP Print simultaneously with IngramSpark?

ALLi's recommendation is to go with both as you get the advantage of exposure to Amazon's vast online audience and marketing tools in conjunction with all the benefits of IngramSpark's reach and systems. But a heads-up: if you do publish your book on both sites in the same format using the same ISBN, set up first on KDP, otherwise it will lead to delays and complications. You might also have difficulty linking reviews between your books.

My plan for this book is an initial 500 copy print run with an offset printer, and simultaneously to go POD with IngramSpark. It's a really flexible combination that will help me achieve my goals because I also love DIY distribution. Yes, that's what we cover in the next chapter.

29

DIY DISTRIBUTION

D IY distribution can be intense, fun and highly profitable. It involves targeting individuals, businesses and retailers yourself or responding in a professional way to their enquiries when they come to you. Here are some of the things I've learned.

Think outside the box

In addition to bookstores, what other businesses or organisations might find value in your book? For example, might vets stock your book on cat personalities? Or real estate agents your book on renovations? Or might a relevant association include your book with their membership fee?

Other potential outlets might include shops in museums, art galleries and other tourist attractions. It's all about finding outlets that would benefit from being able to provide their customers with access to your words.

Understand consignment sales

A consignment sale involves leaving an agreed quantity of books for sale, for an agreed period of time, price point and commission. If the books sell, you receive your share of money from the sales. If they don't, they're returned to you (hopefully undamaged) with no money changing hands.

Consignment arrangements remove a key risk for the retailer which may make them more open to stocking your book.

Retailers open to consignment arrangements include independent bookstores like Readings, smaller retailers, local shops and specialty stores. FYI, Readings only considers consignment requests at specific times of the year, and when choosing what books to take on they 'take into account store demographics and subject matter, author profile, market trends, planned publicity, and book design.'

They also say, 'Please be aware that we are offered many, many more titles than we are able to stock. We only take around 5–10% of the books offered to us, so don't be disheartened if we decide not to stock your book.'

As Readings suggest, even when books are offered on consignment, retailers might still refuse to stock it for various reasons including already being overstocked with titles in your niche, or not seeing enough relevance or 'fit' with their own target customer. It may also be something as simple as being the wrong season ... your book might be more suitable for a summer crowd when it's currently winter.

If going the consignment route, stay on top of admin, invoicing, restocking and your relationship with the manager.

> If I take on a book, I'll do a consignment order of between six to twelve books so I can stack them up, make an impact and give the book the best chance of success.

— CATHY BAYES HUNT, BOOKSTORE MANAGER

What you need to know about dealing directly with retailers

Unfortunately, they probably don't want to deal with you! That's right, though your local store might make an exception if you've been a good customer, many will only take your book on if it comes through a distributor or IngramSpark, and with the required margin of at least 40 to 55%.

It doesn't mean you shouldn't research and reach out to bookstores. I use the search function on the Australian Booksellers Association (ABA) website for this purpose. In doing so I have been able to work with many wonderful independent stores including Avid Reader in Brisbane where I also run workshops. Don't limit yourself to bookstores though, also consider gift shops and other potential outlets for your book. I keep a box of books in the car for just this reason when visiting a new town but am always prepared for rejection.

One of the best things you can do to get booksellers on board is to be visible in the media. It's a bit like the chicken-and-egg scenario. What comes first: does a book being discoverable on shelves propel public and media commentary? Or is it great coverage in the media and on socials that generates demand for a book and gets it on to those shelves? Hmmm. We'll look at building demand in the Marketing section, but right now, let's turn to a bookstore manager for her thoughts.

~

INSIDE ADVICE: CATHY BAYES HUNT
BOOKSTORE MANAGER

Cathy has worked in bookstores for many years, including as manager of Book Face Port Macquarie, a busy shop on the Mid North Coast of New South Wales. Book Face is part of an independent, family-owned group of stores and the company allows managers at the local level to make decisions about local, relevant acquisitions.

How many self-published book titles do you take on in a year?

About 35 titles out of 5000+. It's a very tiny part of our business.

What trends are you seeing?

Whereas fiction manuscripts can sit for years waiting for the right wave to come along (such as Domestic Noir or Gothica), the turnaround has to be much quicker with non-fiction because it's a reflection of society, dictated by what's going on in the world.

Relationship books have always been big and you also see waves of books on specific subjects such as Greta Thunberg, tiny houses, Trump, Black Lives Matter, Covid, indoor plants, gender issues and ... the 'next big thing'.

In the last few years we've finally had enough books on Indigenous subjects to set up a section, which is great. Books like the CWA's *Thrifty Household: More than 1000 budget-friendly hints and tips for a clean, waste-free, eco-friendly home* did a great job of meeting demand for financial as well as environmentally friendly information. Then there are books with touching, timeless messages such as *The Tattooist of Auschwitz* by Heather Morris and Eddie Jaku's memoir *The Happiest Man in the World*.

What makes you take on a self-published book?

- It needs to look great. Some covers can be so busy you don't know if you're coming or going.
- We're much more likely to take on a local author with a good network of friends who will come into the store and support them rather than an author who's just popping in on holidays (unless the book is brilliant!).
- Some self-published works that we've seen do well include local history books, books on bushrangers and local walks, and books that have a relevant tie-in with a local organisation or charity.

What do you wish authors knew before they approached you about stocking their book?

- A minimum of 40% of the RRP will go to the bookstore. Do your calculations prior to approaching us and think long and hard if it's really worth your while having your book in store. For example, we need to sell hardcovers at approximately $55, not $35. So even if you are prepared to discount your book and not make money from it, for us to carry it, we need to be able to make a decent margin.
- A lot of people come in with books about their lives such as their experience as a 'Ten Pound Pom'. If this is you, it needs to be brilliant both in terms of the content and the cover.
- Poetry can also be very subjective, so it is rare for us to take poetry on.
- If you think your book is worthy, you need to be worthy of it. Put your effort into promoting it.
- There's not enough room in bookstores for all books to be front-faced, so you can't assume yours will be. Unfortunately, some self-published books are so skinny that nothing can be written on the spine, which is an issue.

What is the best way for authors to approach you about stocking their book?

- Please don't come in and expect to spend 15 to 20 minutes telling us about your book. It can really put me and the other staff on the back foot, as we already have our day planned, have customers to serve, and might have new stock arriving or be busy with admin. We just won't be as welcoming. Instead, introduce yourself and your book via email first. If we're interested, we will then send you our terms and conditions about consignment so you can see if you'd like to proceed.
- If you do come in, please don't come in with too much attitude. Be humble, as we need to cooperate and work together. One author approached us in a really lovely way. He checked in with us first via email, we agreed to stock his books and he brought them in and then took photos of his books instore that he then promoted across social media. He even wrote to our head office to thank us. That's the kind of person who makes working with authors effortless and rewarding.

Do you do book launches in store?

Not often as it can interfere with our regular customers and it's often too noisy for guests to hear what is being said.

We recommend that authors launch at the local library. That way they can tap into the library's marketing and booking system. There's normally a dedicated room, and tea and coffee is served too.

We do, though, welcome any author who wants to come in for an hour or two and stand (or sit) in the store with a table piled high with their books. This gives them plenty of visibility, and they get to chat directly with interested customers. It's good to have a bit of paraphernalia like posters or bookmarks to add to the display.

What are some things authors can do once their book is instore?

- Take pictures of the book instore and share them on your blog, socials and with the media.
- Please don't call us every day asking how sales are going. Be

considerate and professional in your communications, with a monthly check-in during the early stages.

- Don't berate us when your book doesn't sell. It might just be that there isn't a market for it, or you haven't created enough demand through publicity.
- Keep your records up to date. Don't put the onus on the bookshop manager to stay on top of how many books you have delivered and when.
- Bookstores have limited storage space, so after three months, if your books haven't sold, please take them away. If, however, your books are selling, we will reorder. We like to say that any book we reorder is a bestseller, so you're on your way! We love seeing authors succeed and wish you good luck.

And as authors and self-publishers, we do need good luck. But we also need a good work ethic, to have our head on straight, and to put ourselves in the shoes of others. Which is why I also want you to really be open to the learnings in the next chapter about library distribution.

30

LIBRARY DISTRIBUTION

One of my favourite places to be is my local library: so many ideas and worlds to discover and comfy chairs to sit in while doing so! And what a thrill to see your own books in pride of place on the 'recently returned' shelf, or unavailable because so many people have put a reserve on them; to see an entire set of books out with book clubs and people emailing you after reading them; and to receive not just book sale revenue, but annual lending right payments directly into your bank account for years to come.

Yes, that can all happen to you because it has happened to me. So, how do you go about it? Do these three things:

1. Write a great book for an audience who wants it and produce it professionally.
2. Three months before launch, send early information to library suppliers (also known as specialist library wholesalers and distributors).
3. Generate demand from libraries using the PR and marketing techniques discussed in the Marketing section of this book, so the librarians and their members can't resist ordering copies.

Why is library distribution worth it?

Book sales! According to Australian Library Services (ALS) there are approximately 14,000 libraries in Australia and 2,500 in New Zealand.

Being in libraries gives your book visibility and a level of prestige. If people like it, they will talk about it, recommend it, and perhaps order their own copy or one for a friend.

Libraries may also invite you (or you should be out there offering!) to give an author talk, which generates fresh opportunities for media coverage and further sales. Additionally, it's a way for people to access your book who otherwise might not be able to afford a copy, and it's an environmentally friendly way for people to access your book too.

Finally, if you have more than 50 copies of your book in libraries across Australia, it makes you eligible for PLR and ELR (see Chapter 51).

How do I get my print book into libraries?

The easiest way is through a specialist library supplier.

While some of the wholesale distributors mentioned earlier in the chapter also distribute to libraries, and some libraries may order direct from IngramSpark, most libraries in Australia purchase their books through specialist library distributors. They do this because it's easy and convenient from an administration perspective. Many libraries are not equipped to buy one-off books direct from the author, nor do they like being asked to.

Key Australian Library distributors include: ALS Library Services (ALS), James Bennett, Peter Pal, Keith Ainsworth Books, Westbooks, DLS Books, St Georges Bookseller and Network Educational Australia.

Most of them prefer a wholesale discount of at least 40% and you will also need to be clear as to whether postage to their distribution centre is included or on top of the book price.

How do I approach library distributors?

Each distributor has their own preferred method, so research on their website, then supply the information in the format requested. Be polite. Library distributors don't have to take your book on, so give yourself the best chance of success by writing a brilliant non-fiction book and producing it professionally.

How do I get my ebook into a library?

This is another segment of the industry where change is happening fast. If using services such as Draft2Digital and IngramSpark you'll be able to reach most of the services such as BorrowBox (Bolinda), Overdrive, Bibliotheca (Cloud Library), Baker and Taylor and PublishDrive. Having your book on these services doesn't guarantee a sale though, so you will still need to create demand direct with librarians.

It's recommended you price your library book 2-4 times higher than your normal ebook price to take into account the number of uses and current lack of ELR/PLR payments for digital books (though the ASA is lobbying for a DLR on behalf of authors).

Ways to build library demand for your book

Your library supplier will include details of your book in their catalogue and if you ask and they agree, may even include some of your marketing material such as promo postcards in the deliveries they send out prior to your launch. But it is up to you to build awareness, demand, and buzz with the librarian community.

Some things I've had success with include asking librarians for feedback on initial book cover concepts and, once my books were accepted into the library suppliers' catalogues, reaching out to librarians around the country via email ... yes, one at a time, and yes, call me 'crazy' but it did get the word out.

For my previous titles I've also used Facebook and other social media channels to raise awareness with librarians and pursued author talks at libraries where the demographics made sense. It was all helped along by lots of PR on radio and in print. Publicity is sometimes the key tipping point to successful library acceptance.

Other authors I've spoken with have had their friends around the country request a copy of their book at their local library, while other authors have donated copies with mixed results.

I'll include extensive current links to local libraries around the country and how I did the library outreach for this title in the *Look—It's Your Book! Workbook*. Hopefully the shortcuts will save you loads of time.

But let's hear direct from a library manager to learn more. Please read it being willing to listen, don't kid yourself that you and your book are 'different' or an 'exception'.

~

INSIDE ADVICE: JIM MAGUIRE
LIBRARY MANAGER

Jim Maguire, Library Manager for Port Macquarie Hastings Council, is responsible for running three libraries and a mobile library servicing approximately 80,000 prospective readers in the Port Macquarie Hastings region of NSW. The library's cooperative agreement with the Kempsey Library service adds another 30,000 potential readers. Between this group, they have 180,000 items available to members.

Over the course of a year, the library purchases approximately 60% fiction and 40% non-fiction. Less than 1% of the books the library purchases in a year are self-published.

According to Jim, the average lifespan of a book in the library is between five and ten years, although a percentage are only kept for five years and if the book doesn't get loaned out to a member within two years it is removed. Jim provides the following tough love for indie authors.

What are the best ways for authors to get their book in front of you?

1. Be featured in a library supply catalogue.
2. Get media coverage and send a copy of the coverage to the library with more information on your book and how to purchase it.
3. Offer to do an author talk. This is something we are quite open to.

What's the worst way for an author to get their book in front of you?

Any other way than the three listed above. Walking in off the street and being demanding doesn't work, and emails are likely to be overlooked, as we receive so much correspondence.

What makes you say 'no' to a self-published book?

- The topic, such as if the book is quickly outdated (like computer and tech books), or if it's too specific. For example, we don't really need a book on the mating habits of the Red Terrarium Frog.

- There are a lot of really, really bad self-published books—the covers aren't professional and the illustrations and editing are poor. They just don't look good or read well.
- Librarians are not your friend. We have a set book-buying budget and book-buying policy and will always need to prioritise bestsellers, celebrities, politicians and traditionally published books.
- There are also a million published cookbooks out there, so if it was a book by a local chef, we would probably have to purchase it, but we'd be the only library in Australia who would. A cookbook would need to have a real point of difference.
- It's also hard to deal with an author who doesn't have an ABN, as it makes it difficult for Council to purchase the book.

What makes you say 'yes' to a self-published book?

- It needs to be relevant and it helps to be a local author writing on a local topic, or writing in an area that's attracting a lot of attention or is of general interest.
- When we see it mentioned positively in the media and the book itself looks good and professionally presented.
- As a community library we believe members should have as much say as possible, so if a member recommends and requests it, we will likely get it in.
- When the writer is willing to give an author talk and also has an ABN.

Any other tips?

- If it's a good book and you're really proud of it, get your friends and family across the country to ask their local library to stock it.
- With regard to author talks, there are no guarantees we can get you more than six people. The library will promote it through our website and newsletter, but it's up to the author to do the marketing. We've had some very disappointed authors, but we can't drag people in off the street. We provide the room and refreshments, but over and above that it's up to the marketing

efforts of the author. The good thing about giving an author talk is that we feel obliged to purchase a copy of the book.

- Don't worry about soft or hardcover—we are happy with either, and the softcover is probably better value for us.
- Poetry is really hard to sell.
- Biographies need to be focused on a theme such as addiction recovery, tree change, or other areas of interest; they can't just be a timeline of your life.
- In the end, it's all about the subject matter. Jump on trends quickly, whether it's lifestyle, simple living or something really timely. For example, in 2021 the hot topics we would have been interested in would have been books on disaster recovery, wildlife rescue and Covid, including hobbies people turned to during lockdowns. But that was then. Be ahead of the curve, be different, be great but at least be current.

Any stories to offer hope?

- A sex worker once offered to do an author talk on her book about life and money. We ended up buying the book at her talk, and it was so good and of interest to so many people that we ended up buying a book club set too.
- Your books, *Small Farm Success* and *Honey Farm Dreaming*, looked really professional and were right in the sweet spot of the simple living category. You also offered an author talk that was well attended. The books have been constantly out on loan and our set of your memoir is also popular with our book clubs. The success of those titles is definitely comparable to that of traditionally published books.
- If you can get your book into the media, someone will see it, and someone will request it and then we will purchase it.

∽

So yes, you're going to do everything Jim recommends. And you know what that means? You're going to get orders for your books and you'll need to know how to ship them. Tips on that are next.

31

SHIPPING YOUR PRINT BOOK

W hether selling direct or shipping books to distributors or stores, they need to arrive promptly, undamaged, and in a cost-effective way.

HOW TO SHIP BOOKS

You have a few choices!

Australia Post is convenient as you can set up an account, print labels at home, avoid post office queues and qualify for quantity discounts. If you are selling a LOT of books then membership of SPN makes you eligible to also join the Australian Booksellers Association (ABA) as an associate. This then unlocks the ABA's heavily discounted Australia Post pricing for you.

You can also use IngramSpark to send books on your behalf (at print cost plus postage and handling fee). This option allows you to personalise messages, but you won't be able to include a letter or bookmark. The service can save a lot of hassle and is especially useful if you're away on holidays and don't want to lug books and packaging with you!

Courier networks might also be an option, especially if sending books in larger quantities.

No matter how you end up sending your books, or with who, ensure the package is trackable and let your customer know the tracking number. This saves no end of 'did you send my book?' correspondence and provides a better customer experience.

SHIPPING COSTS AND STRATEGY

Plan your shipping costs in advance. For example, will you offer a flat $10 fee for shipping one book, or will you include shipping in the price? Will you subsidise shipping for orders of five or more copies or charge full freight? Or what about offering free shipping if they buy an entire box?

PACKAGING

When designing your packaging, plan for it to be:

- Protective: avoid damage during shipping by choosing a well-padded bag, box or hard cardboard wraparound (you can recycle your own from cardboard boxes or purchase from a supplier).
- Non-damaging: be careful that the type of pen you use to sign the book or write the accompanying note to your customer doesn't smear. If you are tying the parcel with string, make sure it won't cut into the book cover and damage it or the pages en route.
- Eco-friendly: reuse, recycle and repurpose whenever you can.
- On-brand: if your book is about beauty, think about how to beautifully package it with a decorative paper and ribbon. If your book is about fashion, how about wrapping the book in fabric cut-offs, or, if it's about cars, what about using pages from a car magazine or car classifieds? You can often pick up unsold magazines and newspapers from newsagents for free. And many businesses in the industrial area of your town will have plenty of 'waste' packaging they'd otherwise have to throw in the bin.
- Personal: include a personal note or card, and if you're pre-printing notes or bookmarks, leave room for you to handwrite the person's name and your signature to add a personal touch.
- Cost effective: budget correctly. If you spend $4 just to package the book, will that give you a return?
- Not too weighty: if your packaging weighs too much, it will tip the scales on postage prices, putting you over standard postage limits such as 500 g and 1 kg.
- Easy and fast: writing your return address out by hand on every

package really adds up in terms of time and, who knows, you might need hundreds of them for all the orders you'll need to respond to when your book becomes a runaway success! Instead, it may be worth investing in creating small return address labels so you can stick and run at speed. You can create labels on your computer or online with services like Canva, Vistaprint and Avery. If you design your return address labels with the same colours and font as your book, even your labels become a marketing tool that helps build your brand.

Oh, and be efficient. It's something I learned the hard way. Only compile and fulfil orders at a certain time and only once per day. I even try to stick to the same time so it becomes a daily discipline. It's much more efficient than getting all your packing and shipping supplies out whenever a new order comes through.

So that's how to distribute print books, but how about ebooks and audiobooks? Tips await in the next chapter.

32

HOW TO DISTRIBUTE AUDIO AND EBOOKS

There are four key ways to distribute audio and ebooks, and you can do a combination of some or all of these based on your goals and how much administration time you can afford to spend coordinating and managing them:

- direct to customers from your website
- direct to key ebook distributors
- through ebook aggregators
- via affiliate networks.

AUDIOBOOK DISTRIBUTION

At the time of writing, Australian authors still did not have access to Amazon's audiobook platform ACX, which is why I turned to Author's Republic to distribute my *Honey Farm Dreaming* audiobook. Other services that can help Australian authors with distribution include Authors Direct, Findaway Voices, Libro.fm and Soundwise.

These services can take quite a hefty cut from your royalty, which is why some people use BookFunnel and other companies to deliver audiobooks direct from their own website. BookFunnel also allows you to prepare a shortened file as a giveaway or reader magnet, which you can use as an introduction to or 'teaser' for your work.

Audiobooks are a fast-moving space though so I'm sure more opportunities will be open to Australian authors soon.

~

INSIDE ADVICE: ALLi's GUIDE TO BOOK DISTRIBUTION REPRINTED WITH PERMISSION

In choosing your ebook distribution strategy, you will first need to consider which venues offer advantages for signing up directly, and whether those benefits outweigh the convenience of using an aggregator.

Signing up directly for Amazon's KDP is relatively easy, grants you full and immediate control over your books, and gives you access to powerful marketing tools such as the Amazon Marketing Services (AMS) advertising platform and KDP Select's Countdown Deals for ebooks. Because KDP is so tightly integrated with Amazon's retail operations, there is little benefit to using an aggregator or outside distributor to reach Amazon shoppers.

If you are comfortable with managing multiple accounts and navigating the online interfaces of the major retailers, you may also wish to sign up directly with Barnes & Noble, Kobo, GooglePlay and iTunes (which requires you to use a Mac). Direct access to these sellers maximises control over your ebooks and provides slightly higher royalties.

For the countless remaining retailers, the centralised management of aggregators is a blessing to any indie author, and well worth the small cut of the royalties charged by these services.

Avoid ebook distribution services that try to lock you into exclusive contracts. Most ebook aggregators do not require exclusive agreements, and there is great benefit in being able to leverage the strengths and scope of multiple aggregators. If you do use multiple aggregators, you may need to compare their distribution channels to avoid overlaps.

Ebook aggregators that ALLi recommends are Partner Members: Draft2Digital, PublishDrive and StreetLib.

~

SELLING YOUR EBOOK DIRECT TO CUSTOMERS

Selling your ebook direct to customers means cutting out the intermediary and being paid immediately. Importantly, you're in control of all aspects of branding. You won't be surrounded by competitors' books, and you'll know where your sales are coming from, who your customers are and be able to establish ongoing relationships.

If you have great additional or newer content, you can upsell or include some of it on your website as bonus material, which gives customers another reason to buy from you directly.

Just be aware that if you've signed up exclusively to KDP Select, you aren't permitted to sell direct from your website for a 3-month period. You'll also need to set a price that does not undercut any other channels selling your book.

How to sell your ebook direct from your website

It's easy with a service such as BookFunnel, which, upon the customer buying the book on your website, sends a private link to the customer so they can instantly and securely download their copy.

For ecommerce functionality on your website, you can DIY or have a tech person set up a free service such as WooCommerce (integrated with payment gateways such as PayPal or Stripe) on your site. Alternative ecommerce services include Payhip, Squarespace, Shopify, Selz, Podia and E-junkie, all of which allow digital downloads and sales from your website and some from your emails and socials. (See Chapter 37 for more information on author websites.)

Finally, though PDF downloads are great for summaries and free chapters, if you allow downloads of your main book as a PDF file, it's difficult to control it being shared and copied, unless you lock the file. Doing that will make the PDF only able to be viewed on your website but it provides a terrible reader experience so I don't recommend using PDF as a format for sales.

HOW TO DISTRIBUTE YOUR EBOOK THROUGH KEY RETAILERS

In addition to selling your ebook direct from your website, you can also sell it through Amazon's Kindle Store, Apple Books, Barnes & Noble NOOK, Google Play, Rakuten Kobo and online stores supplied by IngramSpark.

These companies have what you want: a lot of customers! Listing with these online retailers, sites and apps puts your book right where the audience's eyeballs are, but it still doesn't mean readers will discover or respond to you unless you back your distribution up with plenty of marketing. You can enrol in these companies' distribution programs direct or sign up with an aggregator to streamline and do it for you.

Amazon remains the biggest of them all, but Apple is also targeting authors by offering rightsholders 70% of royalties at any price point, which is a different approach to Amazon's. We will take a closer look at the ins and outs of Amazon soon but another thing that Apple Books offers independent authors is access to '250 free, digital promo codes for every ebook they distribute on Apple Books.' You can use these free copies as part of your pre-launch strategy, to build buzz or relationships.

HOW TO DISTRIBUTE YOUR EBOOK THROUGH AGGREGATORS

If you don't want to go to the hassle of uploading directly with each of these big online retailers, the alternative is to use an aggregator to do the job for you.

Key ebook aggregators include Draft2Digital, PublishDrive, StreetLib, IngramSpark and Smashwords, and Apple has a list of other partners they work with too.

Though it will cut into your royalties, the benefits of working with an ebook aggregator include simplicity, because you don't need to keep track of multiple passwords, you won't be bombarded with emails from multiple vendors and your royalty statements will be streamlined. You will save time!

Working with an aggregator also makes it super easy to update your master book file, say, if you want to add a promotion for your latest book or because new information has come to light. They will then send it to all the sites, so you don't need to upload it to each one and fill in all the details yourself.

AMAZON: THE BASICS

Amazon has plenty of resources about their offerings online, but here are some to look out for.

Kindle Direct Publishing (KDP)

KDP is a way to publish, distribute and sell your print and/or ebook on Amazon. It gives you access to publishing, promotional and knowledge tools, including Amazon University, the KDP Community (where you can share learnings with other self-publishers) and the Kindle Create Tool. It also gives you access to Amazon Author Central and Amazon Advertising Services, which we discuss in the Marketing Section of this book.

KDP Jumpstart

KDP Jumpstart is Amazon's online guide to help new authors get started and get going. It also outlines what share of royalties you will be entitled to. For example, at the time of writing, when you price your ebook between US$2.99 and US$9.99, Amazon grants a 70% royalty rate, but if you price your book below US$2.99, Amazon only grants a 35% royalty. Wild, huh!? As mentioned before, Apple offers authors 70% of ebook royalties no matter your pricepoint.

You will also learn things such as if you make your book free as part of a promotion through a different channel, including on your own website, Amazon retains the right to make your book available for free. So be careful how and when you plan promotions.

KDP Select

KDP Select is Amazon's exclusive rights program. Enrolling in this program means you can't sell your ebook anywhere else, including on your own site for the exclusive agreement's 90-day period.

KDP Select gives you access to Kindle Countdown Deals (KCD), Free Book Promotions and Kindle Unlimited (KU), which is Amazon's monthly subscription service for readers in which authors get paid for the number of pages read. In July 2021, the fee was US$0.004297 per page read. So, if you have a book of 260 pages, and there are 2,427 page reads (equivalent to about nine copies of your book), the total royalties would be $10.43 … translating to about $1.16 per ebook. By comparison, if the nine copies of that book had been purchased through KDP at your chosen price of US$9.99, minus Amazon's 30% and a 0.75c download fee based on your book's size, you would have earned a royalty of US$6.24 per book x 9 copies for a total of around US$56 in royalties. Quite a difference, but also still significantly lower than you can achieve through direct sales.

However, despite its size and profile, Amazon does not have to be a part of your strategy. Playing devil's advocate, Jaqui Lane gives us some insights into why Amazon might not be the best place to sell your book, especially for business authors.

INSIDE ADVICE: JAQUI LANE
THE BOOK ADVISER
What are some reasons not to sell your business book on Amazon?

You don't know who is buying your book

If you sell your book through Amazon you'll have no idea who is buying your book, no chance to develop a strong relationship with the purchaser and no opportunity to develop a potential business lead or increase awareness of you and/or your brand. Why would you give away all this critical information when a key part of writing and publishing your business book is about sharing your knowledge and developing a larger, meaningful network?

You lose control of how your book is presented

Amazon has strict rules and requirements about how you present your book. There's very little opportunity for you to make your book stand out from the millions of others on the site. When you develop your own book website, you not only present your book and key parts of it—like the contents page, sample chapters, endorsements, media releases, media coverage—you can also present information about you and your expertise in a way that reflects your own branding and values. This is authentic marketing. And it means that you can drive all your marketing/awareness activities to your site, again giving you the opportunity to engage potential purchasers who may well be potential clients/customers in the future.

You make less money

Self-publishing your business book costs money, so why would you give a significant proportion of the recommended retail price to a third party when, with just a little effort, you can set up your book website to take orders and keep all the money from sales for yourself? Yes, this takes a little more effort on your part and you'll have to organise how to fulfil the orders, but this is quantifiable and manageable, and you'll retain the earnings from your book.

Others can and do 'game' the Amazon best-seller system

Not all books on Amazon are equal. I've had clients say, 'I want to have a best-seller on Amazon.' Apart from asking 'Why?', I explain that there are really simple ways to 'game' the best-seller system. In fact, there are free resources online that show you how to do this, and I know 'best-selling Amazon authors' who do this on a regular basis. Apart from completely de-valuing the whole Amazon Best-Seller tag, this gaming of this system is fundamentally dishonest in my view and does not serve the purpose of my clients wanting to share their knowledge and insights and build meaningful, longer-term relationships for them and their business.

Your business book gets lost in the millions of others

To get great sales from Amazon (or anywhere else for that matter) you have to be prepared to spend time and money marketing and promoting your book. If you're going to do this, which you should if selling a lot of books is one of your objectives, you are way better off driving potential purchasers to your own website where—you guessed it—you can then start developing a relationship with them, as you'll have their contact information.

It was Jaqui who really made me think about what I wanted from this book, after all, I'm not trying to build a massive fan base or reach a huge international audience (though you may be). I'm also not after a quick sale to then sell people on the rest of the books in my series ... because I don't have any (though you may). Really, I just want to help people through their self-publishing journey faster, better equipped and with more chance at success than when I first did it myself.

But I also want to be fairly paid for the year-plus (and also the more than a decade of building up the experience and knowledge) I've spent on this book at the expense of other income and work and life opportunities. Putting an ebook up on Amazon, to reach my limited target market, to earn $6-$8, just doesn't make sense. For me.

So what is another way to distribute a book? That would be through affiliate networks which is the subject of the upcoming chapter.

33

DISTRIBUTION THROUGH AFFILIATE NETWORKS

Have you ever seen online ads promoting ebook downloads for topics like *12 Days to Awesome Abs*, *333 Backyard Shed Designs* or *99 Romantic Ways to Propose*? Often, these types of ebooks are sold by a network of affiliate marketers (promotion and sales agents) on behalf of the author. The affiliates may be people blogging in a similar subject area, minor influencers or just businesses who make their income, not by creating themselves, but by selling the creations of others. Dubious?

I don't have first-hand experience of using affiliate programs to sell my works, but I can see how some ebooks (or adaptations of them!), especially in categories including business and entrepreneurship, health, nutrition and fitness, wellness and personal development, crafts and home renovation projects, may find a global market. The books you release this way might also act as a lead-in to your other works, improving your visibility in your specialty due to the book's appearance on multiple sites.

The best results come from your book appearing on professionally run niche websites that are also relevant to your target audience. These sites often source books from affiliate companies including Clickbank, CJ Affiliate (Commission Junction), JVZoo, Warrior+ and PLR Products.

How do ebook affiliate programs work?

You pay to upload and list your book, then set the book's price as high or low as you like. The higher the book price, the more likely affiliates will put their own marketing behind it, as their cut will be between 50% and 75% of the listed price. Some books, especially those containing plans, sell at very high prices, so your royalty, though low, comes off a higher base.

What are the potential negatives of using an affiliate program to distribute books?

Though your book may be a quality product, it may end up surrounded by a sea of junk. This could significantly tarnish your brand as you also won't have control over how your work is represented or sold.

Affiliate sites can have a hint of get-rich-quick schemes and digital products can be copied, passed on and pirated (in some cases your content with a different cover and author's name) more easily than a print book.

Some affiliate companies also have a 'no questions asked' returns policy, so people may buy and read your book but then return it, the end result being that neither you nor the affiliate gets paid.

∼

There is more in Chapter 55 about affiliate programs and how you can turn the tables, earning a commission yourself by referring other people's books and products to your readers. But something that might be even more interesting for you could be the crowdfunding model. Crowdfunding is what's up next.

34

CROWDFUNDING AS A WAY OF DISTRIBUTION

The ATO defines crowdfunding as 'the practice of using internet platforms, mail order subscriptions, benefit events and other methods to find supporters and raise funds for a project or venture.'

I wasn't sure whether to include crowdfunding in the Publishing, Distribution, or Marketing section, since along with being a way to finance your book, it can be a great marketing tool. But I'm including it here because when you can successfully crowdfund, you've successfully created a distribution network too.

So, what do you need to successfully crowdfund a book? A book (and a story behind your book) that captures the imagination of supporters. You'll also need marketing and admin skills, a bucketload of time and unwavering passion for your project.

Crowdfunding works well for projects including illustrated books (where the author can offer bonus illustrations as personal rewards for bigger backers), books that require extensive research on topics already keenly followed by a large audience and books where your expert skills are in demand. You can see some examples of successful campaigns on the major crowdfunding websites, including Pozible, Patreon, Indiegogo, My Cause, GoFundMe, Kickstarter and ReadyFundGo.

(Disclosure: I've borrowed some of this information from my book *Small*

Farm Success Australia. This is an example of how, as a self-publishing author, you can re-use and repackage your content!)

Successful campaigns often rely on you already having an engaged community. You also can't focus on your own needs; you need to think about your customers' needs and what will inspire them to pledge. Be reasonable and rational about the amount you are trying to raise because in some cases if you don't reach your funding target, you won't get any of the pledged funds.

Plan what you can offer your backers (also known as donors and pledgers) at the different funding tiers. A backer pledging $10 might receive a handwritten thank-you postcard. A backer donating $50 might receive the above as well as a signed copy of your book upon publication and a mention on your website and socials. A backer donating $250 might receive all this plus additional signed copies of your book and an hour-long Zoom call. A $600 pledge will receive all of the above, as well as having you turn up to their book club (if it's in your home city) with champagne, a cheese platter, enough signed books for members, an illustration as a lucky door prize and a personal Q&A session. There are so many unique options you can devise!

Set a budget, too. It needs to incorporate the cost of fulfilling your promises, such as platform fees, books and gifts, postage and any travel costs

Running a crowdfunding campaign is not for the faint-hearted; you'll need to promote the hell out of your campaign and ensure that you can deliver the goods, and I mean that both literally and figuratively!

According to Kickstarter, 'Launching a Kickstarter crowdfunding campaign is a very public act, and creators put their reputations on the line when they do so.' Keep that in mind before heading down the crowdfunding path—you need to be able to deliver, or your reputation and project could take a massive hit.

So, from DIY to distributors to crowdfunding, you now know how to distribute your book. But how do you drum up demand for it? That's what the next chapter on marketing is all about.

PART IV

MARKETING YOUR BOOK

35

YOUR PLAN AND YOUR PLATFORM

Hello fellow author! How exciting! You wrote your book because you had something special to share, and now it's time to share it! This is where you shift focus, from vocabulary to visibility.

With tens of millions of books already in existence, propelling yourself and your book from obscurity to directly in front of your ideal audience is now what it's all about. It's okay if your audience is made up of hundreds of tawny frogmouth lovers, people allergic to mandarins or your local community, just like it's okay if you want to get in front of tens of thousands of small business owners or millions of people around the world who care about the same issues and opportunities as you. In the end, no matter the potential size of the audience, you still need to reach them.

And it is a task. Because it doesn't matter how brilliant your book is or how many years you've sweated over it; without marketing, readers won't know it exists. And, on the flip side, if your book doesn't connect with the audience and impress them enough to generate word-of-mouth recommendations, no amount of expensive marketing will help.

 I'm an author but I call myself a marketer. Authors need to get their head around the fact they're in sales. Everyone is in sales.

— KIM MCCOSKER, *4 INGREDIENTS*

So, how do we go about it?

In truth, the best time to begin marketing yourself and your book is before you even begin writing it. The next best time? As you are writing it. And, if you've written the book and are only just starting on the marketing now—well, you'll just need to work a bit harder!

In Part I we discussed planning your book, defining your audience and creating a manuscript to solve a problem for them. We've spoken about the importance of quality in thought, writing, editing and design—about making your book worthy. And from that knowledge, you have created a product. That product now needs marketing.

 There's no shortage of ways and places to market your book. However, you simply don't have the time or the money to cover all of them. So, you have to work out and focus on priority groups and avenues and create a plan. However, having a plan is one thing, executing it consistently is a completely different thing. I advise clients that they need to be prepared to market and sell their book for a minimum 15-month period: 3 months before their book is published and 12 months after it's launched.

— JAQUI LANE, THE BOOK ADVISER

Think of this part of the book as you would a menu at a restaurant. There will be all sorts of items, some to your taste and others not so much, or just not to your taste right now. Some will be free (like a self-service water refill station), while others will come at a hefty premium (like European white truffles), which you may or may not have the budget or appetite for.

Just as at a restaurant, you won't be able to eat everything on the menu in one go (and if you tried, you and your credit card would likely regret it). You might return to that restaurant and explore more of their menu over time, and it's a good idea to be adventurous, but you don't need to force yourself to choose anything that is unpalatable, overly decadent, that you're allergic to or that is well beyond your budget. You can also just whiz up a lot of things at home as I do!

 When their first copies arrive, every author suddenly thinks, 'How do I get this book into as many hands as possible?'

Everything they've done on strategy goes out the window, and I need to take them back to their initial plan and remind them that that 'everyone' wasn't their initial target market—nor should it be! All business authors want to see their book in an airport bookstore: but that's often (they will admit) an ego stroke. Remember, having your book in an airport bookstore doesn't mean it's getting into the right peoples' hands. As marketing guru Seth Godin says, 'aim for the smallest viable audience'.

— KELLY IRVING, BOOK COACH AND EDITOR

Some of these marketing tasks are one-offs that you attend to before publication, while others you will be doing long after your book hits the shelves. So, roll up your sleeves and let's dig in!

CRAFT A MARKETING PLAN IN FIVE STEPS

1. Define where you are right now and where you want your marketing efforts to take you (in terms of readers, royalties, new clients and partnerships, media appearances and personal brand building etc).
2. Define your unique selling proposition (USP): why you, why this book and how will your target audience benefit from it?
3. Really understand your key target markets and research the best ways to reach them.
4. Create a plan and set a budget (this may include outsourcing some components).
5. Execute and continually review the plan, doubling down on the things that are working.

Sounds easy, but these five steps take up much of the rest of this book and will demand plenty of your time! Marketing is an investment of both headspace and money, and if done poorly, it will drain your bank account and confidence. But when done well, it means you gain not just a book sale but customers and fans for life.

Yes, marketing can be fun and energising and in many ways it's a creative process. But it is a process! The key is to make a real connection, to market your ideas, self and knowledge, not just your book, in a way that leaves people wanting more. So, where to begin?

ASSESS YOUR AUTHOR PLATFORM

An author platform is not something you stand on physically but having one certainly boosts your chance of success.

Publishing expert Jane Friedman defines an author platform as 'an ability to sell books because of who you are or who you can reach'.

A platform takes time to build, as it's about being known in your field of expertise, by people who actually care about your field of expertise. For example, you might be a Nobel Prize-winning food scientist, but if you write a book about folk art, your established platform will be completely irrelevant.

 Building your platform is really a career-building exercise. It never actually ends. Moreover, it's never too early to start, and it's never too late, especially in the context of your book. But you need to understand, you can't buy a platform, and you can't have it overnight.

— KELLY IRVING, BOOK COACH AND EDITOR

The best time to build a platform is throughout your adult life, but if you're starting from scratch, a disciplined approach to platform-building as you write your book can work too.

Each of these elements will be explored in some way in the following chapters, along with plenty of other ideas to give you and your book the best chance of success.

 Self-publishing and the constant marketing required is hard work, but for me, it's all about the writing. If it was about the money, I'd have stayed in television.

— MONTE DWYER, JOURNALIST AND SELF-PUBLISHER

Elements of a good platform include:

- A professional website. This is your face to the world and often the first point of contact many people will have with you.
- Your personality and your preparedness to make things happen.
- The content you have previously created, such as blogs, papers, articles, media mentions and interviews, presentations and speeches.
- Your expertise, all the things you're known for by your target audience, as well as awards, reviews and recognition from others.
- Who you know and what they say about you; basically, this is your social, business and media contacts.
- Your email list—all those people who have given you permission to stay in touch.
- Your social media following—not so much the size, but the level of engagement they have with you.
- Your sales and marketing expertise. Any experience in these areas goes a long way!

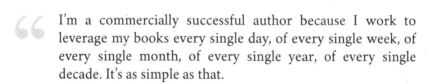

I'm a commercially successful author because I work to leverage my books every single day, of every single week, of every single month, of every single year, of every single decade. It's as simple as that.

— ANDREW GRIFFITHS, BOOK WRITING COACH, AUTHOR
AND SPEAKER

~

Not known for much? Haven't focused on your website? Only have a few social media followers? Or are you already a success, but want to be a roaring one? Read on as we step through all the elements of a successful book (and author!) marketing campaign.

36

YOUR AUTHOR WEBSITE

Your website will be one of your most important marketing tools, and that's why it needs to be your first priority. It can be anything from a basic site used as a promotional tool right through to a sales channel with all the ecommerce bells and whistles.

If you are struggling with what to put on your website or how to update the one you have, I hear you! I sat on a barely useful, poorly branded DIY WordPress site for years. One of my conundrums was that I had no strategy to underpin the website because I couldn't even think through the strategy. I mean, how could I appeal to and be relevant to such a broad range of audiences from business groups, commissioning editors, farmers, corporate types and parents through to people who care about the environment and all kinds of writers of non-fiction? I also had no discipline when it came to updating my site because there was no discipline or planning behind the website itself—except to 'have a presence'. You know what I learned in the end? 'Having a presence' is of no benefit at all if the presence is poorly executed and not on-brand.

While researching this book, I came across specialist author website designer Jin Wang, and I immediately knew he understood the writer's dilemma: that we are not one thing, we are many things and we need a website to encapsulate all of that. Though I could have DIY'd my website again or used a cheaper overseas service, I decided to put my business hat on, support another Australian business and finally upgrade for the launch of this book. I am so glad I did. Having a decent but simple website helps both your audience and you. It elevates your brand and your confidence too.

There are plenty of website designers on the internet, and yes, you can still DIY, especially if you're not in a position to invest in it now. But do pay special attention to things such as your privacy policy and site security or you could face significant fines and hacks. The following advice, reprinted with Jin's permission, is solid regardless of how you create your site.

~

INSIDE ADVICE: JIN WANG
DESIGNER, JIN & CO.

What are the benefits of a tailored author website?

It shows you're a professional and builds your credibility. Your web presence is one of the first—and often only—points of contact for prospective readers, media, commissioning editors, clients and festivals finding out about you for the first time. It's essential to make a good first impression, and the best way to do this is with a distinctive design. Just as books need distinctive covers, so do author websites. Aim for an identity that's tailored to your goals and style; one that visitors will recognise and remember.

Do authors need multiple websites for different books and audiences?

It's hard enough to do online marketing and maintenance for one website, so multiple websites spread your time and money too thin. It's better to put your resources into one property: your author name. Use this site to promote the values behind your writing and create a strong association between those values and your name. Simon Sinek, author and motivational speaker, suggests that people buy what you 'believe', not what you 'sell'. Although the different kinds of books and services you 'sell' may not resonate across all your audiences, what you 'believe' will.

Why is a dedicated book page important?

When people hear of something new, they turn to the web. If you do a search on the web for your name or your book, the results might look something like this: Booktopia, Amazon, Facebook, a book blogger's review. But where are you and your book? Having your own page establishes a primary authoritative source regarding your book, a single page for people to link to, and for you to link from, a place to display your resources and control everything visitors see without competitive clutter.

Do I need to bother with a custom domain name?

Owning your web presence starts with getting the domain name you want. Firstly, it's dirt cheap. With a custom domain, you've also got somewhere you can send people to 'find out more'. When you get press coverage, or after speaking events, it's far easier to drop your domain name—the central hub for your online presence—rather than list your various social media links. So, if you haven't secured a domain yet, do so ASAP before it's taken.

Do I need a custom email address?

If you want to look professional, a custom email address, linked to the same URL as your website, will always be more personal, professional and permanent than a Hotmail or Gmail address.

What about email marketing and newsletters?

Email marketing for authors is all about building an asset you own. Social media is great for transient communication and reaching new people quickly, but it's also crowded and noisy. More important than reach is 'ownership'. You own your email contacts, but you don't own your Twitter or Instagram followers or your Facebook likes. It's easy to set up an email marketing service and many have free plans.

What if I'm publishing for international markets?

Professional author websites offer the flexibility of creating region-specific landing pages. This way, information such as book covers, translated text and purchasing options can be customised to suit the access location.

Do I need ecommerce?

Adding ecommerce converts your author website from a promotional tool to a complete online shopfront. An online store allows sales of single items, like books, all the way to automated billing subscriptions for products like email courses or video tutorials.

A few examples of single products for writers and illustrators are Skype consultations, mentoring sessions, illustrations or artwork, self-published ebooks or print books, workshops, live or pre-recorded events, and resource packs.

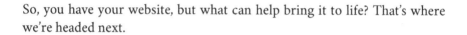

So, you have your website, but what can help bring it to life? That's where we're headed next.

37

PHOTOS, IMAGES, INFOGRAPHICS, BOOK TRAILERS AND VIDEOS

Your book may or may not feature images, but photos, infographics, images and videos will be useful resources for your website, marketing and publicity in general. In this chapter, we'll explore book cover images, developing a photo library, what makes for a great author headshot and why using video can give you an edge.

BEGIN BUILDING YOUR PHOTO AND IMAGE LIBRARY

Mobile phones have made it easy to take great photos on the go. Whatever your subject matter, the more images you can tuck away for future website and promotional content the better. Sure, you can use free images from the internet to make your socials look snappy, but being able to access your own original library of images adds a lot more authenticity.

You can overlay your images with quotes and information from others who have given you an 'Aha!' moment. Drip feed them out via social media over time. You might also want to incorporate the sharing of quotes from your book into your social media calendar too. Set a consistent schedule and release a quote a day or every three to seven days across your socials to tempt, inspire and inform your audience.

BOOK COVER IMAGES

Images of your book cover will appear on your website and in online stores, promotional material, sales catalogues and the media. Make them available for download in the 'About' or media kit section of your website and have them in various formats including JPEG, PNG, TIFF and PDF.

Save them in an easily accessed folder on your phone and computer too, with an obvious name such as *yourbooktitle*frontcover and consider having them recreated as a 3D image to add some extra oomph to your presentations. Sites such as BookBrush make this a breeze to do and if you use the *smart mockups* feature in Canva, you can add your book into all sorts of backgrounds.

YOUR AUTHOR PHOTO

Your author photo matters. For my earlier books, the images (of me on my own, with my favourite sheep, holding a baby goat, in front of a dam etc.) taken by my photographer friend Susan Lowick appeared in media ranging from *The Land* to *The Newcastle Herald* and a regional network of newspapers. The photos added immense impact to the stories the papers ran, just by dint of the space devoted to them.

 Even if you are getting a headshot for a very specific event or book, it's a good idea to try for a variety of different shots and emotions that could be suitable for different purposes down the road.

— KARIN LOCKE, PHOTOGRAPHER

However, being so 'farmy', those photos didn't suit this book, and it was time for an update anyway. So, I searched online for local photographers, going through portfolios until I found one who seemed like he could coax a decent photo from a range of faces. In an hour and a half shoot at my house, photographer Lindsay Mollar also reminded me of the importance of communicating well with a photographer. How? The shoot was happening prior to this book being released and I didn't have the budget to do another shoot post-launch actually holding a copy of the new book. When I mentioned this to Lindsay, he took control, taking a photo that would allow the book cover to be edited in later.

Tell the photographer your endgame. That way it can be a true collaboration.

— LINDSAY MOLLAR, PHOTOGRAPHER

When you plan your headshot, think about how you want the photo to make people feel about you. Should it be serious or humorous? What aspect of you and the book's personality do you want to highlight? Wise or wicked? Conservative or cheeky? How do you want the photo to make people feel: trusting, curious, welcomed, or do you want them to feel like you're someone they could have a laugh with? Does your picture say leader, mentor, survivor, success, joker, serious author, or approachable guru?

 Practically everyone hates having their picture taken, so don't dwell on it too much. Leave it to the professional to help make you look your best. If you've selected a photographer because you like their portfolio, and you've shared with them some examples of what you're looking to achieve, trust that they will be able to create something similar for you. Relax into it.

— KARIN LOCKE, PHOTOGRAPHER

INSIDE ADVICE:
SOPHIE TIMOTHY OF SISTER SCOUT STUDIO

Why do authors need good headshots?

A good author photo helps readers and the media to visually identify and relate to you. It humanises you, personalises your marketing and gives people the space to connect at a deeper level than text alone. If you're trying to publicise your books, it's helpful for all your socials and the media, especially as you're giving the outlet the image they need to go with the story. A good headshot can also add legitimacy and credibility, even though you're not signed with a publisher.

What makes a great author headshot?

When the photo is authentic, relaxed and retains the author's essence. It can't be contrived but does need to show you in your best light. You want to feel a vibe and energy from the image, and natural light can help with this. The photo needs to reflect you and the story you want to tell, plus you want it to look like you, just a polished version. A pensive, looking-away-from-the-camera shot rarely works. It's best to be looking directly at the camera, and therefore out at your audience. Avoid transition lenses.

What should an author wear to a photo shoot?

You don't have to buy something new to look like 'a writer', just wear something smart casual or in keeping with the subject of your book and bring a few changes of clothes or accessories. For example, if you're a chef you might wear an apron for a shot or two. If your book is about the military, you might be in khaki. Sticking to black and neutral colours such as whites, greys, denims and creams can work well.

What's the best way to prepare before a shoot?

Know what you are trying to say and who you are trying to reach. Also, tell the photographer where you want to use the photos such as on LinkedIn or for a speaker shot, or even a banner image (in which case we'd take it with a lot of white to the side to leave room for text).

What do you wish authors knew about photo rights?

Read the contract closely and negotiate on any points that are important to you. In my contract, I retain the copyright, so if you want to reproduce an image (e.g., on t-shirts), edit it or sell it (such as to an advertiser), you can't do so without my express permission. Ensure that the contract stipulates the usage you want.

How often do you think an author should update their headshot?

Annually is a good goal, but at least every two years. Fashion changes and hairstyles can date. A fresh folder of images you can use across the year on social media and your website keeps things fresh, and you won't get bored looking at yourself.

Final tips?

The branding process shouldn't start with a photographer, as we're the last piece in the puzzle—ensure that you've worked with a graphic designer to get all those elements right. Also, media are always wanting an angle for a story. If you know the angle is X, Y, or Z, make sure you and the photographer discuss the best way to get a relevant shot. For example, if your book is about rooftop beekeeping, don't just have a studio photo, get a shot on a roof. Similarly, if you're writing a book about productivity, you might bring a timer or a watch to the shoot as an accessory for some of the images.

 With regard to your author photo, make sure it complements your book cover, so when your photo and the book cover appear together on our poster, there is no clash of colours or patterns. Think about what might be appealing to the eye.

— LEANNE WRIGHT, EVENT LIBRARIAN

INFOGRAPHICS

An infographic is a visually attractive image combining text, data and imagery to communicate information in an easily digestible and fast way. It's basically a visual explainer. You can share information about your book, or specific topics covered within it, in one or more infographics released over time. When executed well, they help build your brand.

How do I make them and what do I include in them?

It's relatively easy with a DIY service like Canva, or a graphic designer could create them for you. Include a combination of some, but not necessarily all, of the following:

- key information about your book (or topic) and where it can be purchased

- statistics
- pie charts, bar charts and line graphs
- a picture of your book cover
- images and illustrations relevant to your book and/or your author pic
- website or contact details
- video and/or audio links.

What makes an effective infographic?

According to Canva, an effective infographic:

- is clear and memorable and includes high-quality graphics
- is visually and textually concise
- tells a story and includes a 'hook', or primary take-away/call to action, that is easy to spot
- contains current and relevant data
- is well-organised with a balance of text, illustrations and space
- has a suitable style and sense of flow.

How do I share my infographics?

Include them in social media posts, in your media kit and on your website. You could also print them up as a postcard or bookmark if that makes sense as part of your marketing strategy.

VIDEOS

Mobile phones make shooting short videos fast and easy. You can livestream or edit them on your phone or laptop, adding subtitles, transitions and music.

You could add a welcome video on your site, film and share short how-to videos, use Instagram Reels or even prepare video courses and presentations.

 There is an option on LinkedIn where you can upload a video clip in the *Cover Profile* photo area. People like to see you, hear your voice and get to know a bit about you. That builds credibility and trust. And who do we want to do business with? People we like, know and trust! People also like to watch videos—they don't always want to read. You can do simple things such as record your book launch so you can repurpose parts of the video later, get images of your book inside a bookstore next to other bestsellers and capture other relevant footage on your phone when you can—you never know when it will come in handy.

— LYNNAIRE JOHNSTON, *LINKABILITY*

BOOK TRAILERS

I'm a sucker for a good movie trailer, especially the pace at which they showcase the best lines, action and just a snippet of the story. But did you know that there's such a thing as a book trailer? It's a video summary of your book and it's designed to be a call to action to either buy it or sign up for more information about it.

Why make a book trailer?

- People are consuming more and more video content on the internet thanks to faster broadband speeds.
- If it's effective, people can jump from watching your trailer on their screen to instantly purchasing it online or heading out to their bookstore to buy it.
- It may help with your SEO ranking.

How can I make a book trailer?

Create a slideshow with captions or use any modern phone to take a selfie of you discussing the book, then edit it with simple video editing software that's likely already on your computer or phone. Or, if your budget allows and your target audience warrants it, employ a production company to script, film and edit the video.

What makes a good book trailer?

It targets your ideal audience with a relevant and interesting story, mentioning the pain points or problems the book can solve for them. It also balances good audio with interesting visuals and has a call to action.

What should I avoid with my book trailer?

Anything that could be seen as an annoying sales pitch, is too long and that offers little value to viewers.

Where do I put my book trailer?

You can put it on your website, YouTube and socials, and link to it from your emails.

Why not to make a book trailer

Because you want to spend the time and money you would have invested in creating the book trailer on a different marketing activity. Or, it's just one more thing to get your head around and you don't have any kids, colleagues or friends who can help. And it's okay, you don't need to do every marketing activity outlined in this book!

～

That's right, you don't need to do every marketing activity in this book, but you'd be letting opportunities get away if you don't make the focus of the next chapter, building an email list, one of your top priorities.

38

EMAIL LISTS AND LEAD MAGNETS

All you wanted to do was write a book, and now I'm asking you to brush up on ways to build an empire of people who want to hear more from you. Why? Because a solid email list is a writer's most valuable asset, enabling you to build a business around your expertise.

 There are three things you need to do. 1. Learn marketing 2. Don't be afraid to sell your books and yourself. 3. Network with your potential readers early via social media and your own newsletter.

— DR HELEN EDWARDS, *HEALTHY PLANET, HEALTHY PEOPLE, HEALTHY HOME*

What is permission marketing?

It's the opposite of spam, which is a good thing because spam is illegal. It's when a customer or fan supplies you with their contact details and gives you explicit permission to contact them by email.

Why do I want my own email list?

- To build deep relationships: turn people who want to hear from you into long-term customers, supporters and fans.
- Direct communication: you will be able to communicate with your audience unimpeded and do so whenever you want to reach out to them (within reason).
- Control: it means you're not reliant on social media giants, who can change the rules, prices and your visibility to fans whenever they like. They can even block your account. When you have your own email list, you are in control of your relationship with your customers.
- Speed: you can quickly reach an interested audience with new products, ideas, events, specials and opportunities.
- ROI: the return on investment from email marketing is typically high in comparison to advertising programs.
- Research: you will be able to see which email subject headers were opened and which weren't, which helps you identify the hot buttons for your audience.
- To learn from your list: ask your audience what questions they have on your topic or get their opinion on what they'd like to see in your next book. Being able to communicate with your list gives you a chance to come up with solutions, create fresh content and expand your offering in a way that is tailored to them.
- To make money: it is normally cheaper and easier to make money from current customers than to find and sell to new ones.
- Flexibility: your emails can be as long or short as you like and won't be constrained by character limits or social media requirements.
- To further build your brand: your emails will be in your own unique writing and visual styles with no competitive clutter surrounding them.
- Convenience: you can pre-write multiple emails and schedule them to go out over a set period of time.

 It's important to build your own following. I once lost 22% of my annual income overnight when Borders and Angus & Robertson bookstores closed. From that came lessons. In that moment of panic (five years after I'd launched my first book) I only had 4,000 followers on Facebook and 45,000 subscribers on my database. That's when I started to ramp that up. Every time I stood on a stage, rather than put my effort into 'Buy my books', I put it into 'Follow me, subscribe'.

— KIM MCCOSKER, *4 INGREDIENTS*

What is best practice in email marketing?

- Opt in: offering your followers the ability to choose to hear from you (rather than signing them up without asking) is not just courtesy or best practice. It's the law in Australia and many other countries around the world.
- Opt-out: you must give people the option to unsubscribe at any stage in the process. You can also offer them the chance to 'opt-down' by letting them choose to receive emails from you less frequently.
- Privacy: never share or expose people's data.
- Frequency: no one likes being bombarded with emails. Receiving them too often is a common reason people unsubscribe. Set a schedule and stick to it. It might be weekly, monthly, or seasonally, depending on the amount of content you have and how often your customer base is happy to receive it. If you're more of a freestyler and don't like to schedule things, just be honest at sign-up and let people know that you will only contact them when you have something you think they will appreciate. In writing this book I realised I'm a freestyler, it might not be good business, but it is how I roll!
- Personalisation: technology means you can use each follower's name in the email they receive. Why is that important? Subscribers are more likely to open an email and feel warmer towards it when it is personalised.

What technology can I plug into my website to help with this?

Key players offer services ranging from simple landing and signup pages through to tools that allow you to automatically send out a sequence of emails (such as a welcome email, followed by an email offering bonus content etc.) when a person first signs up.

Companies that offer these kinds of email marketing tools and services include: Mailchimp, MailerLite (this is what I use), ConvertKit, Drip, GetResponse, ActiveCampaign, Sendinblue, AWeber, ClickFunnels and others.

There are also powerful services such as Kartra that offer holistic solutions. With Kartra, you can create list-builder campaigns to help grow your email list numbers, deliver video content for marketing or as part of an online course or training session, upsell secondary products, set up recurring membership payments and even create your own affiliate program—all under the one system. Yes, you'll pay for it, and yes, it may be overkill for your current needs, but if this is the level of automation and features you seek, then Kartra (and alternatives such as Ontraport) can offer this. I was very impressed with Kartra, and I can see how some authorpreneurs would benefit from it, which is why I've become an affiliate with them.

What do I send to my email list?

Content that will be useful, entertaining and/or inspiring. This might include information, tips, plans, recipes, giveaways and competitions, reviews on products/other books of interest, interviews with subject experts, video summaries, the latest statistics, reports and more.

How do I start building my email list?

- Decide (with your website designer if you're using one) which program/software you will use and integrate it into your site.
- Have a simple sign-up form on your website and include links to that form in your header and footer and on your home page and blog.
- Offer bonus content (also known as 'reader magnets') to anyone who signs up.

- Provide a discount on your book or other products for anyone who signs up for your newsletter.
- Design a course that can be delivered by email. Anyone who wants to do the course will obviously have to provide their email address.
- Reuse your content and make it available as a download. According to ConvertKit: 'A short PDF ebook is perceived to be worth more than the same content in a blog post.'
- Host an online event (such as a webinar), which you can also record so you have even more content to tempt future subscribers with.
- Link to your signup content/reader magnet in all of your marketing.
- Run giveaways or competitions (ensuring that they comply with the laws in your state).

LEAD MAGNETS

A lead magnet is a bonus you offer on a specific landing page on your website in exchange for the reader giving you permission to email them. It can be run quite simply, for example 'sign up with your email and get this', or in a very sophisticated way, involving an entire 'drip' campaign with the reader receiving specific content based on the actions/reactions your previous emails have generated from them.

What can I use as a lead magnet/bonus material?

- Case studies: for *Small Farm Success Australia*, I offered a bonus farmer case study that wasn't included in the book. What might work for your book and audience?
- Top 10 lists: offer a top 10 list of either tips, product reviews or seasonal advice.
- Cut material: select some worthy material edited from the book due to space constraints.
- Bonus material: videos, interviews, audio files, or, depending on your subject matter, crafting patterns, recipes and key contact lists.
- Interactive Excel spreadsheets and charts: for example, a book

about property investing or starting a business might offer access to budgeting and forecasting tools as a lead magnet.

How do I set up a lead magnet on my site?

Your website developer and many of the companies that provide email list solutions have the tools to integrate and run this process.

Planning well ahead means you can promote your lead magnet from within your book, such as with an ad at the end of the book. But one of the other great places to promote lead magnets is through social media. We cover off all things social in the next chapter.

39

SOCIAL MEDIA

You've either been able to avoid it (until now!) or you already spend upwards of three hours a day on social media. What you can't avoid, though, is that when done well, social media can underpin your book's success. It can:

- increase visibility for you and your book
- connect, expand, and deepen your networks of peers, potential readers and clients
- deepen understanding of your brand
- help you sell more books
- assist you with market research
- give you access to people whose contact details you wouldn't normally be able to find
- amplify your voice and message and increase your email sign-ups.

Conversely, when done poorly, it can cost lots of money with little return and can:

- waste your time
- affect your mental health
- detract from your brand
- lead to trolling and negative pile-ons.

Your aim should be to find the right medium for you and the right groove within it. Things are always changing in the space and what's hot right now might be a week-old dinner by the time you read these words. Trends move on, but find your space and give it your best shot.

~

INSIDE ADVICE: JAQUI LANE
TOP THREE TIPS FOR SOCIAL MEDIA FOR AUTHORS

1. Write great stuff and use quality images that help your target audience with the challenges they have. Don't spruik your latest course, program or book all the time. Share knowledge and insights, develop trust, deliver value.
2. Commit and execute consistently over time: only select those social media platforms that you will be actively engaged with for at least 12 to 24 months. The social world is littered with supernovas. They shine brightly for a few months and then disappear. If you really want to build a presence, and respect and engagement with your target audience, it's a long haul. If you're not up for this, don't start. Be honest with yourself so you don't waste your or other people's time.
3. Have focus: there are so many social media channels that there's no way you have the time and/or money to engage/advertise on them all, so work out (research) which ones are best for your target audience. If your research shows that, for example, LinkedIn is where your audience sits, check out groups that relate to your area and join four or five of the most relevant groups while you're in the process of writing your book. Start engaging early. By the time your book is ready for launch, you'll be part of this group and you can share your book launch and promo offers with them without seeming like a stranger.

~

KEY SOCIAL MEDIA SITES

Not every social media site will work for you, your book, your brand and your lifestyle. Different platforms rise and fall in popularity over time and new players are always spreading their wings. Each has a different audience profile, and emphasis placed on the type, style and format of content (such as text, audio or visuals).

Also, you need to focus, you don't need to be on every social site, but you need to be on at least one and do it well.

> I can now reach more people on Facebook than I can with a national TV appearance. Social media has enabled me to reach so many from the bench in my kitchen. When I do my 'lives' on Facebook, I can just chat and cook and over the years have created lovely friendships with people from all over the world.

— KIM MCCOSKER, *4 INGREDIENTS*

Some of the key platforms (and there are many others that do particularly well in other countries, depending on the language) include: Facebook, YouTube, Twitter, Instagram, Pinterest and LinkedIn. You also have Medium, Reddit, TikTok, Tumblr, Snapchat and Clubhouse.

Messaging apps also continue to add new ways for writers to interact with people. Some examples include WhatsApp, Messenger, WeChat and Viber.

What are some tools I can use to manage my social media?

There is a variety of time-saving tools to help you create, schedule and post social media to your different sites. Some of the best-known include Hootsuite, Sendible, Buffer, SproutSocial, SocialOomph and Social Pilot.

Are there any other sites that aren't necessarily social media, but that I could use to raise my profile?

So many! As an expert on your subject matter, you can be active in the online community answering questions and posting articles on your specialty. Building a presence on websites such as Google My Business, Medium, Quora and BuzzFeed may help raise awareness of your book and drive email subscriptions. But you can't be everywhere, so think concentrated and effective rather than scattergun.

~

INSIDE ADVICE: LYNNAIRE JOHNSTON
AUTHOR, LINK.ABILITY
As interviewed by Jaqui Lane, The Book Adviser

How can being on LinkedIn help a non-fiction author?

It enables you to leverage your book, increase sales, build your profile and personal brand, and build engagement with your target audience. It can help you share information and reach people who otherwise wouldn't have discovered you.

Is LinkedIn important for all non-fiction authors, or just authors of business books?

All non-fiction authors can and ideally should make good use of LinkedIn. Why? Because LinkedIn is an ideal platform for sharing knowledge. People are there to learn, and if you have a written a book, you are an expert in your field, so share that expertise with your LinkedIn audience. It will help build your reputation and enhance your credibility as an expert. A spin-off benefit is that people will buy your book to find out more.

What are your top 10 tips for promoting your book on LinkedIn?

1. Start by setting up a good profile. Some people treat LinkedIn as a site for their resume, but if you're an author, you're a knowledgeable person—an expert in your field—who will share information, and that's what you want to get across on your profile.
2. You need good images of your book, including a 3D version. Place the image in several places including in your banner image and in the *Featured* section. Make it eye-catching and it will stop people in their tracks. You can also use a video of you talking about your book, or an excerpt, book review or endorsements.
3. In the *Experience* section, mention your book again and include a short synopsis and reviews as well. Testimonials are great for giving you and your book social proof.

4. Have a link to your website where the book is being sold.
5. Use the 10-second *Name pronunciation* feature to introduce yourself and your book.
6. Publish more educational and informative posts than promo posts (special offers, come to my launch etc.). Work towards a ratio of at least five to one.
7. Longer articles have more longevity than 200-word posts and are often referred on.
8. Mix things up by using a variety of formats such as polls, images, text, videos, posts and articles.
9. Hashtag news topics where it's relevant, as it can help you surf the wave of news stories and increase your exposure, but understand that although adding hashtags is important for algorithms, what's more important is that you are posting useful content and building relationships.
10. Always keep in mind that people want to learn more about what you know, not just about what you have to sell.

How many posts should an author aim for?

Aim for a number that is manageable. I see people post every other day for a few months and then disappear. So, think about what your capacity is to generate long-term content and whether this is the right medium for you. You might decide you can do one short post a week and one article a month —just work out what you can manage and stick with it. LinkedIn is a long game; you won't get a lot of success in the short term. It's like compound interest—the more you put in today the more you will get back in the long term. Ideally, you should show up week after week, month after month.

~

Twitter is all about personality, so when I came across Rachel Thompson's book *The BadRedhead Media 30-Day Book Marketing Challenge* and heard she was also writing the *BadRedhead Media 30-Day Twitter Challenge*, I had to reach out to her for some tips. Her reply, in her inimitable style (which you need on Twitter!), was 'F**k yeah!'.

~

INSIDE ADVICE: RACHEL THOMPSON
BADREDHEAD MEDIA, A FOCUS ON TWITTER
Reprinted with permission from *The BadRedhead Media 30-Day Book Marketing Challenge*

Why Twitter?

Twitter is a great channel for networking and visibility, for connecting with readers, book bloggers, reviewers and other publications who can help publicise your book. It also can send a huge amount of traffic to your website and blog. It's not, however, all that great for sales. If you are counting on any one social channel to sell your book, you are going to be disappointed. THE most important point to remember about Twitter and why you need it as part of your book marketing platform (besides connecting with readers) is that Google indexes tweets, so from a search engine optimisation (SEO) perspective, Twitter carries more weight than Facebook.

The basics

If you're not already on Twitter, go to Twitter.com and see if the name you want is available. You have fifteen spaces total for your handle (aka, name). Preferably, use your name, or add *writer, author, blogger,* or *books* to the front or back. I don't recommend your book's title, because in all likelihood you'll be writing more than one book, and then what? Start smart: use your name or some iteration thereof.

Targeting

As writers, bloggers, authors and small business people, we need to be strategic with Twitter and 'follow' our ideal customer. Are your ideal customers and ideal readers other authors (unless your book is about writing or book marketing, like this book)? No? Then why are you following so many? Yes, I believe we form and join communities to support each other, and that's great. Do that, but don't exclusively do that. See the difference?

What to tweet

Many people are unsure what to tweet about (or post on any social media channel in general) because it feels unnatural and forced, which is why authors end up hawking their books constantly, or small businesses only discuss selling their services. ME, ME, ME. NO, NO, NO. This is a mistake. If you were at a dinner party, or, say, in line at the movies, what would you discuss with the person next to you? Likely, not your book or service (one would hope). You'd discuss topics that interest you, a news story, something you have some kind of expertise in.

What next?

For an extensive list of book marketing ideas and how to action them, please check out Rachel's book, *The BadRedhead Media 30-Day Book Marketing Challenge*. I found her 30 days of assignments irresistible because they hand-hold but at the same time gave me a good shove to boost my all-round marketing efforts.

Also, investigate 'Twitter Tips' (see more in Chapter 52). This might be a way to fund the effort that goes into providing your followers with up-to-the-minute, important content.

∼

INSIDE ADVICE: JENN HANSON-DEPAULA
MIXTUS MEDIA: A FOCUS ON INSTAGRAM

I came across Mixtus Media about two weeks into laying out this book and knew I needed to reorganise things to include them here.

I've enjoyed listening to their wife-and-husband podcast while watching the sunrise at 5.30 am, waiting to pick up the youngest kiddo from activities or unpacking the dishwasher. And when their Instagram 'reels' pop up on my phone, I've nodded my head in agreement and laughed out loud. They provide great content as a lead-in to their paid services (which is a lesson for authors in itself!) and they sure know a writer's marketing pain points. I'm grateful to be able to include Jenn's top five Instagram tips for non-fiction authors here.

1. Set aside an hour each week to create your images and text for

Instagram posts and schedule them using a tool like Buffer. It will save you getting bogged down each day wondering 'what am I going to post?'.

2. Social media is not just for marketing, it's about connecting with other human beings. Connect first and the marketing comes naturally after.

3. You don't need to connect with everyone, just your ideal reader.

4. Unfollow accounts that you feel drain you. Fill your feed with people and images you enjoy.

5. Readers are overwhelmed with options so your book must be worth their time. Though it can work for business authors to give away free books (because their intention in writing their book was to create income from extra consulting and gigs), giving books away free is not a great idea for many non-fiction authors. Instead, build anticipation before and after launch so your audience wants to buy your book and so they put a priority on reading it. Free books often end up unread.

~

Yes, there is a whole lot to explore on social media and it's easy to end up wasting hours if not days on it, so be smart, pick a strategy and stick with it.

40

ARCS AND REVIEWS

An advanced reader copy (ARC), Beta, or galley, is a non-final version of your book that you send out one to three months before your launch for the purpose of soliciting reviews, sales, media coverage and to build buzz.

It is relatively economical to achieve through a POD print run but it's even cheaper to do (due to no printing and shipping costs) if you deliver it as an ebook through a service such as BookFunnel, NetGalley and Booksprout, or by using free codes authors receive through Apple Books and Amazon.

The media, reviewers, book buyers, influencers and book bloggers work on very long lead times. To be able to have their coverage ready to go by your launch date, they need to have your book in their hands well before the public. Sharing your work in advance with important contacts also builds excitement around your launch and can spark collaborations too.

I also use the feedback from ARCs to tweak and make changes so my books are the best they can be on launch day. And if I haven't received permissions from all my interviewees for their quotes yet, I use the ARCs to secure the last of them.

Sending out a completely unpolished and unedited ARC will be detrimental though. You need to put your best foot forward.

What format do I send it in?

Send it as a hardcopy, watermarked PDF or watermarked ebook file (watermarking helps but doesn't totally avoid potential piracy).

Add a small header to each of your interior pages such as: *Not for Sale/Uncorrected Proof/Advance Reader Copy.*

If your cover is already designed, overlay it with the above text. If your cover is not ready, a super simple white cover with plain text (including title, subtitle and author name) is fine.

In an email or on the back cover, include the release date, where people can order the book from, RRP, ISBN and other relevant details.

What else do I send with the ARC?

Your contact details, full author bio and a personal note explaining why you are sending it and what action you'd like them to take, such as provide a review, interview you on their podcast or sign you up for an author talk. A few weeks after sending, if you haven't heard back, follow up politely to ensure they received it and to get their feedback.

GENERAL REVIEWS

Word-of-mouth book recommendations are marketing super fuel.

 Reputations don't work very well in isolation, they need a network of supporters, fans and advocates to spread the word. Getting others to sing your praises is far more effective than you trying to do it yourself.

— GARRY BROWNE, THE PERSONAL BRAND CATALYST AND AUTHOR, *BRAND NEW, BRAND YOU*

Some of this social proof happens in chats with friends—'I just read this great book'—through traditional newspaper/magazine reviews and media mentions, when we're browsing social media and when we're looking at book reviews posted through online bookstores.

You will already have your advance praise rolling in, but the quicker you can build a wave of reviews from an even wider pool of people, the more likely others will see and trust in your book enough to buy it.

WHO CAN I GET REVIEWS FROM?

Even though no one owes you anything, especially a review, there are all sorts of people you can approach, and it's a case of 'if you don't ask, you won't get'. Here are some review sources you might like to target.

- Recipients of your ARCs: politely chase them up to see if they have been able to review your book yet. Add the best reviews to your website, socials and marketing material.
- Sources you have quoted in the book: these might be other authors or experts, as well as writers whose books you have mentioned in your 'Further Reading' list.
- Administrators of Facebook group relevant to your topic. Reach out with a direct message asking if they'd like a review copy.
- Social media influencers: is there someone you already follow and interact with who is passionate about your subject matter?
- Top Amazon reviewers: try to locate the contact details for the top Amazon reviewers in your category. You can do this by checking the reviews and reviewers of similar books.
- Media: including magazine editors, radio producers, newspaper journos and freelance writers who cover your space.
- Trade publications and associations: do you mention podiatrists in your book? How about plumbers or pastry chefs? Find the relevant trade publication or organisation for that industry or group and approach them.
- Celebrities: any who have an interest in your topic.
- Heads of community organisations: especially those who might mention your book in their newsletter/socials to members.
- Select industry peers: who in your business or professional network might appreciate an early copy and be able to help promote it in some way?
- Vocal followers and fans: those who already subscribe to your email list or follow you on social platforms.
- Your editor: ask their permission to use something positive they've said about your work.
- Family and friends: especially if they hold relevant positions. Be aware though that Amazon and other sites may be able to detect they are reviews from family and so might remove them and even give you a warning.

- BookBub: this is a consumer site that offers a way for authors to reach book lovers. It is mostly used by prolific fiction authors and relies on authors deeply discounting their book/s in addition to paying fees and purchasing advertising. It can generate quick sales and potentially reviews but it can be quite difficult for non-fiction authors to undertake a financially successful campaign.

HOW TO ASK FOR A REVIEW

- Get in touch: find the individual's contact details and search for a clue as to the best way to contact them, for example, some people might prefer email, others a direct message on Twitter.
- Politely: no one owes you anything. It takes time to review a book and the person might not have the time or might not be in the right headspace. Always approach people courteously.
- Briefly and pertinently: state what you admire about them or their work and why you think your book might be relevant to them. Offer your book in a format of their choice (e.g., print or ebook).
- Follow up: if you haven't heard back after two weeks, re-send your message as a gentle reminder.
- Don't be a jerk: if you still don't hear back or the person refuses, don't write a tirade in return. Move on graciously.

HOW DO I GET MY BOOKS TO REVIEWERS?

The same way as ARCs (but do extra due diligence when selecting recipients to avoid piracy of your work).

 I wish writers wouldn't send me PDFs of their books with their review request. It's like turning up to a stranger's house with a pizza and a bottle of wine without knowing their tastes, allergies, etc., and asking them to start eating immediately.

— TRACEY ALLEN, BOOK BLOGGER, CARPE LIBRUM

REVIEW ETIQUETTE

When you put a book out there, understand that it's no longer your book: it becomes the reader's, and they will interpret it through their own lens. This might mean people don't understand your intention or humour; they may not like your writing style or the conclusions you've drawn. They might not like you. But they also might LOVE you. They might be grateful for all the days you got up before dawn to write and produce it. And some will tell you and some will not. You should write anyway.

What you shouldn't do, however, is pay for fake reviews from dodgy 'review' companies (they'll most likely be removed by online bookstores anyway). And don't offer someone a gift or reward to review your book as this fits into the 'dodgy' category too.

Should I read the reviews on online bookseller sites?

The jury is out on this, and it might depend on your temperament. Bad reviews hurt, even if you only get one bad one for every ten good reviews, 'negative bias' might lead you to dwell on the negative one. However, if many reviewers say the same thing, it might show you where you can make some changes to improve your book. Perhaps get a friend to read them and filter the feedback to you!

How do I respond to a negative review?

Don't. No matter how hurt, disappointed or angry you feel, you can't please everyone, and you have more to lose than the reviewer. Distract yourself, take a walk, take a deep breath and let it go. Everyone has opinions, even if their opinion is obnoxious. If your book is decent, the positive reviews will soon outshine the negative ones. Also, there are trolls (and competitors!) out there who, by definition, choose to use the internet to provoke or upset people, so some of the negative feedback will be more about them than about you/your book.

 There's a small percentage of writers who pressure and harass reviewers when they receive a negative review. When this happens, other book bloggers come out of the wood-work in support and the author's career quickly tanks. Bad reviews come with the territory and not every reader is going to enjoy your book. If you find yourself tempted to correct a reviewer, just don't. You may regret it later.

— TRACEY ALLEN, BOOK BLOGGER, CARPE LIBRUM

Amplify the good reviews you receive

Include them on your book cover and in your marketing materials, share them on your website, broadcast them on social media and add them to your author pages and to the book's metadata details.

INDUSTRY REVIEWS

Some book critics, book bloggers and industry reviewers refuse to review self-published works, but opportunities still exist, especially with the rise of bookstagrammers (Instagram), BookTok (TikTok) and Book Twitter.

You can also request a literary review from the Arts editors at the major papers, but you might be more successful by pitching (or writing) a feature article for a different section of the paper.

A key place in Australia for reviews is Books+Publishing, it's the go-to news outlet for information on the book industry in Australia and is keenly read by booksellers and librarians. You must submit your book many months in advance of launch. They accept ARCs for review in either PDF or EPUB format.

If you are being distributed into bookstore chains or have a consignment deal, you can also write to the editor of their newsletter to see if your book could be featured, such as in *Readings Monthly*.

When I was having a crisis of confidence with my memoir and needed external validation, I forked out a couple of hundred dollars (and the price has gone up since then) for a review from *Kirkus Reviews*. I was able to lift this line from it for my promotional material:

'A charming but realistic look at the modern farming life' –*Kirkus Reviews*

The full review ended up being selected by the Indie Editors at Kirkus and featured in *Kirkus Reviews* magazine, which is distributed to more than 5,000 (mostly US-based) industry professionals, including librarians, distributors, publishers and agents. Apparently, less than 10% of their Indie Reviews are included in this magazine. What happened afterwards, though, was that I started receiving more and more enticements from them to buy ads. No thanks. I got my expensive ego-stroke, along with an independent review which was a useful addition to my marketing materials.

Even more big-name international companies in the publishing industry now offer review services, but they come with all sorts of fees attached, plus some heavy sales tactics to keep you on the hook. Review your marketing goals before signing up for anything.

But you don't need to pay for a review if you can garner them in other ways. When researching reviewers, I also discovered Underground Writers, a group of Australian volunteers, passionate about writing, who review Australian books. They don't take on many non-fiction titles, but I was lucky that one of their reviewers, Jemimah Halbert Brewster, a reader, editor and writer of speculative fiction, also had a side interest in farming and was willing to review both *Small Farm Success Australia* and *Honey Farm Dreaming*. She provided some of the first reviews on the major sites. Grateful? Yes! You only need one or two breaks to get validation and get going!

Here are some review options for you to investigate if you think they might be advantageous for your topic and audience. Some are internationally focused, while others are Australian only:

- Books+Publishing
- Kirkus Indie Reviews
- BookLife by Publishers Weekly
- Foreword Reviews
- NetGalley
- Good Reading Magazine
- The Indie View
- Australian Book Review
- Aussie Reviews
- MidWest Book Review
- LibraryThing
- Booklist—American Library Association
- Library Journal
- Magpies: Talking About Books for Children.

BOOK BLOGGERS

Book bloggers are an important source of reviews. You can find them through sites including Book Bloggers Australia and Feedspot which lists a

Top 40 of Australian book blogs; The Book Blogger List has a non-fiction category and there is also the Book Reviewer Yellow Pages.

∽

INSIDE ADVICE: TRACEY ALLEN
BOOK BLOGGER, *CARPE LIBRUM*

About how many books a year do you read?

About 75 books a year, and I also participate in annual and specialised reading challenges including Aussie Author Reading Challenge, Australian Women Writers Challenge and the Nonfiction Reader Challenge.

How many self-published books do you review?

I estimate it's around two books a year, which I acknowledge is miniscule. Am I worried about that? Not really. Like every booklover and book blogger, I want to enjoy each book I read, and I don't want to drop my standards just to change that particular ratio. This is a huge topic for book bloggers though: reading what you want or reading what you think you should. Or even reading what you think would enhance your 'brand'. I don't buy in to any of that, but it's a huge deal in the reviewing community.

What sets a good non-fiction book apart from a so-so one?

I've read books that should have been a 5-star reading experience but fell down due to poor writing structure and delivery. Other times, an exciting non-fiction book with loads of potential hasn't delivered due to insufficient research or limited content. Setting aside a book without finishing it is something I've become better at over the years. That's when you mark a book as Did Not Finish (DNF), which means that it's a dud.

What do authors need to keep in mind about reader expectations?

You need to deliver. For example, if you are a regular headache or migraine sufferer and read a book about headaches that doesn't offer any new or helpful information, you're bound to be disappointed. Reader expectations can also be misguided if the marketing of a book hasn't been accurate or worse, has been misleading.

What would make you automatically decline to review a book or run a giveaway for it?

If the author misspells my name, doesn't include a blurb, makes me click on a link to find out about the book or includes typos in a review request email. If a writer can't engage me in an email, why assume they could do so in a book?

What are your top tips for authors seeking a book review?

- Research the blogger's website and make sure your book is on a topic of interest to them.
- Send a personal, engaging and well-written email request. Every blogger is different, but for me, receiving a DM on Twitter or Instagram, or a message on Goodreads says to me that the person can't be bothered to visit my book blog and obtain my contact details. If an author, publicist or publisher can't spare three minutes to go to my site and email me, why should I agree to spend at least eight hours reading their book?
- Ensure you have a terrific and engaging cover design. If it's a budget design or appears to be something slapped together by a friend or family member, I automatically worry that the writing might be second rate as well.
- Given that the average book involves more than eight hours reading time, I use other book reviews as a screening process, as it saves me from wasting my time on a dud. However, if it's a new release without any reviews, I'll have a look at the author's website and try to find out more about the book or the author there, so ensure your website represents you well.
- Readers love receiving books in the mail, and book bloggers are no different. When a book arrives that has been gift-wrapped, or contains a handwritten note or bookmark, it leaves a memorable impression. It's also great for social media posts, which can't hurt, right? I've seen some brilliant book presentations over the years, however it's the themed accessories that relate to the book that

are the most memorable. For example, *Precious Things* by Kelly Doust came wrapped in lace with postcards containing quotes and a precious thing, a candle holder. A book about a virus (pre-COVID) came wrapped and sealed in yellow bio-hazard plastic, and book bloggers received a copy of *The Emporium of Imagination* by Tabitha Bird that came personally wrapped with all sorts of trinkets and vintage treasures packaged by the author herself which caused a sensation in the Australian book reviewing community. These books were from established publishing houses, but the key is personal attention.

What do you wish writers knew about book bloggers?

Often an author has spent years writing their book and is so excited to get it out there that they assume offering me a free copy is all it takes to get me to agree to read it. However, the time spent reading a book and then writing and publishing a review involves a considerable commitment. We have an abundance of books to choose from, so the competition is tough.

On a more positive note, book bloggers love to interact with authors. If we publish a review of your book, come and interact with us. Some of my favourite interactions with authors have been after I've published a review and tagged them on social media. Their excitement about my review is a real joy.

What are blog directories?

A blog directory is a list or index of blog sites. There are specific blog directories for multiple categories of blogs (e.g., cooking, parenting, lifestyle, health) or more specialised blog directories for book blogs. Directories that may be of use to Australian authors include Book Bloggers Australia and Blogarama.

A word of warning though: some owners of directories add bloggers without permission, charge users to access the listings, and sell ebooks with a list of 'willing and eager' book reviewers to self-published authors. This is shady. In many cases the bloggers have no idea their details are listed or being purchased in an ebook and, as a consequence, don't reply favourably or at all to requests. In other cases the information is out of date and the blog site may not have been updated for years.

How do giveaways on your site work?

If I receive a review request for a book that's not for me but that I know will be of interest to other readers, I'll decline to review the title but may offer to support the book by running a giveaway instead. Giveaways can create 'buzz' for a book and often, after a giveaway, I'll see readers decide to pick up the book anyway despite not winning the competition. Giveaways can also result in a favourable review of a self-published book from the winner.

Please don't write to Tracey requesting a review just because she is in this book. Follow her advice and do your research first to see if your title is one she'd actually be interested in.

BLOG TOURS

At book launch time, famous authors sometimes fly around the country to promote their book, going from bookstore event to radio interview and then moving on to a new city the next day for more media and promotional activities. These days, a lot of the same results—minus the costs and jetlag—can be achieved through a blog tour, especially if you are targeting overseas readers.

You can organise the tour yourself, or there are publicists who specialise in organising them, but who might also charge you top dollar. A blog tour can help you reach a new and wider audience for your book and improve your SEO through the establishment of back links from blogs to your website.

When budgeting, factor in the cost of the free giveaway books you will need to offer, plus shipping costs if sending print books. Some bloggers, especially 'influencers', will also charge you for the opportunity to appear on their website or social media channel.

BE A REVIEWER

Yes! Another way to market your book is to be out there on online sites reviewing other people's books. Comprehensively and fairly reviewing books in your category—or taking a quick photo of a title you have read with a pithy quote or two and putting it on your website and socials—is another way to get in front of readers and be a part of the writing community. Just don't plug your own book when you do and avoid leaving poor reviews of competitors' books too; there's no need and what goes around comes around.

~

In the next chapter we review the key author sites where you can maintain a presence.

41

AMAZON, GOODREADS AND COPPER AUTHOR PAGES

To give yourself another chance of internet discovery and to stop other authors or copycats moving in on your turf, claim and maintain your author page at places readers flock to. The key ones are Amazon and its wholly owned little sibling, Goodreads and newer entrant, Copper.

AMAZON AUTHOR CENTRAL

Think of Author Central as a free marketing and research tool. It gives you access to another place on the internet where you can showcase your titles and yourself. It also offers up some marketing intel, showing you 'Customers also bought books by' data so you can see a list of other authors your audience has purchased from. If your print book is distributed in the US, you will also be able to see BookScan data to show you how it's selling.

Another nifty feature is that readers who follow your Amazon Author Page receive an automatic email from Amazon whenever you publish a new book. You will also be able to view your book's Amazon Sales Rank and 'claim your book' upon publication so it is linked to your author account.

How do I create an Author Central account?

- Log in (or set it up if you haven't as yet) to your KDP account and click on the link to *Marketing*.
- Where it says *Author Central,* use the dropdown menu to create your Author Page. At the time of writing, Australia is not an option, so instead select the most relevant site for your audience. You can always add the other regions later.
- Choose *Manage author page.*
- When redirected, *Join for free* using your KDP sign-in.
- Bookmark the page so you can find it again easily.

What do I include on my Author Page?

Your bio, a great author photo, blog posts, video content and reviews. Include advance praise and endorsements too and update these over time as more reviews from media and readers come in. A few times a year add new material (and change it as needed) to ensure it stays fresh and up to date.

GOODREADS AUTHOR PROGRAM

The Goodreads Author Program is free to sign up for, although not all of the promotion and advertising tools come free of charge. I've used it to run a giveaway and to keep track of reviews, as well as to review other books. Goodreads also has great advice in their *Authors and Advertisers Blog* including tips on how to manage your author settings, so take advantage of all the shared know-how.

According to Goodreads, to claim your profile, login as a Goodreads member, or create an account. Then search for your book by its ISBN, ASIN, or title and click on your author name. Scroll to the bottom of the author profile page and click on '*Is this you? Let us know!*'. Then complete and submit the application.

COPPER

Copper is a new app 'designed by authors, for authors'. It was just getting established as this book went to print, so give it the once over to see what you think.

Overall, having a presence on these three author sites increases your visibility on the internet and helps readers learn more about you.

What would you like to learn about next? How about how to use promotional material as part of your book marketing and personal brand building efforts? Sounds good to me. Let's get to it.

42

PROMOTIONAL MATERIAL

I f you have ever read a flyer, been given a free drink bottle, worn a cap emblazoned with a company's branding, taken a branded bookmark from a bookstore, or been given a pen by a real estate agent, you have been the recipient of promotional material. Your book and personal brand may well benefit from the judicious use of promo material too.

In this chapter we'll explore some of the promotional material authors use including advance information sheets (AIS), printed promotional material and merchandise.

Why invest time and money on promotional material? To:

- spread the word about your book and create buzz
- build your brand and show professionalism
- help your target market discover your book
- save you having to repeat yourself and to ensure information (such as the correct spelling of your URL, your name, and the title and sub-title of your book) is correctly shared
- woo and/or thank people
- give people something they can share with others
- enhance events with giveaways and/or good background visuals (such as posters behind your book display).

What to avoid

- Overspending! You need a return on your investment. That return might be book sales, new leads, or new business, or it might save you time in some way.
- Merchandise that doesn't align with your brand, values, or book.
- Poor quality promo materials.
- Environmental and monetary waste.

Let's take a closer look at some of your promo options.

ADVANCE INFORMATION SHEET

An AIS is a one-page promotional sell sheet that includes all the key facts and information about you and your book. They are a standard marketing tool used by traditional and self-publishers alike to:

- build awareness for new books
- create demand from wholesalers, booksellers and librarians
- open up media opportunities.

What is a standard AIS format?

- It's a one-sided A4 sheet, preferably printed in colour.
- You can also make it available as a PDF download from your website and can attach it to your email and Facebook Messenger outreaches.
- It looks best when designed in an uncluttered but visually appealing way, and in keeping with your book's theme and colours. Your book designer may be able to assist with the design, or you can DIY using Canva. A sample design is included in the *Look—It's Your Book! Workbook*.

What do I include on my AIS?

- Cover image.
- Title and subtitle.

- Author name.
- Book summary/blurb.
- Advance praise/testimonial quotes.
- Key details: launch date, ISBN, formats, price and where to get it from.
- Contact details.
- Short author bio.
- Author photo (optional).

Who should I send the AIS to?

- Drop it in to bookstores or forward it as an attachment to relevant retailers, book buyers, libraries and library distributors. (If you're working with a distributor, they might send it out to bookstores for you).
- Send it with advance copies of your book to reviewers, book bloggers and influencers.
- Attach it when you are sending out your media release.
- Make it available on your website.
- Include it when pitching yourself for speaking engagements.

PRINT MATERIAL

The only thing worse than having 4,000 books sitting in your garage is having 4,000 postcards, posters, bookmarks, business cards and life-size cut-outs of you holding your book sitting there with them! However, printed promotional products can have an impact and be helpful to your promotion and administration efforts, and with services like Vistaprint and Canva, you can order small quantities without getting carried away.

Postcards, bookmarks and business cards

From my experience, if you are going to print one thing, make it a postcard or bookmark. Print it one-sided to showcase your book cover and website details, or two-sided to include some extra useful facts or features.

A postcard can double as a bookmark and enables you to include a handwritten note when you're sending out books direct. If you are printing two-sided, make sure to leave enough white space so you can still include a handwritten note. Also, always consider what kind of card stock and/or type of pen you will use so you don't end up with a smudged, illegible mess.

You can hand your postcards out at book signings and conferences, use them to list your upcoming author talks, promote a special offer on them, and stack them up at relevant retailers.

Bookmarks make for an economical and useful handout too and are a great substitute for a business card. And about business cards: in the era of LinkedIn, COVID and mobile phone contact-sharing, business cards have become less relevant. But hey, when you can order 100 for such a cheap price, you can go with or without them, without having to sweat the decision too much.

Posters

You won't need hundreds of these, but a few to put up behind you at author talks or on a table in a Perspex cover, can add to the show. Your book cover, printed A3 size in colour at your local Officeworks or alternative, should do the trick.

Life-size cut-outs

A cardboard or corflute cut-out of you holding your book will certainly make a statement, but is it appropriate for your book and audience? Perhaps if you are speaking at a conference called 'Overkill' and like looking at yourself, but perhaps not if you are the guest at your local Rotary or library book club.

MERCHANDISE

I haven't invested in merchandise for my books because it hasn't made sense for me, my audience, budget or goals, but that doesn't mean it won't be useful for you.

Merchandise can help build buzz and assist you with cutting through all the other marketing messages bombarding your target audience, book sellers and influencers in your space. It might help your book be welcomed more warmly by a blogger, get your book and brand onto other people's feeds on Instagram, or just make you feel more confident when you are promoting your book. However, it is not an essential element for a book launch, and if you do head down this path, it does need to be relevant to be effective.

There are endless types of merchandise out there. Here are some ideas based on different non-fiction categories—you can get as creative and bespoke as your brain and budget allows:

- illustrated books: a gorgeous, signed artwork print
- cookbooks: apron, bottle opener, spice mix, cookies
- craft books: a unique pattern, engraved needles, travel sewing kit
- business book: USB stick, pens, notepad
- outdoor adventure books: torch, carabiner, beanie
- gardening books: seed packet, plant name tags, pots
- travel books: luggage tag, journal, a limited-edition photo print.

Merchandise might also come in handy to build excitement at any of your events, such as through lucky door and quiz prizes.

A SOUNDTRACK

Might the reading and use of your book be enhanced by an accompanying soundtrack to get people in the mood? You could provide it free as a give-away, as an upsell, an additional product and in collaboration with a creative muso or two. A soundtrack might give you another avenue to build your brand, drive publicity and knit an even tighter band of fans, followers and collaborators.

∾

You can also use merchandise to build excitement for your book launch. We cover all things book launch next.

43

YOUR BOOK LAUNCH

Ooh, this is getting exciting! It's launch time! Yes, you'll get to party, but first get down to business by setting a date for your book's release. Setting a date will help you focus on your production and marketing efforts and give you a clear deadline to work towards. It will also enable you to begin taking pre-orders.

When do I set a launch date?

Three to six months before you know the book will be ready gives you plenty of time to capitalise on your marketing efforts.

How do I choose the date?

- Make it convenient for you: look at your calendar and choose a week and month when you have few other work or family commitments. It would be difficult to pull off all the work that goes into a book launch when your employer has a big project of their own planned, or during school holidays if you are also entertaining the kids 24/7.
- Make it topical: is there a date or season of relevance to your book? For example, if you are launching a book about winter

recipes, it makes sense to launch it on the first day of winter. If you have penned a peacekeeping mission or disaster recovery memoir, launch it on a significant anniversary of your deployment.

- Find the gap: bookstores are normally crammed with traditionally published books all trying to be out in time for Christmas. By launching at a different time of the year, such as in autumn, you might be better able to cut through the noise.
- Push it into the New Year: if you are thinking about a November or December launch, perhaps launch it in the New Year so your book doesn't age as fast. It will be seen as a 'new title' for the entire 12 months post-launch, not 'last year's book'.

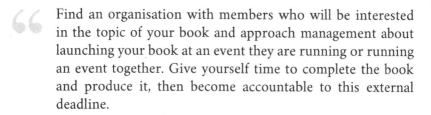

Find an organisation with members who will be interested in the topic of your book and approach management about launching your book at an event they are running or running an event together. Give yourself time to complete the book and produce it, then become accountable to this external deadline.

— BEV RYAN, BOOK COACH, SMART WOMEN PUBLISH

Build in some fat

You might have all the best intentions in the world, but something will come up: you might write slower than expected, your editor and/or book cover designer might be booked solid with other clients, and fiddling with your files can lead to all sorts of technical glitches. Give yourself some leeway. Producing a book is a long process, especially if you intend for it to be a quality one.

I launched my books officially one to two weeks AFTER I'd made them available through IngramSpark. Why? To build in some fat in case something went wrong; I just didn't want the pressure of everything coming down to the wire and finding myself at my book launch without having final copies in my hands. It also gave me space to drum up PR and set up extra marketing activities ahead of time.

Start promoting the date

Now that you have a date, your marketing machine can step up a gear.

PRE-ORDERS

Pre-orders are pre-sales of your book to individuals, bookstores and libraries. The sales can be made through your own website, online retailers, or your distributor. The books are then sent out in time for the launch date.

Why encourage pre-orders?

- It's a great way to capitalise on any marketing you do for your book pre-launch. For example, someone may have seen a social media post you did during the course of writing your book and thought, 'Ooh, that sounds like a book I need!' By being able to place a pre-order, it means you capture their interest and sale in one go.
- To get your book off to a great start. Racking up a large number of pre-orders on online sites might help you race up the online charts on launch day, and that means algorithms will give your book even more visibility. It also means more reviews of your book may appear online in the weeks after its launch, which is the social proof you need to inspire further sales.
- The process of assigning your ISBN and filling in your metadata and release date gives your book visibility on key sites and to key retailers and librarians, even before it is available for sale. They'll also be able to order it and have it in stock when your launch publicity hits.
- It allows you to start selectively promoting your book, even before your actual launch day. For example, I settled on my cover design more than 3 months before official launch date and uploaded the cover image with a 'Pre-Order Now' stamp and immediately began capturing sales. I was also able to use the image to run a marketing campaign to build buzz around my launch date and to help publicise my ability to do presentations on the topic.
- If your pre-orders are strong, it may trigger you to increase your

print run or initial order, which may mean you will receive a better price per copy.

- If listing your book with Apple Books, you can also place a Promotional Feature Request that, if accepted, could see your book promoted to readers.

How far in advance do you invite pre-orders?

Around three months is good.

What is the difference between the publication date and on-sale date?

You set these dates as the same, but according to IngramSpark, the 'publication' date is the official date your book is available for purchase by the public, and the 'on-sale' date is the date booksellers are officially able to begin selling your book (although in reality they might have pre-ordered the book and received their copies a few days before this as IngramSpark's system begins printing and shipping ten business days before the on-sale date to fulfil pre-orders).

What to be wary of with pre-orders

- Don't try to game the system just to obtain 'bestseller' status on launch day. For example, let's say you get your mother's knitting group to all buy your book through Amazon or Apple on launch day. The algorithm will then note that elderly female knitters have an interest in your book, so they are going to start recommending it to other elderly female knitters rather than the real audience you wanted to reach, for example, young renters with an interest in portable garden beds!
- Don't change the price during the pre-order campaign. Plan your pricing strategy and be consistent, as it avoids online sites offering customers the lowest price advertised throughout the period. Yes, they can even price-match against limited special offers you make available on your own site. If planning to enrol in Kindle Unlimited, wait until after your pre-order campaign to do so.
- IngramSpark advises that 'Many indie authors and publishers opt

to do 'fast-to-market' releases, especially for topical books. This is the beauty of self-publishing! However, keep in mind that if you give yourself less than a month from the time you set up and distribute your title through IngramSpark to the on-sale date, it shortens your window to accumulate pre-orders.'

Email your list and contacts to boost your pre-order sales

When Kathryn Heyman launched her traditionally published memoir *Fury* (it's great by the way!), she sent out an email to her list highlighting how 'the first week's sales are crucial in the life of a book'. She included links to where people could buy and order the book and as a thank you, offered anyone who sent their receipt in from their first-week purchase an invitation to a virtual writing class. She also tempted potential purchasers further by offering one person the chance to win a half-hour online writing session. What a great way to get people motivated to buy early and give her book some extra impetus, buzz and to rise up the bookstore bestseller lists.

PHYSICAL BOOK LAUNCH

Why bother with a physical book launch?

- To celebrate: to have some fun and bathe in just a little bit of author glow.
- To focus media attention: local media are usually happy to mention book launches if you send them a story and image, and sometimes they will even attend on the day.
- Sales: if people have made the effort to come to your launch, they're likely to buy your book and ask you to sign it too. (It's much harder to achieve sales at an online launch).
- Content: announcing the launch gives you fresh content for your website and socials, while the launch itself gives you a deadline to aim for and the potential to snap some great photos of your adoring fans—even if it's just a few of your best friends.

> Book launch events are especially integral to the success of business books. They are a point at which to focus attention and engage potential readers (before, during and after the launch).

— JAQUI LANE, THE BOOK ADVISER

Where do I hold it?

- Subject-relevant and/or unique locations: choose a location that makes sense for your chosen subject matter and your target audience. If your book is about flower arranging, perhaps you could hold your launch at a nursery or farmers' market. If it's about stock trading, maybe a funky cafe near the stock exchange or a bank vault.
- Your local library: this can be a great, free solution, and the library might also help promote the launch through their own channels.
- A bookstore: while it can be harder to secure for an indie book, it's not out of the question. My local store hosted the launch for two of my books and it was great—they even made me feel extra special by giving me a window display. It also meant I didn't need to worry about handling sales, as they took care of that part. And it was lovely to hear from the manager that I'd sold more books during my launch than that of a big-time best-selling author!
- At your book club: your own book club provides a ready-made audience. It's a place where you will feel comfortable, and it will be a real celebration.
- Wherever there is a ready-made audience: are you a member of an association or networking group such as Rotary, a business chamber or a special-interest group? If not, can you get an invite to one as the special guest? Tying in to an already established event means getting people there won't be a problem.
- Your home, or the home of a friend: this can take some pressure off, as well as being budget-friendly. It may also be a drawcard if your friend's pad is known on the social or business scene.
- Virtually: many book launches were forced online due to the pandemic, and it is likely to be a trend that will continue into the

future given the flexible format and ability to re-use and re-package the content created for it.

~

INSIDE ADVICE: JAQUI LANE
THE BOOK ADVISER—VIRTUAL BOOK LAUNCH TIPS

What does a virtual book launch look like?

Well, it's pretty much exactly the same as a physical book launch in terms of the preparation, planning and organisation, it's just that it's online, and if you haven't been active online with any of the sharing platforms, you're either going to need to skill up or hire someone to run it for you.

In fact, I think that virtual launches are better than physical launches. Why?

- They cost less (no room hire, catering, video and audio equipment hire).
- You can invite as many people as you like, and it (mostly) won't cost you any more money.
- You can have a global audience.
- Launch event engagement is more interactive.
- Post-event engagement is way easier.
- It's still relatively new, so there's a different buzz about virtual launches.
- They're more environmentally friendly.
- You can interview key people mentioned in your book no matter where they are, and you can interview different people at different launches.

What platform/s should I use?

Zoom and StreamYard are two of the most popular platforms, but there are many others, especially in the live video space (e.g., YouTube Live, Facebook Live, Periscope, You-Now, Instagram Live, Be.live and Twitter).

A great thing about these tools is they provide a recording of the event that you can send to those who registered but did not attend, and you can also edit the recording and re-purpose it for social media.

Do I need a guest speaker?

As with a physical launch, this is a question for you. I always prefer to have a guest speaker or two at a book launch. It's way better to have someone else talking about your book and its value than you as the author. If your preferred guest speaker isn't available on the day, get them to record a presentation in advance and show this.

How long should my virtual book launch be?

I'd recommend 25 to 45 minutes with additional time AFTER the official event for a short Q&A/engagement time (10 minutes max). Make sure individual presentations within the launch are no longer than five to six minutes each. 20-minute presentations by a single person simply won't work in a virtual launch environment.

How do I structure my virtual book launch?

Your virtual book launch should contain relatively short set pieces with some audience engagement elements. A 30-minute virtual book launch might look something like this:

- Pre-launch log-in timer: 10–15 mins before the event.
- Welcome from Emcee: 2–3 mins.
- Author presentation: 5–6 mins.
- Engagement piece: 3 mins.
- Guest speaker presentation: 5–6 mins.
- Launch of book: 2 mins.
- Thank you and engagement piece: 3 mins.
- Q&A: 5–7 mins.
- Short info session on where to buy the book (with slide), special launch offer (mention launch offer code and time limit).
- Formal end (book purchase options slide stays up).

What else do I need to pay attention to?

- Hope for the best and plan for the worst. Have a back-up plan in case the internet gets wobbly or cuts out, and be prepared for your slideshow, links or video presentations to not work as planned.

- Secure someone else to undertake the back end set-up and management of the event. As the author and major presenter, you need to be totally focused on your audience, NOT on the tech!
- Make sure your camera is at the right height, that the lighting in the room you will be in is well-positioned (lighting in front of you not behind or overhead) and that your background is appropriate and not distracting.
- DO NOT sit at a desk as you would in a virtual work meeting. You are presenting, not discussing.

Remember: your book launch is just one part of your book marketing campaign. If you want to market and sell your book, think of your book launch as the start of a marathon. It's a critical punctuation point, but what really matters is executing your marketing and promotional plan over the entire course so that you reach your goal at the end of it.

⁓

What's another way to reach your goals? A whole chapter on the opportunities presented by publicity awaits!

44

PUBLICITY

The best way to make your book newsworthy is to write a newsworthy book. But there are also things you can do along the way to increase your chances of media coverage. For example, think about and create publicity opportunities as you plan and write your book, not just as you're sending it to the printer.

For *Small Farm Success Australia*, I interviewed farmers from every state in Australia, not just so it would be relevant and interesting for readers everywhere, but because I knew it would make the book interesting to the media in every part of the country too. I followed up with targeted pitches and stories for newspapers and radio in each region where a farmer was mentioned or interviewed. The outreach earned great coverage. But it's not too late if you are only coming to the publicity party now.

It's a simple formula really:

- Target the right media outlet.
- Use the right hook (an idea or different take on a normal topic that sparks interest or reveals your information in a compelling way).
- Make sure you aim it at the right audience for your book.
- Deliver it using whatever format the publication, editor, journalist or radio host prefers. This might be a short email with

an irresistible heading, a media release, a pre-written story, a brief phone call, or a copy of your book with talking points).

- Approach them in an interesting and polite way.
- Be reliable and flexible. This makes everyone's life easier and/or more enjoyable. Deliver what you say you will, provide great photos, be available at a moment's notice for interviews and offer up short, vibrant quotes.
- And finally, follow up! Media people are busy, and emails get buried, so follow up in a polite and friendly manner, perhaps even with some extra ideas and angles. Keep at it until you get a breakthrough.

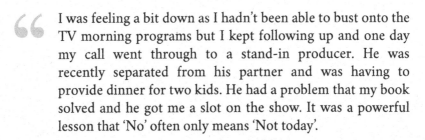

> I was feeling a bit down as I hadn't been able to bust onto the TV morning programs but I kept following up and one day my call went through to a stand-in producer. He was recently separated from his partner and was having to provide dinner for two kids. He had a problem that my book solved and he got me a slot on the show. It was a powerful lesson that 'No' often only means 'Not today'.

— KIM MCCOSKER, *4 INGREDIENTS*

If you don't feel confident about contacting the media, think of it as doing them a favour. They are continually faced with the task of having to fill hours of morning TV and talkback radio time, endless columns of print and scrolling screens full of content. Why not fill it with your book!?

Will publicity make my book a success?

Publicity is a key piece in the marketing puzzle, but it is still rare for people to rush out and buy a book just because they heard about it once. People usually need to come across your book in multiple ways, through multiple media, before they will commit to purchase—so it's easy to see how librarians and booksellers who receive not only your AIS but who then also hear you speaking on the radio or see you in the paper, might be prompted to order your book. A secondary aim of getting publicity for your book is to gather media contacts who will be responsive to you when you are ready to promote your next book or project.

What to avoid when doing publicity

PR consulting fees can add up quickly and though it's tempting to think one appearance on a breakfast TV show (if they can get you a spot) will launch you into the bestseller lists—it won't.

You also need to be truthful. False claims, lies, half-truths (also lies!) and exaggerations will be exposed for all to see.

Importantly, do not launch a major PR campaign for your book before copies are readily available. Yes, be out there building your profile, but if feature pieces about your book appear before it is on sale, you won't be able to capitalise on the interest.

How do I find contact details for the media?

If you are actively engaged with your subject matter, you will already know which traditional media journalists and online media writers are likely to have the most interest in your subject. Track down their contact details using the internet. There are also plenty of freelance writers out there who can be a conduit to getting your story into the media.

Do I need to hire a publicist or PR firm?

This depends on your goals, skills, and budget. Book publicity specialists are great at coming up with angles and have established contacts, but as a writer, you also know how to put sentences together, and deeply understand your subject matter, so are equipped to reach out yourself too. If you're nervous or unsure about being interviewed by media, media training courses are widely available too.

Create a media kit (which can also double as your speaker's kit)

A media kit is few pages of information you can host on your site or send as a PDF to the media and people who want to book you for a talk. It includes:

- your bio and contact details
- author photo and/or short video
- image of the book cover
- a collection of the best reviews

- key details about the book, including where to purchase it (this could be your updated AIS)
- a list of interesting topics and stories you can speak to and/or suggested questions the journalist may like to ask you.

Repurpose your content to use in publicity

- Cherry pick, edit and use some of the content in your book to share with magazines and newspapers, guest blogs and podcasts. Try not to share exactly the same details with competing outlets: they will each want something fresh and unique to them.
- Pitch magazines and trade papers with story ideas, such as a Top 10 list related to your subject (e.g., Top 10 challenges facing university graduates, Top 10 budgeting tools, Top 10 summer dress styles).
- Keep your eyes on the news and if something relevant happens in your subject area, piggyback off it. Contact media, offering your take or an opinion piece on the situation. This will keep you relevant and in the public eye.

Tips for radio interviews

Think about who the audience is and what they would be interested in hearing, not just what you want to say. Prior to the interview, print out a list of key quotes, statistics and takeaways/key messages to prompt you if your mind goes blank mid-interview. And if you're not in the studio with the presenter, stand up—you'll sound more dynamic.

 The biggest thing is to understand what your point of difference is—what do you do better than your competitors? What insights do you have that are unique? Aside from that, being responsive, reliable and having great quality photographs are also key. Media are time poor so the easier we can make their lives then the faster and more effective cut through you'll have in developing a strong media profile.

— SCOTT EATHORNE, BOOK PUBLICIST, QUIKMARK MEDIA

List yourself on 'expert' sites

In Chapter 6 there was a list of sites where you could find experts to interview. Well, now that you have written a book, you're an expert in your own right, so list yourself on these sites too!

Promote the publicity

Use any resulting clips and mentions from your PR outreach widely across your social media. Send clippings to librarians who you think might be interested in your book, and if you will be appearing in a local paper, alert the local bookstore, who might be willing to order your book knowing that some promotion of your title is imminent.

 Relevance at a moment in time is about being visible and top of mind when the moment occurs. If you let your book and your knowledge sink into oblivion ... no one will call on you when the topic is hot again.

— GARRY BROWNE, THE PERSONAL BRAND CATALYST AND AUTHOR, *BRAND NEW, BRAND YOU*

Keep at it

Play the long game. It's not just about sales at launch; consistently promoting your book and yourself as a reliable, media-friendly author over the ensuing weeks, months and years will build relationships, coverage, sales and will help you maximise current and future opportunities.

One of the ways to achieve publicity is to promote your author talks, so how do you go about booking them in and delivering them? We will talk about that next.

45

AUTHOR TALKS

I might be an introvert and a shocker at parties and small talk, but I love giving talks and presentations. It's fun finding out why people have come along and by the time I start presenting I'm on a fabulous high. In addition to entertaining and informing readers, author talks can:

- drive fresh publicity and awareness for you and your book—in multiple regions
- get your book into new outlets
- create new content for your website and socials
- earn you money through appearances, book sales and ongoing payments through PLR, ELR and The Copyright Agency
- boost your confidence
- expand your networks
- unlock potential collaborations
- give you a platform to directly engage with readers: just listening to your audience's questions may give you some ideas for fresh content or even a whole new book!

Where are author talks held?

All sorts of places. Libraries, bookstores, festivals, associations, clubs and networking events such as Rotary and business breakfast meetings. Then you have schools and universities, book clubs, conferences, online events, TEDx and even online from your loungeroom.

Is payment involved?

This depends on what you're trying to achieve. Some libraries and organisations allocate money to special programs and can afford an author payment, while others do not. I do a mix of well-paid and unpaid talks, depending on the circumstances, including who the audience is, the time and costs involved in travel, the preparation time required, and other benefits such as book sales, potential high-paying consulting gigs and media opportunities that may arise from the talk.

Some conferences pay top dollar for guest speakers, while others expect that your exposure to their audience is enough compensation. But if their audience is paying them, they really should be paying you. There is more about paid presentations, courses and workshops in Chapter 52.

Writers and illustrators deserve to be fairly paid for their work. Creators need to value their own talents and be brave enough to ask to be paid fairly. Talks and workshops take considerable preparation time including the authors' intellectual property.

— AUSTRALIAN SOCIETY OF AUTHORS

The ASA lists current recommended rates for public appearances on its website (including for in-person panel appearances and keynote speakers). They also suggest negotiating an additional fee if a recording is made based on the length of time it is available for access.

Some other things I have learned from doing author talks

- Local government websites offer a great range of contact details for librarians, as well as department heads who might be responsible for organising talks for the local business community.
- Pitch talks to capitalise on relevant dates such as Seniors, Refugee, or NAIDOC Week; the day the Federal Budget comes

out; World Environment Day; Coffee Appreciation Day and innumerable other days celebrated on the calendar.

- Keep your eye on government programs that may be relevant to your subject area as they sometimes offer grants, such as during Small Business Week, for talks and presentations.
- Prepare well and make your first talk fabulous! The effort is worth it, as you then only need to tweak it for future talks.
- When planning holidays, research libraries and groups in the area and reach out in advance.
- Keep a glass of water handy when speaking.
- Print a copy of your speech (but don't read from it) in case you need to refer to something or lose your way. I find having key points up on a screen prompt me, without letting the audience read everything word for word.
- Be generous with your energy!
- Embrace feedback. Ask people to fill out an evaluation form so you can learn how to improve and get ideas for future talks. Include a space for their email if they would like to sign up for your newsletter list.

Leanne Wright, an Events Librarian with Port Macquarie Hastings Council in New South Wales, organises a bursting calendar of author talks and has seen plenty of good and not-so good ones in her time. She suggests self-published authors look at author talks as a marketing opportunity that may also lead to, but not guarantee, book sales. Here are some more of her insights.

~

INSIDE ADVICE: LEANNE WRIGHT
EVENTS LIBRARIAN

What kind of numbers do you get for author talks at your library?

From 10 to 110. 20 is a good number.

How do you like to be approached by authors?

- Send an email initially with a clear subject line, for example, 'Author Talk suggestion: *subject of your book*'.
- In the email, briefly state that you are offering to do an author talk and include a brief blurb on the book, a brief bio, an image of the book cover and your availability.
- If you want to be paid to do the talk, you should state this upfront so the library can let you know if it's feasible. It is not common for us to pay for talks, as public libraries are run on tight budgets, though we do sometimes pay for children's authors who are on the circuit.
- It's great if you can suggest a date for your talk that aligns with an event that is relevant to your topic such as World Environment Day, Seniors Week, Nurse Appreciation Month, etc.

Why would you say 'No' to an author talk?

- If there are already too many booked in. Ideally, we wouldn't have more than four in a month, as it dilutes the audience.
- If the expectation of the author is too high and they come across as high maintenance, for example if they expect us to guarantee an audience and do all the marketing.
- If the time requested is during December and January, as we just don't tend to get the audience in those months.

What makes a good author talk?

- The person giving it needs to be engaging.
- Ask up front why people have come, as this helps you understand whether your audience is interested in the topic, or whether they are writers themselves and more interested in the writing process. Then you can skew your talk as you go.
- As people arrive, be polite and say hello, thank them for coming, and ask them what their interest is. Try to avoid being on your phone as people walk in!
- Humour is key. Be able to laugh at yourself and tell some funny

stories. This is especially important if your story covers heavy material.
- You can scatter in some short readings from the book that connect back to the story you're telling, but not too many.

Where do author talks go wrong?

- When the talk is too long and just goes on and on.
- When the author tries to do a really hard sell on the book.
- When the author's attitude is wrong and they don't appreciate that the audience has given up their time to come to the talk.
- When the author relies too heavily on PowerPoint. Pictures can be beneficial when they align with your talk, but relying on a PowerPoint and merely talking to it when the audience can read what's on the screen for themselves, means that it just falls flat. You also don't want your presentation to sound like you're just reading a report. Add colour with your voice, gestures, eye contact and a conversational tone.

What are some ways authors can plan their talk?

- Begin by thinking about how you want people to feel when they leave. Informed? Entertained? Uplifted? Motivated? Sad? Joyful? Intrigued? Then use that as a basis for planning your talking points.
- A good length is 45 minutes, with 15 minutes for questions.
- Don't assume people have read or will read the book, so focus your talk more on the story behind the storyteller. People want to know what inspired you to write the book, what you learned from writing the book, what surprised you about the process, and how you did it.

How can an author help promote the talk?

- An unknown author can be very hard to promote. We offer to promote authors on Facebook, in our monthly newsletter, on our

website and with posters displayed in the library itself, but
everything else is up to the author.

- Once the date is set, the author should advise the local paper,
  ABC radio station and other outlets about the upcoming event.
  Do this well in advance and provide them with all the
  information they need on the talk so it is easy for them to cover
  or pre-interview you.
- Once we've set a date for your talk, provide us with a good high-res
  photo and a short blurb on you and your book. It can help if you
  have two different blurbs— one of 100 words and another of 300
  words—as that gives us something to work with for different media.

What are the best ways for authors to sell books at a talk?

- When you arrive, set up a table with a nice book display. Include a
  sign that clearly states the price of the book and the types of
  payment you can accept.
- Have a call to action at the end of your talk so you can strike
  while the iron is hot. Let people know they can purchase the book
  after the Q&A.
- It is best to have some kind of credit card transaction system such
  as Square or an EFTPOS machine as the library cannot provide
  this service. You can also bring a cash float for anyone who wants
  to purchase using cash.

Any other tips?

- Sometimes an audience member will hijack the conversation
  during the Q&A. Be prepared for that with a gentle response such
  as 'That's really interesting, but what was the question again?'
  Sometimes, though, authors try to completely control the
  conversation, and that can backfire. Try to go with the flow of
  peoples' interests, and then bridge back if necessary.
- I know an author who donated 10 copies of his book as a book-
  club set and offered to go and speak at the book clubs too. It
  worked for him, as he had a business that benefitted from those
  interactions, so it wasn't just about book sales for him.

- Be nice to the librarians; don't treat us like the hired help.
- It's harder to sell books at online events. You may need to offer a discount code, or if it is a paid event, suggest the organiser package your book into the cost of the ticket.
- Be honest as a writer. Be honest as a presenter.

~

And be honest with yourself. Some people really don't present well or have a complete aversion to speaking in public, so perhaps advertising will be more your thing. If that's you, breathe easy, we cover advertising next.

46

ADVERTISING

Book advertising is only worth doing if you get a return on investment (ROI). Though advertising in glossy magazines, television, radio and on the sides of buses might make you feel important, the resulting book sales will likely not.

However, achieving a decent ROI using online advertising, although not guaranteed, is much easier! Here are some other reasons online ads may work for you.

- Online ads are more economical: you can pay per click or per view.
- You can target your audience: by age, gender, location and interests, on sites they're already comfortable with and trust.
- Online ads are measurable. You can track the success of your campaigns in real time. This gives you the flexibility to see what's working and what's not, and make changes as needed.
- A dollar spent on online marketing will almost always achieve more direct sales than that same dollar spent on other media. And other media will likely cost you hundreds if not thousands of dollars just for one ad. The only time this rule might not apply is if your print ad is in a very targeted newsletter or magazine with a particularly engaged audience.

The main online services used for book advertising are Facebook and Instagram Ads, Google Ads and Amazon Marketing Services (AMS). There are plenty of free and fee-based online courses, guides, gurus, and books devoted to online book advertising strategies and I include a list of them in the *Writing Resources* section of my site. Unfortunately, many are geared toward prolific fiction writers rather than non-fiction writers. Also, just because you run a campaign, it doesn't mean you will experience success.

> I spent almost $2000 on ads and a consultant, targeting markets in North America and Europe, calling for people to either buy the book or submit stories for a new edition. I reached over 2 million people. I sold zero, ZERO, books and I got two story submissions. It generated lots of traffic to my website and Facebook page, but only a handful of new likes. I was shocked and dismayed. After lots of soul searching, more advice and opinions, I came to the conclusion that, whilst I could have done some things better, maybe there just wasn't a market for what I was selling—not in physical book form anyway. I realised it might have been different if I'd created a blog or a podcast. Or, at the very least, an ebook. Sometimes you just need to know when to call it. But despite everything, self-publishing my book was a deeply satisfying and soul nourishing learning experience, and I'd do it all again with the right project.
>
> — TINA MORGANELLA, ACCREDITED EDITOR, AND SELF-PUBLISHED AUTHOR OF *WEAR A MASK, CUPID!*

Some authors, again, mostly fast fiction authors (but also non-fiction targeting an international audience), have a strategy of pumping thousands of dollars into online advertising, believing that if they spend $5,000 and bring back in $5,800 that it's a worthwhile ROI. But it requires the right books (you'll need more than one for this strategy to pay off), for the right audience and takes a lot of courage, money and diligence tweaking ads and measuring results, to get results.

Rather than straight out advertising, be strategic.

> LinkedIn has a feature called Sales Navigator. It's essentially LinkedIn's database that you can pay to access and then

search by all manner of categories. This is an AMAZING tool to leverage the power of LinkedIn in terms of growing your network and connecting up with people who you genuinely want to connect and engage with and who might be interested in your book, content, knowledge, etc. Of course, you need to know how to do this and it's a medium-term program but, again, for authors of business books, it's an extraordinarily powerful and completely under-rated resource.

— JAQUI LANE, THE BOOK ADVISER

I will be trying some limited online advertising for this book, and will update the results on my blog so I can share any learnings with you.

~

Most successful books and authors aren't successful just because they focussed on advertising, or PR, or author talks. For many it's because they worked out the power of collaboration. Yes, you don't have to do everything on your own, collaboration can be a wonderful marketing tool. To find out why and how to go about it, read on.

47

COLLABORATIONS

W hen you team up with others it means it's no longer little ol' you against the world! Hooray for that!

Some of the benefits of collaboration are shared resources, research, knowledge, skills, contacts, enthusiasm, joint marketing, promotions, and budgets. Working with others will invigorate you, helping you achieve your goals faster and better than you might have been able to on your own. So, how do you get started on a collaboration?

Begin by creating a list of all the people, organisations, and businesses you know or know of who might be able to help contribute to, raise awareness of, buy, promote, or sell your book. Come up with reasons why they might want to collaborate with you: win-win ideas so all parties benefit in some way. Then start connecting. Here are some ideas as to how a collaboration might work for you and your book.

- Piggybacking: when a large organisation runs a campaign, can you run a satellite event under its umbrella? For example, I run workshops and give talks during Small Business Month, showing people how to identify unique content in their personal life or business, that they can then publish in relevant ways.
- Co-branding: this is especially an option for leadership books whereby a company pays for co-branding of the cover, their

Chairman/CEO writes the foreword and then the book is distributed to staff.

- Author collabs: include promotions for other authors in your socials and newsletters in return for reciprocal promotion. Devise an arrangement with other authors or aligned businesses whereby you sell their products at your events and vice versa. Or how about joint-publishing a box set of mini-ebooks, with other specialty experts contributing essays, how-to information, tips or deep dives?
- Local businesses: might a local restaurant host a reading with a degustation menu to suit your book's theme? Is there a local product or hamper company that might package your book with other items, or you package their products with yours? Is there a business in town that would let you do a window display?
- Giveaways: devise giveaway promotions of your book in return for coverage.
- Charities: is there a relevant charity you can organise a fundraising event with?

A collaboration might even involve you becoming a spokesperson for a company, or a recipient of a sponsorship deal from them. For example, might you be a good fit as a spokesperson for a company or product that aligns with your values and specialty? Can you think of a company that might like to tie in with your book's message, or who might like to reach your audience?

If you've written a book about your year in Antarctica, perhaps a deal with an outdoor adventure company might be the go. Or are you a crochet guru who a craft store might want to co-brand with for a crochet kit or to do demonstrations instore?

Might a company want to sponsor your speaking tour or get your help promoting their own products when you're out promoting your book?

Think about what products and organisations you have synergies with and work out how you can both benefit through association.

∿

Successful collaborations deepen relationships, extend your reach and open new opportunities for your book. But what else can you do? There are some more marketing ideas in the next chapter to get you thinking.

48

OTHER MARKETING IDEAS

U se your imagination to devise ways to drive awareness and sales for your book. Here are some prompts to get you thinking.

REVEALS

There are all sorts of moments during the creation of your book when you can reach out to your audience and build the buzz. Reveals are a big part of this. You can even do a reveal of a reveal, such as revealing two cover options and asking your audience to help pick the winner. Other things you can reveal include who you're interviewing and salient quotes from them, your author photo, any new piece of information that helps to build a story around the writing and release of your book, and of course, a reveal of your expression when you unpack your first box of books!

AWARDS

Winning a legitimate award creates opportunities for media coverage and social media bragging rights. It can also help raise awareness of your book in the trade, will boost your confidence and adds the halo effect of general prestige to your title. Many awards offer winners a sticker that can be placed on your book cover, which helps a buyer trust it will be worth the read.

However, there are a lot of shonky awards that are more about helping you part with your money than giving you an award party! These types of awards are fronts for money-making schemes targeting naive and hopeful authors seeking external validation. Be on the lookout for high entry fees, slippery sales tactics, obscure contracts, and the upselling of other services (funnily enough, such as award stickers for books!).

Writer Beware is a wonderful site that provides updates on many of the latest scams and ALLi regularly updates an awards program ratings table. Awards are listed in one of three categories: Caution, Mixed and Recommended. You can check this table to see if the award you are thinking of entering might be a profiteer or otherwise suspect in some way.

Another potential marketing strategy is to run your own award program for your specific industry. This is a huge move and will require a lot of resources, but if the industry or niche you are in is award-less, maybe you can build community and generate publicity by putting on your own!

POLLS, SURVEYS AND STATISTICS

Polls, surveys and statistics are an engaging way to create content for your audience and stay in the public eye. For example, you can design polls for your website, or put out questions on social media to encourage interaction and feedback, and perhaps use the responses and results as a way of getting media attention.

You can also use a short summary of fresh statistics and research released by third parties (giving due credit to the source of course) to remain relevant. For example, for the media, come up with a zippy subject line and then in the body of the email say, 'Commenting on data released today by X, (your name and title/ description) said (add intelligent and interesting commentary)'.

CONVENTIONS, EXPOS, MARKET STALLS AND POP-UPS

Conventions, conferences and expos can draw huge visitor numbers around defined interests, whether it be medical or professional services, boats, cars, home improvement, investing, travel, food and beverage, fashion, fitness, leadership, quilting, pets or cosmetics.

Find the right event and you will find your audience.

The cost of stands at these events can be exorbitant, but perhaps there is another writer or business with whom you can collaborate. Or you might even be able to book a spot as a guest speaker or be an expert on another company's stand in return for having your books front and centre.

On a different level, I had a stall at festivals and farmers' markets for years and often saw authors set up a table to sell solely their books. I always admired their courage and was secretly grateful I had not just books but also a table full of honey, beeswax balms, turmeric, and other farm produce to hide behind. What was interesting though, was that I saw the same authors again and again. Their bookselling stall was working for them.

You can also organise a pop-up stall in a shopping centre. Some people will avoid you like the plague, but if you have posters, stacks of books and a wide smile, there will always be someone who wants to have a chat. Don't worry if they're boring or more interested in telling you about themselves: a crowd attracts a crowd. You may even be able to collaborate with other authors to make the promotion more fun, and time- and cost-effective.

As I was putting this book to bed I ran into Monte Dwyer (ex-weather presenter, journalist and author) behind a pop-up table of books at our local mall. A fantastic salesman, he now finds shopping malls—though pricier than farmers' markets—better for his bookselling strategy due to the protection provided from the vagaries of weather.

A strategy selling at events, markets and shopping malls won't work for all books, but for a small investment of cash and a day of your time, testing the market like this gets you and your book out there in the public eye.

BULK SALES

Are you in a position to offer bulk sales for conferences, meetings and asso-ciations? Or how about a special print run for a business organisation whereby you change the cover to their corporate colours or have one of the company's key leaders write a special foreword?

 If you are speaking at conferences, first negotiate your speakers fee, then, in a separate negotiation, suggest they purchase bulk copies of the book to either package into the conference cost or for goodie bags. The company will often have a training budget and a marketing budget, so you can tap into both.

— ANDREW GRIFFITHS, BOOK WRITING COACH, AUTHOR
AND SPEAKER

❧

INSIDE ADVICE WITH JAQUI LANE
THE BOOK ADVISER

Approach companies that have a linked interest in your topic that could use the book as a special promotion, giveaway or lead magnet of their own. There are only so many keep cups, pens, and caps that companies can give away. Think about companies/groups that your target audience is well represented in. Here are some actual examples from my clients: a book on step parenting was of interest to a childcare group; a book about patient safety for nurses and doctors was of interest to a medical insurance company; a book about working from anywhere is of interest to a caravan manufacturer; a book about funding and commercial advice for startups as SMEs might be of interest to universities and start-up/scaleup hubs.

Most authors think about selling one book to one person. Selling hundreds of books to one company changes your book sales dynamics significantly, especially if you can secure these orders before you hit the print button.

Another benefit of bulk pre-sales is that they bring down the unit price of all your books so you make more money from the get go.

And bulk sales can apply to eBooks as well.

❧

STUNTS, GIMMICKS AND HOAXES

Can you have some fun with your book, or pull off a relevant stunt to attract attention? What is there about you and your book that, with a bit of creativity and humour, could cut through for media attention? You don't have to be Banksy shredding just-sold art at an auction or do anything too outrageous, but how can you get attention for your book in a smart and savvy way?

WRITERS' FESTIVALS

I love the vibe of writers' festivals—so many creative thinkers to listen to and ask questions of, while surrounded by crews of smiling volunteers and beaming patrons. But for self-published authors, the odds of being invited to speak at one are not in your favour.

> We receive upwards of 700 pitches per year and with approximately 100 places in the program, it is not possible to include all interested writers. Though if a book speaks to us and is relevant to the themes of the program, then it is added to the list for consideration.

— EMILY BRUGMAN, PROGRAM MANAGER, BYRON WRITERS
FESTIVAL

I've been to a few festivals as a patron, but as a self-published author (and prior to this book's publication), I've only been invited to speak at one ... but go on, encourage your fave festival to bring me in for a talk or workshop and let's shake things up.

Your odds may improve if you are an author local to where an event is being held. For example, Angela Bennetts, Festival Director, *Words on the Waves Writers' Festival* on the Central Coast, NSW ensures there are opportunities for local authors but advises writers to get in touch well in advance as programming decisions are made more than half a year ahead.

In the end, you might not get a speaking gig at a festival, but you may make new friends and bookish connections, learn lots and leave motivated and ready to grow. I'll have a list of writers' festivals on my site if you want to attend one for inspiration ... or, better still, to be the inspiration.

BEGIN WRITING YOUR NEXT BOOK

WHAT!?! You likely haven't even finished the writing and marketing of this book yet, and already I'm telling you a great marketing strategy is to write and launch another one. That's right, there are many benefits to starting your next book.

- You've already warmed up your writing muscles, so you'll be keeping them in top condition.
- As a second-time author, you benefit from the experience of writing and publishing your first book. Your next book will be even better.
- Launching another book, especially in the same genre, will

normally help lift your backlist sales. It makes better commercial sense to be able to sell more than one product.

- It's easier to sell a new product to someone who's already a customer. Also, much of the background marketing work you've done for your current book, such as your website and social media presence, can be utilised for your next.

∼

Whatever marketing activities you pursue, track and measure the success of them. Let's head down that track now to find out why.

49

TRACK AND MEASURE YOUR SUCCESS

Measurement is key to understanding what elements of your marketing campaign are working. After all, how will you know where to best spend your time and money if you don't know what's getting results?

Track mentions on the internet

Set up *Google Alerts* for your name and the title of your book so you can track when new mentions appear on the internet. This will alert you to fresh blogger mentions and some (but not all) media coverage.

Measuring sales directly from your own website

If you have Google Analytics or an alternative plugged into your website, you'll be able to see where your visitors are coming from, the actions they're taking and which outlets and pages are referring them.

When you receive an email out of the blue from someone, always ask how they heard about you and your book. Track their responses, so you can focus on doing more of what's working.

Measuring social media success

Track which posts have the most interactions and how many followers you have gained month on month. What has driven likes and sign-ups? What is the best time of day to post? Which topics and images achieved the most engagement?

 I've come to respect words enormously. I have 750,000+ followers on Facebook and you'll see how I use words: emphasising some, putting gaps between others. I want to know, 'Are these the best four words I can string together to grab someone's attention?' And then I let the market tell me. Some posts will only get 40 likes, some will get 4,000. And then I analyse. What time did I publish? What words and images did I use? What will I try next?

— KIM MCCOSKER, *4 INGREDIENTS*

How to measure bookstore sales of print books

A service like this isn't necessary for a book like mine, but Nielsen Book-Scan Australia offers a *Live Title Tracking Sales Data Report*. This report shows how your title is selling in bookstores and where it ranks in the official Australian bestseller charts and within its own category. If it's selling like hotcakes, it may be the data you need to decide to order a reprint to fulfil demand, it may also help you work out which of your marketing campaigns are having the biggest effect on sales.

How to measure Amazon, Apple, Kobo and other ebook outlet sales

Tracking is easy through your dashboard on these sites, or through your ebook distributor's dashboard.

How to measure IngramSpark sales

You can track print and ebook sales through your IngramSpark dashboard. Ingram does not disclose from which retailers your print book sales come through though as Ingram says it is proprietary information.

Does your marketing measure up?

Compare your original goals with your current results. Hopefully, you'll be streets ahead, but if not, change things up! But be realistic: some books just aren't the hits we hoped for. Learn what works and what doesn't so you can implement new strategies for your next book.

So, we've come to the end of the marketing section, but this is not the end of your book's journey. In many ways, you're just getting started. Why? You've put all that effort into building your brand and writing, publishing, distributing and marketing your book. Now it's time to capitalise.

That's the FABULOUS thing about being a self-publisher—any opportunities and money that flows is now flowing your way.

The next section will show you how to leverage your book to amplify your message, personal brand and income.

PART V

LEVERAGE YOUR BOOK

50

RIGHTS SCHEMES: PLR, ELR AND CAL

I n this section we look beyond book sales to see how you can leverage your book, and perhaps even build a business around it. We'll start with the rights schemes that have been mentioned earlier. The key Australian schemes are as follows.

AUSTRALIAN LENDING RIGHTS SCHEMES

If selling your book into libraries and/or educational institutions, it's a no-brainer to sign up for the Australian government's Public Lending Rights (PLR) and Educational Lending Rights (ELR) schemes. It costs nothing to join except your time to fill out the online forms and could result in hundreds or many thousands of dollars in payments.

Though you join upon publication of your book, there eventually needs to be at least 50 copies (per title) available in libraries to be eligible for a payment.

Submissions for new title claims close on 31 March each year. If you miss the date, books are not eligible for back payments. Ebooks are currently not eligible for the scheme, but this may change.

Speaking from experience, it's wonderful to receive an annual notification that the book you worked so hard on is sitting there earning money because people are still borrowing, enjoying and getting value from it!

COPYRIGHT AGENCY LTD (CAL)

Another rights payment is known as CAL. I only recently signed up (it's free) with the Copyright Agency and received a $600+ CAL payment in my first year. I'm hoping to increase this figure going forward. The more works you have in print (such as published articles), the more potential for ongoing income.

The Copyright Agency collects and distributes copyright fees for the copying and sharing of text and images, for example, when schools, government departments and businesses reuse text and images (such as photocopying a handout). Beneficiaries of the scheme include journalists, publishers, surveyors, visual artists, photographers, cartoonists, illustrators, and authors. That's you!

You're not just limited to PLR, ELR and CAL payments though. There are plenty of other rights and opportunities you can pursue too. They're covered in the next chapter.

51

OTHER RIGHTS AND OPPORTUNITIES

No longer just a consumer of books, you're now a writer of them too: a producer! What a great feeling! And an even better feeling is realising that as the product creator and holder of the IP, you can leverage your product in whatever way you see fit and in the ways the market is prepared to pay for. Here are some ideas you might like to pursue.

EXCERPT SALES

Yes, you can share excerpts of your book from your website as a lead magnet to entice purchasers, but you may also be able to earn money and wider promotion by either selling or giving media outlets the right to reproduce it.

The trick to choosing which excerpt to share is to make sure it gives readers a great all-round read but still leaves them wanting more. You can also give other authors the right to excerpt some of your work to reproduce in their works.

I've found the best way and value for me as an author is to offer a slightly edited excerpt to relevant publications free of charge in return for promoting my book. Interestingly, the resulting article might also then qualify for a CAL payment. However, if you're a business writer or working in a specific subject area, you may be able to charge a fee per word, especially if being published in an industry journal or magazine.

You might also hear the term 'first serial rights'. These are the rights to publish an excerpt before the book is published. This works well if you have a chapter from a particularly interesting or controversial memoir. These are well received by the big newspapers' weekend magazines.

FOREIGN SALES, TRANSLATIONS AND FOREIGN LITERARY AGENTS

Is your book one that might be embraced in another country? Memoirs where the author shares a heritage between countries and books ranging from craft through to history may well find a solid readership overseas. That's fine if it's in an English-speaking country, but what if your audience speaks Arabic, Punjabi, Polish, Mandarin or Malay?

That's where foreign literary agents and translation services come in.

My book *Honeycomb Kids* was picked up by publishers in South Korea and Turkey of all places! I had no idea how to handle the enquiries, so I turned to the internet and searched for 'foreign literary agents', finally finding one who I thought had similar values and represented authors like me. In this case, the agent didn't 'bring in' the business, but she was able to 'handle' the business, which I was so grateful for.

The key to working with overseas publishers, literary agents and translators is to ask around your writing community, do your due diligence and check with an advisory service such as the ASA to ensure that the contract you're signing is fair and legitimate.

You can also go it alone and organise your own translation and distribution. Translations can be expensive though, and although artificial intelligence programs such as Google Translate and other services do a basic job, you really need a human to ensure that your translation hits the mark. But first, ask yourself this question: are there enough people who might buy and read your book in that language to make a translation worthwhile? If so, great! Once it's translated, it will be relatively easy to upload it through Amazon, IngramSpark, Apple and other sites.

LICENSING

Licensing is a business deal whereby you sell specific rights to an individual or corporation to use and repackage your IP over a certain period and for a specific fee. Here's how it might work.

Licensing your book in other markets

I'm currently working on a licensing deal with an agricultural journalist in the UK to bring out a UK version of *Small Farm Success Australia*. It will be based on my original book, but with relevant UK-specific information and case studies included. I plan to do this for the US and other key markets too. For this book, I'd love to work with a successful Australian indie author to bring out a book on the ins-and-outs of writing and self-publishing fiction such as romance, mysteries and sci-fi.

Can you license your book in some way or develop a series from it?

TV, movie, podcast, and documentary rights

Have you written a true crime book or a powerful memoir? Are you approaching or have you been approached by professionals wanting to license your work for other formats? It's time to get yourself some professional advice because there's big money to be made for the right to reproduce your work in these mediums. Maybe we'll be seeing your story on TV, at the movies or on a streaming service soon!

Product tie-ups

Have a hit on your hands? Companies may be interested in licensing your brand to apply to relevant products ranging from toys to clothes, cosmetics and food. Perhaps your book could even spawn a monthly magazine.

Licensing for creatives

For creatives and authors of books where you have generated your own art, companies such as Art Shine Industries may be able to point you in the right direction with ideas and pathways to further commercialise your work.

∽

Inspired? The next chapter will illuminate even more opportunities for you and your book.

52

COURSES, APPEARANCES, CONSULTING, WORKSHOPS, COACHING AND MEMBERSHIP PROGRAMS

H ave you ever signed up for a course? Bought a ticket to listen to someone speak? Engaged a consultant to help you or your business? Well, now it's you who people might want to hear from.

Writing a book makes you an expert. Sure, you might not want to embrace these opportunities, but for authors who do, you can earn more income from the following offerings than you ever could from book sales alone.

Here are some ways you can leverage your book and play in the big (or at least, bigger!) league.

 Your book is a rich resource of quality content you can leverage. But that means you have to write a quality book first.

— KELLY IRVING, BOOK COACH AND EDITOR

SPEAKING ENGAGEMENTS

Whether it's speaking to a few people at your local Probus Club, a graduating high school class, a group of high-level executives or thousands at a convention, speaking engagements are a way to raise awareness of your subject, book and expertise—and get paid too.

The key word though is 'engagement'. Your audience wants to be engaged, not spoken at. They want to learn about you, and from you. And, you need to keep it real.

> Psychology teaches us that vulnerability builds trust and deepens relationships, yet in business we perpetually apply a slick veneer and wonder why it's so hard to develop loyal, lasting customer relationships. Corporate communications and fears of damaging our careers have trained us to avoid telling the full story in all its messy, compelling glory. It could be that we're so close to our own stories that it's hard to know when real authenticity is needed to build that vital bond of trust and believability with customers.
>
> — MARK JONES, AUTHOR, *BELIEFONOMICS*

Some authors, especially in the business sphere, make a large amount of money from their talks through a combination of speaking fees, book sales and the new business they win as a result. Depending on your topic, there could be many non-traditional opportunities. For example, if you're in the health and wellness space, perhaps you could barter an extra few days at a health retreat in return for a presentation to guests. But you need to be great, so read books on topics like how to deliver Ted Talks, and watch them too. Learn from the best.

What formats do speaking engagements take?

In person or online, you might speak directly to the audience, with or without PowerPoint slides, with a Q&A at the end. You can also appear in a more informal 'in conversation' arrangement, where a well-prepared host asks questions so it's more of a back-and-forth chat. You could also get a spot on a panel, taking questions, and sharing your opinion alongside other experts and guests. These can be so much fun to do!

Speaking bureaus/agencies/bookers

Research online and you'll find a range of talent managers and agencies specialising in promoting and booking presenters.

How do I negotiate payment?

Review the ASA's current speaking rates and those of your peers. Be clear on your website if you charge for speaking engagements and when you receive or reach out for opportunities, be upfront about your expectations.

How can I get over my fear of public speaking?

All it takes to banish a fear of public speaking is a well-prepared and practised speech, says me. But for others, glossophobia, the fear of public speaking, triggers a huge amount of nerves, angst, doubt and procrastination. What can you do?

Speak to a counsellor, take a course or do a workshop. There are numerous private trainers (some even with Medicare-assisted funding), as well as Toastmasters International.

Start small and practise. Try your speech out on your dog, cat, or a random tree in the park. Just get started, and gradually develop your confidence and capacity.

~

INSIDE ADVICE: KIM MCCOSKER, *4 INGREDIENTS* PUBLIC SPEAKING TIPS

What I have come to believe make for a great speaker are the following attributes:

- Be real: you will be asked questions, so know your topic well.
- Add humour: who doesn't love a giggle?
- Know when to end: finish talking before the audience finishes listening.
- Prepare: spend time beforehand, know your audience and tailor your messages aligning them with the theme of the event.
- Nail your opening: the first words to leave your lips matter the most. In this instance your audience will either believe you and come with you or start to doubt you.
- Stand tall: let your body language, from your hand gestures to your facial expressions, complement your message.
- Use silence: silence is a very powerful weapon, so let those

pregnant pauses linger a little after key moments in your speech. This allows time for the message to sink in.

- Care: care deeply about your topic because if you don't, why should your audience?
- Adjust your tone: it will help you hold your audience's attention.
- Confidence is contagious: even if you are nervous, smile, take a deep breath and tell yourself 'You've got this!' And get out there and make it happen!

∿

CONSULTING AND COACHING

For some consultants, the reason they produce a book is so that they can use it as a lead-in to sell their other services such as consulting or coaching, either one-on-one or in a group.

Sessions can be offered in a variety of ways, including phone calls, Zoom-type calls and in-person. They might be one-offs, semi-regular, or scheduled at the same time and day each week or month. Having access to a service like this can be great for clients who just want to ask a few one-off questions, as well as for clients whose needs are for a much longer-term relationship.

∿

INSIDE ADVICE: KATH WALTERS
BOOK COACH

If you are passable at maths, you'll realise that you would have to sell 330 books at $30 each to make $10k. Hard work. And that's if you self-publish and get all the money yourself. If you have a publisher, you'd have to sell 3,300 copies to make $10k on the average 10% royalty.

So, here's how to make $10k from one book.

You are a coach, trainer or speaker, so you have a program that you sell for, say, $10k.

You meet a prospective client and GIVE them a copy of your book. Which they love. And so they buy your coaching or training program, or book you to speak. Bingo, one book = $10k. Even if your program is $3k, it's still a fabulous return on investment.

I made around $400k off the back of my first book: *Sticky Content: Mastering the Delicate Art of Content Marketing*. My second book—*Overnight Authority: How to Win Respect, Command Attention and Earn More Money by Writing a book in 90 Days*—is breaking all records.

What is your rule of thumb for return on investment from a coaching program? Mine is 10 times (I have to get back 10 times what I spend.)

Can you see your book's IP going to any of these places? This is how a book can be turned into a business. There are other ways to capitalise on your book too.

WORKSHOPS

How is a workshop different to a speech?

Workshops are longer than speeches, running from a few hours to a full day, and even across entire weekends or 5-day retreats. People are usually willing to pay more to attend a workshop, as there is an expectation of interactivity, activities and a higher focus on the attendees' development and networking opportunities.

Who attends workshops?

People and businesses who want to learn more from you and put your ideas and actions into practise themselves.

How much can I charge for a workshop?

This depends on your subject matter, the audience it relates to, what's being charged by your peers and the venue in which you're holding it. You might also choose to collaborate with other speakers to put on a unique half-day event, offering yourselves as a package deal to corporates, community organisations, or direct to the public.

My concept is very simple: someone has to be the most expensive, why not make it you? But if you *are* going to be the most expensive, you also have to be the best.

— ANDREW GRIFFITHS, BOOK WRITING COACH, AUTHOR
AND SPEAKER

COURSES AND TRAINING

As an expert in your subject matter there will always be people who want to hear, learn, or be further entertained by you. They might want deeper, more specific, personalised or interactive engagement. And, you can deliver it to them! How?

You could do it in person at a venue of your choosing, or through a third party such as a client-organised event or community college.

You can offer courses online, on your own site or via email, as a guest host on a related site, or on a marketplace platform such as Udemy, Mind-Valley, Skillshare and Coursera. And you can do these live or recorded, or a combination of both.

What software can help me build an online course?

You can use one of the marketplace platforms above or there is a wide variety of services built for just this purpose, including Teachable, Thinkific, Heights Platform, LeanPub, Kajabi and Podia. You can also use WordPress plugins LearnDash and LearnPress.

Running your course on an independent platform rather than setting it up on one of the learning site marketplaces will cost you more to set up initially and comes with a tech learning curve, but you will benefit from a higher profit margin, flexibility, ownership of your IP and from having complete control of your brand and customer base. More important than the platform though, is that your course delivers transformation for the participant. Plan the learning outcomes first, then work backwards to outline the course content, and then pick the platform.

— MEL BRUCE, MARKETING COACH AND SPEAKER

Lindy Alexander is the founder of The Freelancer's Year, a site and community for writers wanting to make a living as freelance writers. She launched her first online courses in 2020, one titled *Foundations of Freelance Writing* and the other *Write Earn Thrive*, a course aimed at helping established writers hit $100,000 a year from their freelance writing. Let's go behind the scenes to learn how it's worked for her.

∾

INSIDE ADVICE
LINDY ALEXANDER, FOUNDER, THE FREELANCERSYEAR.COM

Why did you decide to offer an online course?

I was coaching freelance writers one-on-one and lots of them were coming to me with similar queries, challenges and issues (mostly around how to find high-paying clients) and I could see that there would be a way to help more people by offering an online course and community that would support them and cheer them on.

What has been the most successful marketing tool/process you've used to convert visitors into subscribers into course buyers?

My first intention was always to be as generous and useful as possible to freelance writers. I wanted to openly share information and strategies that worked for me. I didn't really have any intention of converting people, but I knew that an email list was important if I wanted to keep in touch with people. I think blogging every week for 4+ years had a huge impact on people feeling that they knew me, trusted me and wanted to experience the same results as me. Therefore, they've bought the course.

What do you wish you knew before beginning the process?

That it's not just one launch and you're done. If you want this to be a viable income stream, you need to set up systems so that you can launch a few times a year (as well as potentially setting up an evergreen funnel). For me, the tech side of things has been the most difficult—I'm not technologically minded and tend to be more big picture than detail-oriented, so I struggled with all the different components and how they fit together.

What's the most important attribute for an online course?

For it to be actionable (no fluff) and to actually deliver what it promises.

What software/technology/platform did you use to build your course?

I started on my WordPress site and used Mailchimp, Lead Pages, Stripe/PayPal, MemberPress, ScreenFlow, Vimeo, Chatra and Deadline Funnel, but I've since moved to the all-in-one platform Kartra. It's so much easier!

How long did it take to set the course up and get it to the live stage?

I procrastinated for a long time—I told my list I was going to run a course, but didn't launch it until about 18 months later.

Why did you decide to run and sell the course from your own site rather than a site like Udemy?

I wanted to have control over it. I never considered Udemy or anything similar.

How often do you refresh the course?

I did a little refresh in the first year and then a total overhaul based on lots of new information and strategies I've been testing out this past year.

What are your top five tips for someone thinking of creating an online course?

1. Start with an audience. This can be an email list, IG followers, FB followers, YouTube subscribers, whatever, but at the most fundamental level you need people to know about you and your course so you have an audience to sell to.
2. Validate it. It's really tempting and easy to assume that you know what people want and need and get excited about building a course, but the only way to prove that there is a need for your course is to validate it first (and the easiest way to do this is to

pre-sell it, so you create one or two modules, launch the course at a special introductory price and then create the rest week by week). Lots of people may say they're interested in what you're offering, but until they pull out their wallets, you really don't know if the course will sell or not.

3. Don't underestimate how long it will take. The tech. The content. The recording. The editing. The marketing. The updating of content. It all takes much, much longer than you think.

4. Don't be put off by other people in your industry running similar courses. There is SO much potential for edupreneurs, and no one will be teaching exactly what you're teaching.

5. Go for it.

❧

MEMBERSHIP PROGRAMS

What is a membership model?

It's when your audience pays a weekly or monthly fee to support your work, and perhaps have input into it, and so they are given special access to it.

The membership model has become a popular way for creators to monetise interest in their work. It especially suits writers, artists, vloggers and podcasters, but it also works for people who pull together information in specific areas (such as gigs and opportunities in specific industries) and email them out regularly.

People also join for access to and interaction with a community where information is shared on a topic of specific interest to them.

What are some membership sites used by creators?

There are quite a few including Patreon, Drip by Kickstarter, Podia, Memberful, Hy.page, Apple and Spotify. Even Twitter now has a 'tips' feature where people can tip you for the services and information you offer.

What kind of content might I include?

People love exclusive content. Depending on your subject, it might be a new 4WD trail or recipe you've explored, a bonus interview, a fresh cartoon or image, a unique new pattern or how-to video. Supporters also like access to Q&A sessions and to a group of likeminded people, and you can offer early access to events and products, as well as discounts, bonuses and exclusive merchandise.

~

Want to go even deeper? Tune into the next chapter. It's all about podcasts.

53

PODCASTS

P odcasts are a fantastic way to learn all sorts of things while being entertained, but you can also be a guest on one, host a podcast yourself or license your content for someone else to produce.

Podcasts aren't for everyone or every topic, and it's crowded space, but they are yet another channel through which you can build your profile and promote your book, business or interests.

The best podcasts really dig deep into a specific topic. The topic might be true crime, leadership, politics, writing, motivation, life balance or making money. Or, the podcast's success might be built on the particular personalities hosting the podcast and their unique take on their peers, life-style and current affairs.

Podcasts can be daily, weekly, or monthly. Or they might be launched as a one-off series.

Why podcast?

- To increase book sales.
- To maximise the potential of your work.
- To grow your brand while building and strengthening your community.

- To go deeper into and expand on your subject in ways that a printed book can't.
- And, to market the book, and potentially improve search engine results.

How do I make money from a podcast?

You can derive revenue from advertising, sponsorships and memberships, and different platforms such as Patreon, Spotify and Apple offer a variety of ways to monetise your content. Ad insertion companies like Omnystudio and Acast can help in the process.

What technical solutions are out there to help me create a podcast?

So many! A few of the better-known ones include Audacity (which is free!), BuzzSpout, PodBean, Captivate, Blubrry and Castos. There are also local providers who can help with the strategy and production needs of your podcast.

What else will I need?

- A plan, as well as time, patience, money, and skill.
- A good microphone, mike stand and a screen for your mike to improve sound quality.
- Headphones.
- A quiet room.
- A website to promote your podcast from (this could be your own, or on Patreon).
- And when it's all ready to go, you'll need to get it listed on the major sites including Apple Podcasts, Spotify and Stitcher.
- Staying power. Podcasts often aren't 'discovered' until you've built up a large amount of quality content and a long episode list.

Where can I find more information?

There's plenty of information on the internet, but beware, there is lots of bad advice there too, and sometimes authors give well-meaning advice that has worked for them but may not be right for you. And of course, there are podcasts on podcasts! ALLi's publication *Podcasting for Authors* is a good place to start.

~

INSIDE ADVICE: DANI VEE
WORDS AND NERDS PODCAST

What's the most important attribute for a podcast?

Quality content—it needs to be your top priority. Audiences may forgive unstable Wi-Fi or an inexpensive microphone, but the content must be engaging and appealing. I'd like to think that a great podcast engages your audience on multiple levels through a combination of humour and deep, vulnerable discussions. A good podcast should inspire you to take action in some way.

What have you learned about audiences?

Prior to creating content, you need to have some idea of who might listen to your podcast. They may vary and be transient, but if you have a good idea of who's tuning in, you can work out how best to appeal to them.

Do values and beliefs have any place in a podcast?

Yes. It's the values and beliefs of the host that make a podcast unique, which in turn draws a certain type of listener and guest to it. It's important to be yourself: if that's vulnerable, curious and funny, be that person.

How do you sustain enthusiasm for the show after so many episodes?

People often wonder how the podcast can sustain so many episodes, but the truth is, the conversations on the podcast nourish me in ways that I could never have imagined. It's important to stay inspired though.

Does it need to be a solo effort?

No, being open to collaborations can lead to great things. For my show, that's meant experimenting and embracing co-hosts, livestreams, group chats, different formats and focuses, letting people 'take over' the show and going off on specific tangents (such as our *Publishing Insider* podcasts where we get insights from everyone from agents to major marketers).

What's one tip you can give someone starting up a new podcast about structure?

Variety keeps things lively, but a similar structure for interviews gives a sense of familiarity and flow to each show. For example, I end every podcast by asking my author guest, 'Why do you keep writing?'.

What general tips do you have for someone appearing on a podcast for the first time?

I'm really interested in organic and authentic conversations. I only provide the questions beforehand if requested because I want it to feel like we're having a coffee at a cafe. People relax, and the best conversations are the ones where you throw away the questions! Know your book, think about what you want to say about it and prepare for some deep questions! Also, headphones please!

What would you say to a writer who hasn't yet listened to your podcast?

Whether it's mine or someone else's, a good podcast can inform, entertain and inspire. Why wouldn't you want to get an ear and heart full of that? The last few years have been weird times, so if you can escape into a book, or a podcast, or by baking a cake, do that.

~

A podcast is not the only potential spin-off for your book though, read on to discover why.

54

SPIN-OFFS

There are all sorts of ways to parlay your prose into profit. Here are some other ideas to get you thinking.

WORKBOOKS, JOURNALS, TEMPLATES AND PLANS

Does your book lend itself to additional items, such as workbooks, journals, templates, plans, goal-setting notepads or other stationery?

I decided to add a workbook to my offering when I realised I had so much more useful information—checklists, sample emails and templates—that could be of huge benefit to readers but which weren't really suitable to include in this book's format. Yes, I've had to invest a lot more time, and consider things like IP, design and production, but I think it's well worth it and will provide me with another revenue stream and readers with real value. Do you think you could add further value for your readers through a workbook too?

METAVERSE, VIRTUAL REALITY AND WEB3.0

Might your book have a second life in the metaverse? Is your book rich enough to morph into not just a game, but a virtual reality experience? Joanna Penn from The Creative Penn has plenty of ideas on her site about where web3.0 could go for authors.

SIMILAR MESSAGE BUT WITH A MORE TARGETED AUDIENCE

Can you rewrite your original book to specifically target an even more niche audience?

That's what US-based author Phil M Jones, author of *Exactly What to Say*, did when he brought out a book specifically targeting the property industry. His spin-off book, *Exactly What To Say—For Real Estate Agents*, sold 25,000 copies within a short space of time and the franchise rolls on with *Exactly How to Sell* and many more.

BRANDED MERCHANDISE

If people buy your book, and then buy into your thinking and style, they might also want to buy related products.

Merchandise works best when it's of real use to your audience. And, it works best for the planet if you think about its lifecycle and make it as eco-friendly as possible. Merchandise can be a money maker, but it needs more thought than just going through a catalogue to work out what quote, image or URL to plonk on a mass-produced product.

Some common types of merchandise include posters, prints and fabrics, and slogans on t-shirts, tote bags, pens, mugs, hats and aprons. But here's your chance to get creative. Written a book on gardening? Create seed packets or your own line of pots. Writing about local history? Coasters featuring historic images or a map and app with a walking tour of the town might suit. Have a business book ready to go? Perhaps produce a goal-setting journal or commission an artisan to handcraft premium timber pens. Get some ideas for merchandise by speaking with local creators and makers.

BUNDLES

What associated products can you bundle with your book, or become a regular supplier of? Here are some thought-launchers:

- Craft book: pre-cut material, kits and special dyes.
- Pottery book: pottery tools, clays and glazes.
- Gemstone book: bags of select crystals.
- Cookery book: herb and spice mixes.

You know your topic the best though. What will work in your niche?

APPS

Do you have an app that might make a great companion to your book and offer your readers some type of deeper interaction, solve their problem, or entertain them?

Though they can be costly to develop, successful apps build deep customer relationships, and attract a fee for each download and in-app purchase so can drive further revenue around your specialty. Do lots of homework though to prove your idea is viable before heading down the app track.

SPECIAL EDITIONS

Does your book have the potential to also be released as a limited or special edition? Your special edition might include bonus material, handmade binding or premium paper. Think creatively; if your book is about knitting patterns, perhaps you could hand-knit some one-off covers!

Or, perhaps you can add extra content such as illustrations or interviews, and sign these copies.

You can also release a limited edition with bonus content and sell it as a Non-Fungible Token (NFT). Yes ... it's a whole new world!

If you are contemplating a special edition, use the same title but add *Special Edition* or *Limited Edition* to the title. It will also need a new ISBN. To ensure that it comes up in Amazon searches and the reviews of the original edition are combined, email Amazon and ask them to link the editions.

NEW EDITIONS

Things change!

If what you have written about is in a fast-moving area, plan to release a new edition every couple of years (or sooner) with updated information. Some books, like *Guinness World Records* are updated annually. What a great marketing strategy: a base set of information with constant new information to add, market and tempt readers with. These type of books come with ready-made sales, as every person and organisation who made it into the latest edition will buy at least one copy as a keepsake.

For your book to qualify as a new edition, include at least 10% updated and fresh content.

Craig Lewis and Cathy Savage are great examples of self-publishers who have experienced success bringing out new editions. This pioneering self-publishing couple have written and published more than 25 individual titles with multiple editions sold of each for a total of just under 2.5 million books. That's right, they've sold just under 2.5 million copies!

As a backlist publisher, they update and bring out multiple editions of their bestselling titles. For years the couple travelled Australia as full-time travel writers and photographers, mostly writing about Australian bush travel, camping and 4WD adventuring. Just some of their titles include:

- *4WD Treks Close to Sydney* (8th edition).
- *Australian Bush Cooking: Recipes for a Gourmet Outback Experience* (approximately 50,000 copies sold).
- *Australian Bush Pubs: A Celebration of Outback Australia's Iconic Watering Holes* (2nd edition and working on a 3rd, with 50,000+ copies sold).

∽

INSIDE ADVICE: CRAIG LEWIS AND CATHY SAVAGE
BOILING BILLY PUBLICATIONS

Cathy and Craig steered their first book into Dymocks George Street because Cathy had the courage to walk in and show it to the buyer. They were one of the first self-publishers to get into the store, and the company set up an account with them for that book, and then continued to order and reorder. With their early success, they needed to hire a storage unit to store their books, but after years of dealing directly with wholesalers and some-times having to chase $30,000 to $50,000 a month in unpaid invoices, they were approached by Woodslane Press, who offered to act as their ware-house and dispatch arm. In 2008, a distribution agreement was finalised and in 2010 Woodslane bought into the Boiling Billy imprint, taking care of the publishing side including printing and marketing.

The couple credit their success to working as a team, with Cathy doing all the fact-checking, editing and business, and Craig focusing on the writing and photography. Let's hear from the pioneers themselves.

Why self-publishing?

Self-publishing has given us the freedom to live our lives and run our business in a way that suits us. The publishing industry is rife with unfulfilled promises. It's kind of like why we wanted to build our own house and why we went to the sawmill and even cut our own timber for it: we like the sense of control. We weren't keen on the big corporate wheels churning away, and in the early days the major publishers just didn't see a market in what we were doing. We took the risk when we worked out we could make money from selling just 2,000 copies of each title.

What is your writing process and timeline like?

The books are all a bit different, but as an example, our *Australian Bush Pubs* was a cumulative book and probably came together over about five years. We'd be out on another project, but if we heard about a pub close by, we'd zip out of our way and take a photo and go inside and chat with the locals. Then we'd do a gap analysis, working out what gaps we had in the book, such as 'We need two more pubs in SA', or 'There's a good pub in the NT we haven't been to yet.' So, we'd jump in the car, head off for a month, have a few beers at the first pub, get up at dawn to take pics and then drive a few days to the next pub and do it again. We made lots of notes and then when we got home, we'd start fact checking and putting it all together. When we bring out a new edition, we do our research again. We sometimes find that a pub burnt down or shut down, so we select new pubs to fill the gaps so that the book stays up to date. We're generally working on two or three books at a time. Craig does the layout and design using InDesign.

How are sales going?

This month we sold nearly 4,000 books without doing anything exceptional. That's because we've built up such a big list, and our titles continue to sell. What is interesting is that we're seeing disruptive technologies, like apps and online forums, take a bite into travel publishing. These mediums supply fresh, regularly updated, user-populated content and are quite cheap, as people are paying less than $10 for an app, whereas a book might cost you $50. We're looking at the next phase for us right now in light of this, and whether it might involve licensing content, publishing new titles, or other options.

What marketing strategies have worked for you?

- Setting up stands and running seminars at practically every caravan and camping show on the east coast was massive for us. We'd be up on stage speaking to 300 to 400 people and then they'd follow us back to the stand where Craig would answer questions while Cathy sold the books. At one camping show we sold about $10,000 worth of books and sold another $15,000 worth at a trade show. Customers would come back year after year and either ask us to sign their book or buy the latest edition.
- We offered pre-orders to the wholesalers, giving them an extra 2% discount if they put their order in early. That brought in bigger sales right at the beginning of new book launches.
- We also advertise our other books inside each book.
- Cathy was constantly on the phone selling to outdoor retailers.
- We made ourselves available for interviews, and so would regularly get calls from media like ABC Radio who'd ask us for comments on camping for Easter and similar subjects; this helped build awareness of our books and brand.
- We donated entire sets of books to local libraries and made plenty of sales too, so we now have thousands of books in libraries across Australia and our PLR payments are fantastic.
- Overall, writing useful books in one field of interest was one of our best strategies. We would do things like use the cover flap for a map, legends and symbols which made understanding the content easy, and the cover flap could also be used as a bookmark. Producing books that served their purpose well was a great loyalty marketing tool.

What are your top tips?

- Be single-minded. Sit up until 3 am in the morning to finish a section off, then get straight back into it the next day. You need to put in the hours.
- But also, be lazy whenever you can. For example, we write straight into InDesign because why would we write 450 words in Word when we can look at the design space and see that only 200 words will fit.

- Work out a way to capitalise on your book; there's no point writing 15 books and only selling one edition of each of them.
- Put yourself in the shoes of your reader. Do they want paperback, or hardcover, or spiral-bound? For a guidebook, we might do a print run of 5,000 copies, with 3,000 spiral-bound for 4WD buyers so it can lay flat and fold back on itself when they're out on the trail, and 2,000 stitched copies that bookstores prefer to sell.
- Use spectacular imagery. People are visually bombarded all the time now, so selling content is hard without great imagery to go with it.
- Cents matter in a print run; does your book need as many pages as you think? That said, the bigger the book, the more likely it is to stand out in the bookstore.
- Experiment with POD and print runs for different books if it makes sense. We released a POD book way back in 2006 and it sold 100 copies this month (more than 15 years later!) without us needing to stock or ship it.
- Stay away from dustjackets. The book retail industry is so difficult with returns, and the dustjackets come back from retailers torn and dirty.
- Don't tie up capital in books that are going to be sitting around not making you money. It might be better to do three print runs of 3,000 books over a year rather than 9,000 upfront. And don't get sucked in by printers trying to upsell you with how low the per book cost will drop if you just order an extra 2,000 copies.
- If you're not getting paid on time by a wholesaler, chase them. Cathy was always on the phone saying, 'Time's up, where's the money?'

Best piece of advice from another writer?

Craig: It was someone who was also travelling and writing in the early days and he would tell me that people would come up to him all the time and say 'you must be so lucky to do what you do'. But he'd tell them, 'It's not luck, you've chosen to work in a city or an office, that's what you chose to do. I chose to do this, no luck involved.' And my mum said to me before she died, 'If there's no opportunity, make one.'

Worst piece of advice from another writer?

It was from within the publishing industry in the early days and it was that 'You can't make money self-publishing.' Self-publishing has paid for our house and life over the last 25 years. One year Craig said to the accountant that the goal that year was to achieve $250,000 in sales, and the accountant looked at us and said in disbelief, 'Righto.' That year we did $275,000 as self-publishers.

What are you most proud of about your books?

So many things. Our book on outback pubs has become almost like a passport. People take it with them on their journey around Australia and get the publicans to autograph it. There's even a couple on YouTube who take a picture of the book and the publican at each stop. It's great customer marketing. And it's great to see people emulating the photographs we've taken, setting up in the exact same spot.

Then there's the progression we've made ourselves, starting off with a tiny little black and white DocuTech book right through to full-colour books in hardcover that we design ourselves. And the fact that we have done it for so long, the two of us.

But mainly, it's that we've empowered people to go to places they didn't even know existed.

～

Wow! What a powerful legacy. And it's the type of legacy that you, as a committed author and self-publisher, can create too. We still have another opportunity to cover on your road to empowerment though, so let's explore the world of affiliate programs.

55

AFFILIATE PROGRAMS

Not everyone needs to or wants to make money from writing a book, but if you're in the 'Yes please, make me some money' camp, affiliate programs can tip some extra earnings into your account as well as help your readers. It's basically another way to monetise your site, blog or ebook by generating sales and leads. And you can also set up an affiliate program for your own books and products and have people refer business to you, for which you reward them too! Let's explore the opportunity some more.

What is affiliate marketing?

It's when you help promote and sell another company's products or services and receive a small payment for doing so. It doesn't mean you need to stock or ship products; all you need to do is direct people to the product using a special link that 'links' the sale back to you.

Why become an affiliate?

Joining one or more affiliate marketing programs is a way to increase your income while helping your readers and followers find and buy relevant products easily.

It's not for everyone, as you can also provide these links as a service without being in an affiliate program. But if you are treating your writing as a business, affiliate marketing is something to investigate. Every dollar will count in your publishing enterprise and there is just no need to leave money on the table, especially as you're providing a curated referral service that takes time and thought to offer and deliver.

Over time, the affiliate links you set up might help you cover the cost of your website hosting or help you claw back some of the publishing costs of your book. Or, even make you rich!

How? Once set up, the links tick away in the background earning you money while you sleep, even if it's just a few dollars here and there, or oodles due to the amount of traffic you attract to your blog and socials. Sure, that might be the realm of major 'influencers', but perhaps that's who you already are—or who you aspire to be.

What are some examples of affiliate programs?

If you've ever found yourself on a 'Top 10' site, you've probably come across an affiliate marketing program. Many bloggers, product comparison and product review sites earn money by directing their followers to certain products, from dehumidifiers to software programs, yoga mats to sporting goods, silk pillowslips to cosmetics. If you click a link on one of these sites and go to the retailer's site and buy it, it's likely the website or blogger that sent you there will be paid a commission.

ALLi's Affiliate Program

ALLi recognises affiliate programs as a legitimate source of revenue too and incorporates them into their activities. That's right, if you click on the ALLi link on my site, in my resources section or in the ebook and go on to sign up as a member of ALLi, they will credit me with a percentage of your joining fee, which I can then use to help pay my own membership fees (for which I thank you because it really means something to me). Once you're a member, you'll be eligible for the affiliate program as well.

What are some ways authors might use affiliate links?

Though it's great when a person buys a book direct from your site, it might not be the way they want to buy the book. Perhaps they don't want to share details with yet another website, or perhaps they want to try and save on postage by purchasing other books at the same time from their favourite online bookstore. Or they might be used to purchasing and reading ebooks straight from Apple Books, Kobo, Amazon or another provider. And in the UK, there's Bookshop.org (hopefully a similar site in Australia soon too!) which links readers, authors and independent bookstores, so your reader might prefer to support an organisation like that. So, what to do?

Many online bookstores run affiliate programs, so if you are selling your book through any of these outlets, it might make sense for you to also sign up with these sites as an affiliate. Why? Because you can earn money directing customers to buy your book on these sites, and even if they don't end up buying your book and instead buy a competitor's book (the horror), you'll at least benefit from a commission on that sale. Yes! You can earn money from your competitors' books. Is that ethical or nice? I'm not sure, but it is possible. Also, at least you pointed a potential reader to a book they decided might be better for them.

If you are going to direct traffic to online bookstores, I say spread the love and link to multiple bookstores so your potential reader has a choice of which link to click on and so that you can support independent stores too, not just the goliaths.

And yes, the affiliate fee is an extra commission paid on top of your normal royalty.

Still don't think affiliate programs are relevant to you? Here are some scenarios that might make sense for you.

- Written a travel guide or a memoir about a special place? Does it make sense to have some relevant affiliate links through to travel booking sites?
- Written a guide to walking Tasmania? You might have a page on your website listing your Top 10 recommended walking socks with a link as part of an outdoor retailer's affiliate program.
- Written a smoothie book? On your website, you might run an honest Top 10 comparison of different machines and blenders, all linking through to a whitegoods retailer.
- Written a fitness book? Lots of sporting goods and sporting-wear brands offer affiliate programs.
- Written a book on gardening? List, describe and link to your favourite gardening tools and accessories.
- Maybe you think your readers would benefit from a course you've attended on an education site such as Udemy—or maybe

you're creating your own course and putting it on Udemy or another site. Or you want to reward affiliates for sending people direct to your new course. Whatever way you go, you can potentially benefit by integrating affiliate links. Many online education sites offer affiliate programs. In fact, there are SO many companies offering affiliate programs across a huge range of areas it's mind-blowing.

I'm still dipping my toes in the water, and you'll note I haven't signed up to be an affiliate for products in health and wellness, fashion, cars, sporting goods or other areas that have no relevance to the core information in this book. It just wouldn't make sense. But I have signed up for affiliate programs that provide services that I use and believe in, and that I think may make sense to you as a reader, writer and someone who is also interested in publishing. They include: ALLi, Amazon, Booktopia, Publisher Rocket, Kartra and ProWritingAid (and I will include an update of which ones on my site for full disclosure). What affiliate programs might suit you and your topic?

What companies provide the software and programs to run affiliate programs?

The big ones include Impact, Share-A-Sale/AWIN, ThriveCart, CJ Affiliate (Commission Junction) and Rakuten Advertising. You can browse on their sites to see the retailers and products they support.

Kartra also lets you set up an affiliate program on your own site and for your own products, while ClickBank is an affiliate marketplace for digital material such as ebooks. You could source books and guides to sell on your own website or list your book on it, though this will only work for certain styles and types of work and it's not a site I have used.

Affiliate sites and Australian Consumer Law

Australian Consumer Law states that you must legally disclose if you have affiliate links on your website or in your book. It's not just a fair and moral obligation, or about forming and maintaining trust with your readers; it can land you in legal hot water if you don't do it. You can also be banned by sites such as Amazon if you don't have proper disclosures. I've included a disclosure in the front matter of this book, display information on my website and have been open about the services throughout this text. Keep everything above board, it's the right thing to do.

What are some best practices?

- Don't be a shonk. Only provide links to trustworthy, useful services you really believe in and use. If the company or product changes and it no longer meets your standards, drop your links or find a better product or company to refer to.
- Be helpful. If you can save someone typing in a link, providing a link does just that—even if you get paid for it.
- Be selective. Make your links useful and appropriate to your readers. If your book is about sneakers designed in Australia, you wouldn't run ads or links to foreign shops selling scarves.
- Avoid clutter. When there are too many choices, it will distract from your actual content and either be confusing to the reader, overwhelming, or they'll feel like they're being sold to by a spruiker. Please stop, it's not good for you, your brand, or your audience.

I think that's a good note to end this chapter on—a reminder that it's not just you on this journey—your audience are on a journey of their own too. If being an affiliate doesn't make sense for you, but especially if it doesn't make sense for your audience, don't pursue it as a strategy. In the end though, I think a book needs a heart, more than it needs a strategy and in the next and final chapter, I would like to share a bit of mine with you.

56

FROM ME TO YOU

Phew! We've covered a fair bit, huh?! Thanks for coming with me this far. But there's always more to learn and explore when it comes to being an author and self-publisher. I hope though that this book has provided you with the basic information you need to begin, as well as many jumping off points to other information sources and organisations, so you can complete your book and complete it well. Here are just a few final tips from me to you.

Stay fun

You weren't required to take on the challenge of writing a book—you chose to. Even when it's a slog and things go wrong or don't come along as fast as you'd hoped, centre yourself, but more importantly, find, feel and share your internal and external smile. As my husband frames it, 'You don't have to write a book. You get to!'

Be brave, it's more fun than being terrified

If you're feeling a bit wobbly after reading this book and are not sure you can do it, I'm here to tell you that you can. You just really need to want to. I've created a companion workbook (available for purchase on my site) which simplifies some of the writing and publishing steps so you can get started today. Yes, a lot goes into writing and producing a worthwhile book, but it's true of every other venture worth doing too.

Pets, kids and liquids

If you have any of the above, never leave your work open and your keyboard accessible or you may find chapters deleted or multiple nonsensical phrases such as 'mhehahohw' added. This translates as 'kid/pet paws woz here.'

Liquids of any type, whether they be smoothies, wine, tea, water or coffee will break your keyboard and heart when upended. Keep them at arm's length.

Writing and publishing don't need to be expensive

If possible, plan software purchases and marketing material buys around the big sale dates such as mid-year or Black Friday and Cyber Monday. You can score huge discounts at these times. Don't be sucked into buying things you don't need, do take advantage of free trials, and make use of the discounts offered by organisations such as ALLi, ASA and SPN.

Avoid

Avoid at all costs what I call the shonky, wonky, donkey.

- Shonky vanity publishers, shonky awards, and shonky over-priced providers.
- Wonky words and covers. Use professionals, even if they tell you things you don't want to hear.
- Donkey pace. Stop browsing, dawdling, second guessing and procrastinating. Be brave, not fearful. Get started. Get writing. Get finessing. Get finished. Push through to break through!

Track your steps

Make a note of every step you take as you publish, so it's easier for your next book. It's amazing how quickly you forget all the little things that add up to a successful launch and campaign. Also, just like hiking out of the Grand Canyon, giving birth or running a marathon (not that I've ever done the latter), if you don't write down how many hours it took and how much pain it caused, you will forget and do it again.

Piracy and plagiarism

I was gutted to see that within a week of my memoir being launched there was a site on the internet offering it free to readers. I couldn't believe it. However, I've since learned that most of these sites are specifically set up to either phish information from outraged authors or to download malware onto readers' computers. Don't worry, these types of sites will not eat into your book sales. If the site appears at the top of the search engine results for your book, just write a few extra blog posts or get people to mention your book on their site so authentic links to your book rise above the fraudsters' efforts—it won't take long. If you are really concerned, ALLi and the UK Publishers Association provide a discount to a copyright takedown service that you may want to engage on your behalf. But as Seth Godin once said, 'Your problem is not piracy. Your problem is obscurity'.

Follow up

Even though it can feel uncomfortable, always follow up. If I hadn't, there'd be half the interviews in this book, half the advance praise and half the opportunity and potential ahead.

Practise

Everything you write is practice. Even if the idea and book you are working on right now doesn't end up as the breakthrough you dreamt of, you still need to write it so you will be ready and more able to write and publish the next one. It's all practice so start practising.

Keep up the momentum

All it takes to write and market a book is one small action every day. Momentum will help you keep faith in the project too. Eventually you will have not just any book, but *your* book, in your hands. Even when it seems too hard, too long a road, beyond you. Just. Keep. Going!

Your book is everything, but it is also nothing

Don't give your book too much power. Keep your ego in check.

Be kind

Be kind to other writers, be kind to the people you interview, be kind to your readers, and most importantly, be kind to yourself.

Give yourself the benefit of the doubt: you can write this book, and you can write it well. You will be able to find the right knowledge and professionals to help you make it the best it can be. Sure, first drafts suck and you'll make mistakes along the way, but making mistakes is the fuel you need to learn and grow. Oh, and there will always be a typo or something that could be better. Go on, be kind.

Further reading and resources

A list of my favourite writing books and resources (I wouldn't have got this far without them!) is available free in the *Writing Resources* section at www.annafeatherstone.com.

I'd love to hear from you

We come to writing for different reasons, write with different styles, and at different paces. We write with different dreams and hopes, our curiosity leading us in different directions. Yet, for all these differences, we are the same: we have something to share, and we want to share it well. It is my hope this book will contribute to your success in doing just that.

If this book helps you on your journey, now or in the future, I'd love to hear from you. I'm really looking forward to that. Also, if you have any ideas for content you'd like to see, please get in touch.

Thanks, from me!

Really, thank you. Thank you for supporting me in doing what I love. I feel honoured and so very grateful. If you want to leave a review on online sites or share information about my book on social media, that would be great too. Best wishes to you, thank you again and I hope to be reading your words soon! *Anna*

ACKNOWLEDGEMENTS

Thank you to Rachel Smith, founder of Rachel's List. Our collaboration on a mini self-publishing masterclass was all the spark I needed to finally get this project off the ground. Sometimes a little nudge is all it takes!

The indomitable Susie 'Juice' Jones took on the painful role of first reader (the early manuscript was a shocker), providing thoughtful advice and just enough encouragement to stop me tossing the project into the too-hard basket.

Stoic editor Geoff Whyte then took on the swamp of the first draft, salvaging it with well-applied structure, ropes, pulleys and tough love.

Copy editor and proofreader Tina Morganella added shine and sparkle, and to indexer Sherrey Quinn, I'm so grateful for your flexibility helping craft a wonderful index given the constraints.

I couldn't have asked for a better cover designer. Tess McCabe was great from the start, creating great initial design concepts, offering wise advice and graciously assisting with so much more, including development of the workbook.

A big thanks too, to all the people who allowed me to interview, quote and learn from them. Extra gratitude to Andrew Griffiths, Cathy Bayes Hunt, Cathy Savage, Craig Lewis, Jaqui Lane, Jim Maguire, Jin Wang, Kelly Irving, Kim McCosker, Leanne Wright, Tim Heard, Virginia Lloyd and Valerie Khoo for all the time you spent on this.

To the members of online groups including Australian Binders, ALLi, the Australian Writers' Centre and the Vellum user group—what an amazing writing community you are!

And to Darcy Campbell and Janek Drevikovsky, thanks for the gift of your writing and editing expertise in the final weeks.

There's also no way I could have completed this book without carers (aka all-round great people) Cass Davies, Kathleen Elliott and Annette Hatherly and the wonderful office team at Mid North Coast Home Instead, who helped care for my gorgeous Nonna Bear a few hours each week so I could get some time on the book. And Cass proved again her multi-tasking magnificence by proofreading and jigsaw puzzling at the same time. So grateful to you Cass and I look forward to seeing your first book come to be.

Thank you too, to Pete, Dawn, Olivia and Lucy Martin, I could write volumes about your kindness. To Sofia van Mill for giving me a break from the day-to-day by taking me on energising walks and talks; and to Sue Brangwin for all the pottery fun.

To one of my favourite *huwoms* on the planet, Jodie Kennedy, you bring grounded grins, generosity, kindness, warmth, sparkle and neurons wherever you go! And to Christine Beury, Susie Jones, Leanne Sheraton, the Warriner and Tyrell clans and Daryl Brenton, you're basically hearts, hope, hugs and happiness on legs.

And bear hugs and the hugest love to the local fam bam (hahaha, never last, except in books): Darcy, Zac, Josie, Nonna Bear, Franjipani (thanks for being you and for everything you do and are), Markle Sparkle, Panjack, Tink, Margie, Ross, Liam and Oliver, and Nicole, Sean and Lil.

And in the greatest understatement ever—thank goodness for Andrew, hey!? Longest boyfriend eva! Still 'this much'. xox

INDEX

F

J

K

I'm here to help!

Companion Workbook

Want to speed up the self-publishing process? Don't want to create everything from scratch? The **Look – It's Your Book Workbook** is full of checklists, worksheets, sample promotional material, templates (for interview requests, permissions and more). I wish I'd had a resource like this when I was producing my books! The workbook is available exclusively from **annafeatherstone.com**.

Talks, Presentations and Workshops

Yes! I'm available for fun, upbeat and informative paid presentations on a variety of topics including finding your unique idea and story, sharing your story through various mediums, and of course, book writing, publishing and marketing!

Private Consults and Mentoring

Have some burning questions to ask? Seeking clarity on your book idea? Need help moving past any blocks, getting to the next step, or would like a referral? Consultations and mentoring sessions are available to book via my website.

**More info at
annafeatherstone.com**

Speed up your author journey.